Get Ready for

International Business

English for the workplace

Teacher's Book 2

With Digibook

Jaimie Scanlon
& Dorothy E Zemach

MACMILLAN

Contents

Get Ready for International Business 2 Introduction

About the course

Get Ready for International Business is a two-level speaking and listening course designed for pre-professional university or college students or students just starting their professional careers. As the course aims to prepare students for the business world, it can be used with students who have little or no previous professional work experience. *Get Ready for International Business 2* is suitable for students at a low-intermediate to intermediate level of English (level B1 of the Common European Framework of Reference).

The emphasis of the course is on providing students with the skills to communicate effectively in English in a variety of business situations, both social and work-related. The course comprises 12 topic- and function-focused units. In each unit, students are guided through a series of motivating, student-centred activities aimed at building their skills and confidence to communicate successfully in the global business world.

The topics and functions in *Get Ready for International Business 2* provide students with a variety of business-related contexts in which to practise the vocabulary, language structures and business skills presented in each unit. The unit foci include meetings and discussions, reading and writing emails and CVs, giving presentations, interviewing and handling performance reviews.

Unit structure

The unit structure aims to give students mastery of the target language before moving on to the next unit. Unit content is loosely graded with regard to difficulty, so students build up to more complex language and skills as the course progresses. The exercises in each unit provide guided practice followed by more open-ended, independent tasks which allow students to apply the language and skills in a realistic context. There is some slight variation in structure from unit to unit, as each one presents content in a sequence that best maximises students' learning potential. A typical unit may have the following format:

Listen and practise / Read and practise: Students begin the unit by listening to a short dialogue or reading a text related to the unit focus. Dialogues are between two or more main characters. Students engage with the listening and reading texts in a variety of ways including completing comprehension questions, fill-in-the-blank exercises, predicting, and practising dialogues in pairs while substituting additional information.

Unit language and skills: These sections present the key functions, vocabulary, structures and skills foci of the unit. The first set of exercises includes abundant guided practice activities in the form of individual tasks and communicative pairwork. As well as this, additional listening exercises lead students to work towards mastery and internalisation of useful topic-related target language and skills. As students progress through the sections, they learn additional topic-related vocabulary and structures to complement and build on the content presented in the earlier exercises. Here, too, students engage in individual tasks, guided pair practice and listening activities.

Viewpoints: This section focuses on common business practices and ways in which they may differ from culture to culture. Students read or listen to people from different cultures talking about a particular aspect of business, for example, discussing business stereotypes and generalisations, decision-making, email habits or presentation styles. The level of the *Viewpoints* section is slightly higher than that of the rest of the unit to allow for vocabulary-building and extension, as well as to address the needs of multi-level classes. Exercises include open-ended group discussion tasks.

In business: At the end of each unit, students complete a business task related to the unit themes and content. These student-centred tasks provide an opportunity for students to apply the unit language and skills in a useful, realistic context. For example, students work in groups to plan a business meeting, hold a decision-making meeting, prepare and give a presentation about on-the-job use of English, or compile personal information into a CV. Through these tasks, students build the confidence to participate successfully in a variety of common business situations.

In addition to the 12 main units, the Student's Book includes three review units, one after every four units of the book. The review units allow students to consolidate the language through a variety of fun puzzles, games and interactive activities.

Student's Book Introduction and strategy review

Page 4 of the Student's Book provides an introduction to some of the characters that appear on the *Viewpoints* pages. Students match the quotes to the characters after studying the *Viewpoints* sections. Additional notes and answers are provided within the *Viewpoints* Teaching notes. Page 5 reviews the conversation strategies first introduced in Level 1 of the course. You may wish to remind students of these strategies from time to time or before and after extended speaking tasks. More detailed guidance is provided on page 5 of this book.

Teacher's Book

The *Get Ready for International Business* Teacher's Book includes the following:

- Unit aims
- Getting started warm-ups
- Teaching notes
- Review unit answer key
- Grammar reference answer key

- TOEIC® and BEC practice answer key
- Tests 1 and 2
- Tests 1 and 2 answer key
- Photocopiable activities
- Audioscripts

Unit aims: The bulleted unit aims at the beginning of each Teacher's Book unit are intended to provide teachers with a preview of the topics, functions, vocabulary, language structures and business-related skills students will learn in the unit. You may want to write the specific aims for each lesson at the beginning of class to give students a general idea of the lesson objectives.

Getting started: Each Teacher's Book unit includes several fun, interactive warm-up ideas for starting the unit. Unit 1 includes ideas for presenting the Strategy review on page 5 of the Student's Book. In other units, the activities are designed to review key concepts, vocabulary and language skills from the previous unit.

Teaching notes: The teaching notes section provides step-by-step lesson procedures and instructions for each activity. You need not feel constrained by these procedures, however. The notes are intended to offer alternatives for presentation and practice of the unit content and options for expanding and supplementing the material. The notes include suggestions for implementing the activities with lower- and higher-level students as well with multi-level classes. In addition, the teaching notes sections include the following features:

- Vocabulary and expressions – a list of challenging words, phrases or expressions from the unit
- Answers – answer keys to all of the activities in each unit as well as suggested possible answers for some of the open-ended tasks
- Extension activities – ideas for quick optional in-class activities that allow students to practise language and skills in a fun, engaging way
- Culture notes – useful tips and information about aspects of business culture related to the unit themes
- Language notes – explanations for complex language structures or terms, and additional ideas for expanding the language component in the unit
- Teaching tips – teaching suggestions and techniques for more effective presentation of the unit content

Review unit and Grammar reference answer keys: The answer keys (pages 75–78) include answers and possible answers for the Review unit and Grammar reference activities. You can ask students to complete the Review units in class, and then hand out a photocopy of the answer key and have them check their own (or a classmate's) answers. Similarly, you can refer students to the *Grammar reference* section in class during the course of the unit, or set the practice tasks for homework at the end of the unit.

TOEIC® and BEC practice answer key: On pages 79–81 you will find the answer key for the Practice for the TOEIC® and BEC practice activities from the two editions of the Student's Book.

Tests: There are two photocopiable tests. Test 1 (pages 82–85) covers the vocabulary, language structures and concepts presented in Units 1–6 of the Student's Book. Test 2 (pages 86–89) covers the material presented in Units 7–12.

Test 1 and 2 answer key: On pages 90–91, you will find the answer key to Tests 1 and 2. Each test comprises a *Listening section* (24 items – one point each), a *Language and Vocabulary section* (51 items – one point each) and a *Speaking section* (worth a total of 25 points). The scoring for the first two sections is self-explanatory; you should subtract one point for each incorrect answer. Please see page 89 for the *Speaking section* scoring guidelines.

Photocopiable activities: There are 14 supplementary photocopiable activities (pages 92–110), one or two to accompany each Student's Book unit. The photocopiable activities are fun, interactive pair, group, and whole-class tasks designed to motivate students and reinforce target language. They can be used during the course of the unit to complement a particular lesson, or at the end of a unit for review. Instructions for each photocopiable activity are included in the teaching notes.

Student's Book audioscripts: The audioscripts for each listening activity are included on pages 111–143. They are photocopiable, and you may wish to reproduce them and hand them out to students for additional dialogue practice or vocabulary building.

Digibook: for classroom presentations

You can use the Digibook disc that comes with this Teacher's Book for classroom presentations. The Digibook contains three parts:

- a digital version of the Student's Book main units and review pages
- the audio files for the listening activities; and
- a copy of the audioscript as a pdf file.

You can use the Digibook tools to highlight text, to zoom in and out of sections, and a reveal tool allows you to cover up part of the page. When you click on a listening activity an audioplayer allows you to play the audiofiles. When you select 'audioscript' from the main menu, you access the audioscript in a pdf form, which you can print out.

Welcome to the company! 1

Unit aims

In Unit 1, students learn about:

- Introducing a colleague
- Conversation topics
- Self-introductions
- Small talk
- Making introductions
- Viewpoints: Breaking the ice
- In business: An ice-breaking session

The aims for each class can be written on the board to orient students to the unit content and objectives.

Photocopiable activity (1a)

p92

Classroom language

1 Prepare one copy of *Classroom language* for each student.

2 Read the sentences aloud and ask the class to repeat in chorus. If you like, follow up by calling on individual students to read the sentences aloud.

3 To practise the language, you can ask students to work with a partner or in small groups to perform short skits in which they use several of the sentences, and then have them present their skits to the class. As a variation, students can perform the skits but not say the sentences from the photocopiable. Instead, audience members call out the appropriate sentence.

4 Encourage students to keep their photocopiable in their notebooks and bring it to class each time. Do not let students use their native language to express the ideas on the photocopiable. If they do, point to a copy to remind them to use English.

5 As an extension, have students work with a partner or in groups of three. Divide the sentences evenly among the groups. Ask each group to write their phrases on a poster board or large sheet of paper. They can draw illustrations or cut out pictures from magazines and glue them onto the paper. Then hang the posters around the classroom to serve as a reminder for future classes.

Getting started:

Strategy review p5

Before you begin this first unit, it will be useful to do the Strategy review on page 5 of the Student's Book. Here are some activity options for reviewing the three strategies:

1

Controlling language

- Before class, prepare a brief self-introduction about yourself. Include basic personal information to help students get to know you, for example, your family, your hometown, your educational background, your hobbies and interests, etc.
- Ask students to find a partner and tell them to open their Student's Books to page 5.
- Read the instructions aloud, and ask them to practise reading the phrases. For lower-level classes, read the phrases aloud and ask students to repeat them after you.
- When students are comfortable saying the phrases, tell them that you are going to give them some information about yourself and that they should take notes. Explain that they should raise their hands and say *Excuse me* to stop you if they don't understand something, or if they need help.
- As you give your prepared self-introduction, use a variety of strategies to elicit the controlling language phrases, for example:
  - Begin reading quietly, so students need to ask *I'm sorry. Can you speak more loudly?*
  - Read very quickly, so students need to ask *Can you speak more slowly?*
  - Use vocabulary or proper nouns (such as the names of people in your family or schools you've attended), so that students need to ask for spelling.
  - When you finish your self-introduction, ask students to make a poster of the phrases to put up in the classroom. Continue adding useful classroom language as the need arises.

2

Checking and confirming

- Ask students to do a simple sketch of a place they know well, for example, the street they live on, a room in their home, the school cafeteria, etc.
- Put students with a partner, and tell them NOT to show their drawings to each other.
- Ask students to practise reading the phrases. For lower-level classes, read the phrases aloud and ask students to repeat them after you.
- Explain that students are going to take turns describing their sketches to their partner. The partner should listen to the description and draw the same picture.

- Remind students to use the phrases for checking and confirming. Give them about five minutes per student for their descriptions.
- When students finish, ask them to compare their drawings to their partner's original and discuss any differences.

3

Reflecting and reacting

- Before class, copy the nine phrases from the three-columned table on page 5 onto the board. Be sure to write the phrases in random order in a list form.
- Copy the table onto the board with just the three expressive faces at the top of each column but leave the columns blank. Ask students to copy the table into their notebooks.
- Ask for volunteers to read the list of phrases aloud. Model the appropriate intonation for expressions like *Wow! That's amazing!, Oh, no!, That's a shame.*, etc.
- Give students about five minutes to sort the phrases on the list and write them in the correct columns in the table in their notebooks.
- Tell students to open to page 5 in their Student's Books and check their answers.
- To finish, tell students that the phrases on page 4 can help them communicate better in English and participate actively in class. Encourage them to refer to the phrases and use them as often as they can.

Photocopiable activity (1b) p93

Pair introductions

1 Divide students into As and Bs. Prepare enough photocopies so that each Student A has a copy of the A sheet and each Student B has a copy of the B sheet.

2 Ask students to complete the questions on their own. They they should write a follow-up question under each completed question. They may write two questions if they like, to allow for different responses. Give a few examples of different ways to complete question 1 from both A's and B's sheets:

A: *What's your favourite food? How often do you eat it?*

What's your favourite kind of music? How many CDs do you have?

B: *Do you know how to dance? When did you learn?* (or, *Would you like to learn?*)

Do you know how to ride a motorcycle? Is it difficult? (or, *Do you want to try?*)

3 Tell students to ask and answer the questions with a partner.

4 Bring the class back together and ask each student to introduce his or her partner and say one or two interesting things about him or her.

Listen and practise: Introducing a colleague p6

Vocabulary and expressions

major
new employee
pleased
political
religious
salary
tech support
trainee
Would you like to say a few words?

1

- Read the instructions aloud. Ask students to discuss the photo with a partner.
- Ask students to tell you where they think the people are and what is happening.
- Elicit that they are in an office, and that a woman is being introduced to her colleagues at the company.

2 1.02

- Ask students to look again at the photo in Exercise 1. Ask some guiding questions, for example:

  What kind of company is it?

  Where are they?
- Read the instructions and the answer choices aloud. Then play the audio.
- Ask students to compare answers with a partner. Then go over the answer with the class.

> ***Answer***
> To tell some employees about a new employee.

3 1.02

- Before you play the audio, ask students to read the speech silently and predict the missing words. Elicit ideas from several students.
- Read the instructions aloud. Then play the audio once or twice as needed, and ask students to complete the speech.
- Ask students to compare answers with a partner. Then go over the answers with the class.

> ***Answers***
> introduce, working, pleased, addition, few words

- Before students practise reading the speech, give them some additional fluency practice. Play the audio again, pausing after each sentence to allow students to repeat. Encourage students to use the same intonation and speaking pace as the speaker on the audio.
- Put students with a partner to practise reading the speech. Explain any unfamiliar vocabulary. Walk around the class as students work, listening in and offering help as needed. Remind students to take turns.

4

- Read the instructions aloud. Then go over the pronunciation of the names and information.
- Ask students to practise the speech. Remind them to take turns.
- Once students are familiar with the speech, put them into groups of four. Ask pairs to take turns standing up and roleplaying the introduction, choosing the information to insert. Encourage them to look up and make eye contact with the other pair as they give the speech. Continue until all students have had a chance to give the speech.

5 1.03

- Read the instructions and the answer choices aloud. Elicit a few guesses from students. Make sure students understand that they can choose more than one answer.
- Play the audio and ask students to check their guesses. Then go over the answers with the class.

Answers

c She will talk about her background.

d She will talk about her personal interests.

- Ask for volunteers to tell you what specific information Amy gives about her background and interests (She has done volunteer work in Nepal; She enjoys travel; She lived in France; Her father is British).

Conversation topics p7

1

- Read the instructions aloud. Ask several students to read the topics listed in the table aloud. Go over any unfamiliar vocabulary.
- Introduce the concept of 'small talk' (conversation – usually between people who don't know each other well – about light topics such as personal background and interests). Explain that some people may be more or less comfortable discussing certain topics depending on their culture, beliefs or personality. This exercise is designed to help students think about what topics may make them comfortable or uncomfortable.
- Give students about five minutes to enter their responses in the chart. Walk around the class as students work, offering help as needed.
- Put students with a partner or in small groups to compare their answers. Then elicit some of the topics students would feel comfortable and uncomfortable with.

2 1.04

- Read the instructions aloud. Then play the audio once or twice as needed.
- Ask students to compare answers with a partner. Then go over the answers with the whole class. Ask students to tell you how they could tell whether the speakers were comfortable or uncomfortable, for example, by listening to their tone of voice, hesitation, the nature of the topic itself, etc.

Answers

	Woman	Man
a nationality	✓✓	✓✓
college name, major	✓✓	✓✓
b height / weight	✓✓	x
age	✓✓	x
c single / married	x	✓✓
info about family	✓	✓✓
where born	✓✓	✓✓
d job	✓	✓✓
salary	x	✓✓
e political situation	✓✓	✓✓
f religion	✓✓	x
hobbies / interests	✓✓	✓✓

Self-introductions p8

1

- Ask students to look back at the table on page 7. Ask for volunteers to share some of the topics they double ticked, and write those topics on the board.
- Read the first bulleted instruction aloud. To help prepare students, use the topics elicited on the board to make some notes for a self-introduction about yourself, for example:

  Your college's name and your major: *Leeds University, Biology, graduated in 2008*

  Information about your family members: *parents live in Bournemouth, one older brother (age 35), two sisters (ages 27 and 29)*

  Then ask students to listen as you model a brief self-introduction using your notes from the board.
- Give students time to make notes for their own self-introductions. For lower-level classes, you may want to give students additional time, and allow them to write out their self-introductions in full.

- Depending on students' level and your class size, you may choose to divide the class into groups, or ask students to present to the whole class.
- Point out the model language to help students get started. Encourage students to look at their notes for reference, but also to make eye contact with their classmates when they speak.

Small talk p8

Vocabulary and expressions

Mechanical Engineer
originally

Culture note

Some students may be unfamiliar or uncomfortable with the concept of making small talk. In some cultures, it is uncommon to strike up a casual conversation with strangers, however, in many Western cultures, making small talk is an important social (and professional) skill. Take time to discuss the concept of small talk with students. Explain that many English speakers may begin conversations with strangers, for example, at a party, in the doctor's office, in a lift, etc. Teach some useful topics and phrases for starting a small talk conversation, for example:

The weather:

Nice day today, isn't it?
Looks like rain/snow.
It's chilly/hot today, isn't it?

General comments or questions:

Have you been to this convention before?
Great party.
Are you having a good time?
The food is great, isn't it?

Teaching tip

Expanding conversation skills: Before you begin this lesson, it will be useful to spend some time introducing some specific strategies for helping students to have longer, more interesting conversations. For example, teach students the following:

- **Finding something in common:** Try to make a personal connection with the other person by commenting on things you have in common. For example:

  A: *What do you like to do in your free time?*
  B: *I like bicycling and running.*
  A: *Really?* ***I enjoy running, too.***

- **Follow-up questions:** Try to extend the conversation by asking follow-up questions about the topic. For example:

  A: *Where are you from?*
  B: *I'm originally from Berlin, but I live in Hamburg now.*
  A: *Oh, really?* ***How long have you been in Hamburg?***
  B: *About five years.*
  A: *Wow!* ***Do you like it?***

- **Answer + 1:** When answering a question, expand your answer by adding one more piece of information about the topic. For example:

  A: *How many brothers and sisters do you have?*
  B: *I have two older brothers. +* ***One brother lives in Seoul, and the other one lives in New York.***

1

- Read the instructions aloud. Then give students time to read the statements and the responses.
- Ask students to work alone or with a partner to match the statements and responses. Walk around the class as students work, offering help as necessary.
- Go over the answers by calling on two students to read each statement and the correct response.
- For additional practice, ask students to work with a partner to come up with one more possible response for each statement. Alternatively, ask them to choose one of the statement/response pairs, and write a continuation of the conversation. Then ask them to perform their conversations for the class.
- For higher-level classes, teach additional phrases for responding when one finds something in common with another person. Point out the phrases in Exercise 1: *I do, too; My brother is, too; I am, too.* Then write the following on the board to introduce the additional phrases:

Affirmative sentences	*Negative sentence*
I do, too. = So do I.	*I don't either. = Neither do I.*
I am, too. = So am I.	*I'm not either. = Neither am I.*

- Encourage students to use the new phrases in subsequent exercises in Unit 1.

Answers

a 4
b 1
c 6
d 5
e 3
f 2

2

- Ask students to work alone to unscramble the questions. Alternatively, add an element of competition by asking them to form teams, and then having them race other teams to unscramble the questions first.
- Go over the answers with the class by asking students to write the correct questions on the board.

Answers

a What is your name?

b What do you do?

c Where are you from originally?

d What kinds of things do you like to do?

e Why are you studying English?

- This exercise provides an opportunity to review *Wh-* question intonation. Write some questions on the board and ask students to practise the contrast between the falling intonation of *Wh-* questions and the rising intonation of *yes / no* questions, for example:

What is your name? ↘	*Is your name Susan?* ↗
What do you do? ↘	*Are you an Engineer?* ↗

3

- Put students with a partner to ask and answer the questions in Exercise 2.
- For lower-level classes, ask the class to brainstorm possible follow-up questions for each question.
- Walk around the class as students work, offering help and support as necessary. Encourage students to keep their conversations going as long as they can by asking follow-up questions.

Making introductions p9

1 1.05

- Read the instructions aloud. Then play the audio and ask students to follow along with the conversations on page 9.
- Ask students to read the discussion questions aloud. Then ask students to discuss the questions as a whole class. Alternatively, ask them to discuss the questions with a partner or in small groups. Then go over the answers with the class.

Answers

a Conversation 2 is more formal. Some of the phrases are more formal than in Conversation 1, for example, *I'd like you to meet …* vs. *This is …* ; *A pleasure*. vs. *Nice to meet you*. Conversation 1 is more informal; it is more relaxed and friendly and has some shorter sentences.

b *This is …; I'd like you to meet …*

c **Conversation 1:**

He's an exchange student.

He's studying in Madrid.

David, Amy's just started working with me.

David is really into rock music.

Conversation 2:

Michael, this is Amy Lane, our new management trainee.

Michael is working on a new marketing campaign for Asia.

He's also in charge of our tennis club.

- For additional practice, put students into groups of three and ask them to practise the conversations. Encourage them to stand and roleplay the conversations, shaking hands and making eye contact.

2

- Read the instructions aloud. First put students with a partner, and ask them to ask each other a few basic questions to get to know each other. Tell them that they can use the questions from Exercise 2 on page 8 or their own questions.
- When students finish, ask pairs to combine to form groups of four. Ask two students to read the model exchange. Then ask for one or two volunteer groups to model their introductions for the class.
- Walk around the class as groups work, reminding students to find something in common or ask follow-up questions.

Viewpoints: Breaking the ice p10

Vocabulary and expressions

cheek

fit in

furniture

make the first move

outgoing

rare

1

- Ask students to think about what people in their culture say and do when they meet someone new. Ask for volunteers to share their ideas. Elicit ideas for what people say and do in both formal and informal situations.
- Read the instructions aloud and make sure that students have checked any potentially challenging vocabulary in the reading passages.
- Give students time to read the passages silently. For lower-level classes, read the passages aloud and ask students to listen and read along. Alternatively, ask students to read the passages aloud.

- Draw the following table on the board:

Travis	Teresa	Yumiko

- Ask for volunteers to give sentences to summarise what each person says about meeting new people. As students offer their ideas, write notes in the table on the board. Ask students to say which person they are most similar to and why.

2

a

- Put students into groups of three or four. Ask for volunteers to read the discussion question and list of behaviours aloud.
- Give groups time to rate the behaviours. Encourage them to discuss their ratings and to say why they would or would not do the behaviours. Walk around the class as students work, listening in and offering help as needed.
- When students finish their ratings, open the discussion to the whole class. Ask the questions and elicit responses from several volunteers.

b

- Continue the whole-class discussion with these questions, asking for volunteers to share their ideas while you write them on the board. Alternatively, ask students to continue to work in their groups. If supplies are available, give each group a piece of poster paper and a marker for their lists, and ask them to present their lists to the class.
- To finish, have the class come up with a list of *Dos and Don'ts* for meeting people and making small talk at a party in their culture.
- Ask students to complete the matching task on page 4 in respect of Travis Johnson.

> ***Answer***
> Travis Johnson: C

In business:
An ice-breaking session p11

- Before you begin this lesson, read the three sets of In business task activity instructions, so that you can be prepared to answer students' questions. Make sure you have the materials on hand for each of the activities. You will need the following:

  Group A: small cards and tape or small sticky labels (large enough to write a name on)

  Group B: small strips of paper, or small cards (large enough to write a question on)

  Group C: no materials needed

Scenario

- Ask a student to read the *Scenario* aloud for the class. Explain or elicit the meaning of *ice-breaking session* (a group gathering to help people get to know each other, often through various games and activities).

Task 1

- Divide the class into three groups. If your class is large, divide each group (A, B and C), so that there are no more than five or six students per group. Distribute any materials groups may need for their activities.
- Tell each group to look at the appropriate page in their Student's Books (Group A – page 84; Group B – page 93; Group C – page 103).
- Give groups time to read the activity instructions and prepare their materials. Walk around the class as students work, explaining the activities as necessary. For lower-level classes, assign a more advanced student in each group to read the instructions and explain the activity.
- Check that all groups understand their assigned activity. Encourage groups to practise explaining the activity with their group members once before they move on to Task 2.
- Collect the labels and questions, as they will be distributed to the other groups.

Task 2

- Ask students to form new groups of three with one member from each larger group (A, B or C).
- Ask students to take turns explaining each activity. Walk around the class, listening in and checking that students understand the activities.

Task 3

- Ask groups to return to their original three groups from Task 1.
- Read the instructions aloud. Help clarify the instructions for each activity as necessary. Distribute the labels and questions, so that each group has the necessary materials to do all three activities.
- Remind groups that they will have 10–15 minutes for each activity. Walk around the class as students work, listening in and offering help as needed.
- If you have a small class, you may want to do the activities with the whole class. You may want to assign, or have the class choose, two or three students to lead the class in each activity. Alternatively, you could allow time for each group to make their own questions and labels.
- After 10 or 15 minutes, stop the first activity and ask students a few questions about the experience, for example, *How did you feel doing the activity? Was it a useful ice-breaker? What did you like about it? What did you dislike? Why?*
- Have groups move on to the next activity, stopping after 10 or 15 minutes to ask the questions above.

Follow-up

- When the class has completed all three activities, lead a whole-class discussion using the follow-up questions at the bottom of the page.

An important visitor

2

Unit aims

In Unit 2, students learn about:

- Starting a presentation
- Presenting information: Openings / introductions
- Guiding a visitor: Making suggestions
- Viewpoints: Stereotypes and generalisations
- In business: An orientation for foreign students

The aims for each class can be written on the board to orient students to the unit content and objectives.

Getting started

Begin this unit by reviewing the strategies students learnt in Unit 1 for making small talk and introductions. Before class, write a list of small talk topics on the board, for example:

films

hometown

hobbies and interests

part-time job

last weekend

music

- Put students with a partner and tell them that they will have two minutes to have a small talk conversation with their partner. Partners should first introduce themselves, and then they should choose one of the topics on the board and talk about it. Students should begin when you say, *Go!*. Remind them to find things in common and to ask follow-up questions.
- After two minutes, tell students to stop. Then ask them to change partners and repeat the process with a new topic.
- Ask students to change partners three or four times.
- To finish, ask for volunteers to introduce one of the classmates they spoke with to the rest of the class.

Listen and practise: Starting a presentation p12

Vocabulary and expressions

background

computer security

cut costs

data protection

installing

slide

values

vision

1

- Read the instructions aloud. Ask students to discuss the photo with a partner.
- Ask students to tell you where they think the people are and what is happening.
- Elicit that they are in a conference room, and that a woman is giving a presentation to employees about the company's future.

2 1.06

- Ask students to look again at the photo in Exercise 1. Ask students to predict some of the things they think the woman will talk about, for example, sales goals, organisational change, future plans, etc.
- Read the instructions aloud and call on a student to read the answer choices aloud.
- Play the audio and ask students to mark their answers. Then elicit the answers and ask students to explain how they arrived at their answers.

> ***Answers***
>
> **a** T
>
> **b** F

3 1.06

- Before you play the audio, ask students to read the presentation opening silently and predict the missing words. Elicit ideas from several students.
- Read the instructions aloud. Then play the audio once or twice as needed, and ask students to complete the passage.
- To check answers, ask students to read the sentences aloud, inserting the correct information.

> ***Answers***
>
> to talk to you, message, to cover three, After that, Finally

- Before students practise reading the passage, go over some important points for giving a presentation to a group, for example,
  – take a deep breath and relax before starting
  – stand straight and tall
  – speak loudly and clearly
  – make eye contact with the audience.

  Model these skills by reading the first few lines and applying the skills above.
- Put students with a partner or into groups to practise reading the presentation. Ask students to stand and roleplay giving the presentation to an audience. Remind them to use the suggestions above for giving presentations. Walk around the class as students work, listening in and offering help as needed. Remind students to take turns.

4

- Read the instructions aloud. Go over any unfamiliar vocabulary.
- Put students into groups of four, and ask them to take turns giving the presentation, inserting the new information. Ask students to stand and encourage them to use the suggestions above.

5 1.07

- Read the instructions. Ask for volunteers to read the answer choices aloud. Elicit a few guesses.
- Make sure students understand that they can choose more than one answer.
- Play the audio and ask students to check their guesses. Then go over the answers with the class.

Answers

b Are there any questions so far?

d Let me start by giving you some background.

- To finish, ask for volunteers to tell you what specific background information Lisa gives. (Two years ago, the company expanded business in Europe and Asia; They now have production plants in the US, France, Japan and Singapore.)

Presenting information: Openings / introductions p13

Vocabulary and expressions

automatic/manual
benefits
fuel economy
make/model
reducing waste

1 1.08

- Read the instructions aloud. Give students time to read the partial phrases in the table.
- Elicit the type of information included in each of the four parts:

  Opening – a greeting, your name and job

  Subject – the main topic of the presentation

  Message – the main point of the presentation/what you will say about the topic

  Outline – how many topics you will talk about and in what order
- Ask students to predict the missing words or phrases. Elicit some ideas from the class.
- Play the audio once or twice as needed. Then ask for volunteers to tell you the answers.

Answers

a subject today

b main point

c is divided into

- For lower-level classes, ask students to repeat the phrases after you. For higher-level classes, ask them to practise with a partner. Then give students some topic prompts to choose from, and ask them to work together to write a presentation introduction using some of the phrases in the table. For example:

  My subject today is saving energy (office safety, international marketing, etc.*).*

  My message today is that we need to stop wasting energy.

  I'm going to cover three areas today: recycling, saving electricity and saving heating fuel.

2 1.09

- Read the instructions aloud. Before you play the audio, elicit some words or phrases students might hear for each part of an introduction. For example, for *Opening*, they might hear *Good morning*; a person's name or company name, etc.
- Play the audio once or twice as needed. Then check answers with the whole class. Ask students to tell you any words or phrases they heard that helped them get the answers.

Answers

a opening	**d** subject
b outline	**e** message
c opening	**f** outline

3

- Read the instructions aloud. Then ask students to read the phrases aloud.
- Ask students to form pairs to classify the phrases as parts of a presentation. Walk around the class as students work, offering help as necessary.
- To check students' answers, copy the headings onto the board and ask for volunteers to come up and write the phrases under the correct headings.

Answers

Opening	Subject
I'm Andrew Thomson. I work for ABT industries.	Today I'll describe … This morning I'm going to talk about …
Message	**Outline**
The main thing I want to say is this, …	There are two parts to my presentation … I'm going to talk about three things …

- For additional practice, ask students to continue working with a partner. Ask them to choose phrases from each column and add their own information to put together a presentation introduction. Then ask them to share their introductions with the class. For example:

  I'm Andrew Thomson. This morning, I'm going to talk about an exciting new product. *The main thing I want to say is that* our new product is different from anything our competition offers. *There are two parts to my presentation: First,* I'll talk about how we developed the product. *Then* I'll compare it to the competition.

4

- Read the instructions aloud. Give students time to read the list of topics and subtopics. Go over any unfamiliar vocabulary.
- Remind students that they can look back at the phrases on page 13 if they need help, and encourage them to be creative when thinking of company names and information to include in their introductions.
- For lower-level classes, you may want to prepare a written example before class and write it on the board or on an overhead projector or slide to help students prepare. For example:

  Good morning. I'm ________. I work for Green Dream Environmental. Today I'm going to talk to you about saving the environment. My main point is that we can save the environment if everyone helps. I'm going to cover three areas today. First, I'll talk about …

  You may also want to give students a target length for their introductions, for example, six to eight sentences.
- Walk around the class as students work, offering help with spelling and vocabulary as needed. When students finish, give them time to practise their introductions with a partner before moving on to Exercise 5. Use the example above to model how to look down and refer to notes, then look up when speaking. When students practise, ask them to focus on maintaining eye contact with their partner.

Teaching tip

Presentation skills – reading from notes: Students may not be accustomed to giving presentations, especially in English, so they may feel more confident reading the information verbatim from their notes. It's important to train students to look down and use their notes for reference only when they need them, and then to look up at the audience when speaking. Ask students to practise this skill several times before they practise their presentation in larger groups.

5

- Read the instructions aloud.
- Ask students to form groups of four or five to give their introductions. Ask them to stand and remind them to use the strategies they have practised for giving presentations – making eye contact, standing straight and tall, speaking loudly and clearly, etc.
- Walk around the class as students work, listening in and taking note of any presentation skills or strategies that might be useful to address later.
- To finish, lead a brief class discussion about students' experiences with the activity. Ask a few reflection questions, for example:

  How did you feel giving the presentation introduction?

  What do you think you did well?

  How could you improve it?

Guiding a visitor:
Making suggestions p15

1 1.10

- To lead into this lesson, tell students to imagine that you are a visitor to their area from another country. Ask the class to suggest interesting places to go and activities to do. On the board, write any useful phrases students use to make their suggestions, for example, *How about …?, You should …,* etc. As students offer their ideas, respond using some of the phrases in the right-hand column in Exercise 2. This will preview the language students will learn later.
- Ask students to look at the photos and ask if anyone knows the places shown. Explain that the photos show popular sightseeing spots around Manchester. You may want to give some brief cultural information about each location. (See culture notes overleaf.)
- Read the instructions aloud. Before you play the audio, ask students to predict some possible words or phrases that might help them get the answers, for example, Likes: *sounds great, good idea, I'd like to go there,* etc.; Dislikes: *not sure, don't know, not interested,* etc.
- Play the audio and ask students to mark their answers.
- Ask students to compare answers with a partner. Then go over the answers with the whole class. Ask for volunteers to share any words or phrases they heard that helped them get the answers.

Answers

Arndale Centre: likes

Chinatown: likes

Old Trafford: doesn't like

The Printworks: doesn't like

Manchester Museum: likes

U of M Library: likes

Royal Exchange Theatre: likes

Culture notes

Places around Manchester

Students may be interested to know a bit of information about the places pictured in Exercise 1. Here is some useful background information.

Arndale Centre: Europe's largest city centre shopping mall. It has 38 million visitors every year.

Chinatown: Home to many Chinese shops, bakeries and supermarkets. It's the third largest Chinatown in Europe and the second largest in the UK next to London.

Old Trafford: Home of Manchester United Football Club, one of the most famous football teams in the world. Rio Ferdinand, Wayne Rooney, Ryan Giggs, David Beckham, Bryan Robson, Bobby Charlton and George Best have all played for the team.

The Printworks: An entertainment venue containing many bars, restaurants and a cinema with an IMAX screen. The building originally housed a large printing press, hence the name.

Manchester Museum: Is owned by the University of Manchester and houses over 6 million items. It is free to the public and is a resource for academic research.

University of Manchester Library: The Library is on Deansgate in Manchester and was opened to the public in 1900. It houses extensive collections of books and has a beautiful interior.

Royal Exchange Theatre: Is located in the city centre in St Ann's Square. Shakespeare's plays and the plays of many others are performed there. It is also said to be haunted!

Tips for entertaining a business visitor

- If it is an international visitor, do some cultural background research before the visitor arrives, so that you can be aware of any possible dietary restrictions or cultural or religious customs.
- Find out ahead of time what the individual visitor is interested in doing. Common activities are dining in local restaurants, theatrical performances, sports events, visiting historical sights, etc.
- Give a small token or gift. This can either be merchandise from your company (clothing, pens, etc. with the company logo) or a locally made item.
- For dining, suggest several options you know are good (try out any new restaurants before your guest arrives). Make sure there are vegetarian menu options. Make reservations ahead of time to avoid having to wait a long time.

2 1.10

- Read the instructions aloud. Then ask students to read the suggestions and responses aloud.
- Ask students to look at the list of responses and tell you which ones indicate that the person likes and dislikes the suggestions. (Likes: *Sounds great, Absolutely, I'd love that, That sounds great*; Dislikes: *We could do, but …, It's a nice idea, but …*)
- Play the audio and ask students to draw lines to match the responses to the suggestions.
- Check answers by asking pairs of students to read the suggestions with the correct responses.

Answers

Why don't we go to The Arndale Centre? – That sounds great!

We could go to Chinatown. – Absolutely!

How about visiting Old Trafford? – We could do, but …

We could go to The Printworks. – It's a nice idea, but …

Why don't we go to the Manchester Museum? – Sounds great!

How about going to see a play at the Royal Exchange Theatre? – I'd love that!

- Put students with a partner to practise the suggestions and responses. Encourage them to roleplay the situation, rather than simply reading the phrases, and to choose responses that reflect their own interests, i.e., if they are interested in trying local food, they should choose one of the positive responses. For lower-level classes, elicit some possible ways to complete the two negative responses before pairs begin practising.

Language note

Responding politely to suggestions: It's important to teach students that in English, it is not polite to give a direct negative response to a suggestion, especially in business situations. For higher-level students, you can teach some additional ways for students to respond when they dislike a suggestion, for example:

Hmm. I like that idea, but I wonder if we could save it for another time.

That's a good suggestion, but I'm not sure I'm up for that today.

That sounds really interesting, but I'm a little tired. Would it be all right if we did something else?

3

- Ask students to work with their partners from Exercise 2, or ask them to change partners.
- Before you begin this exercise, elicit some activities visitors to a new place might enjoy doing, and list the activities on the board, for example:

go sightseeing
try local food
shop for souvenirs
see famous or historical sights
learn about local culture

- Gives students time to think of places in their area where visitors can do the activities on the board.
- Ask for two volunteers to read the model conversation, and ask them to continue the exchange with one student offering suggestions and the other responding. Then ask pairs to practise the conversation, changing roles at least once.
- To extend the practice, ask students to change partners several times and practise the conversation. Students can also choose other locations they know, for example, places they've been on holiday.

Photocopiable activity

pp94–95

Suggestions roleplay

1 Ask students to work in groups of four or five. Prepare one copy of *Suggestions roleplay* for every group. Cut out each card and place them face down in the centre of each group.

2 Explain that students will take turns drawing a card and reading the scenario. The other group members will offer suggestions. If necessary, write the suggestions language from page 15 of the Student's Book on the board: *Why don't you … ; How about -ing; You could …*

3 The student who reads the scenario should respond to each suggestion. Again, you can refer students to page 15 or write the language on the board: *Absolutely!, It's a nice idea, but …; That sounds great!* etc.

4 This can also be done as a written exercise, either in class or for homework. In this case, each student should be given one card and should write out several suggestions, using different introductory phrases each time.

Viewpoints:
Stereotypes and generalisations
p16

Vocabulary

efficient
formal
high-tech
image
punctual
traditional

1

- Before you begin this lesson, write the words *stereotype* and *generalisation* on the board. Ask students to talk with a partner or in small groups about what they think those two words mean, and come up with some examples. After a few minutes, elicit students' ideas. Then work with the whole class to come up with a definition of stereotypes and generalisations (oversimplified – and often inaccurate – opinions or images of a particular nationality or group).
- Ask for volunteers to read the adjectives aloud, explain – or elicit an explanation for – any unfamiliar vocabulary.
- Give students time to think of their responses.

2

- Ask students to form pairs or small groups to compare their answers to Exercise 1. Remind them to share their reasons for their answers. Walk around the class as students work, listening in and making sure all students are participating.
- When students finish their discussion, elicit some responses from the class. Lead a class discussion about the stereotypes of various countries or cultures and the possible reasons for them. Discuss the fact that stereotypes may be positive or negative, and that making generalisations about any group of people may be harmful because these images are most often untrue.

3 1.11

- Read the instructions and the questions in the table aloud. Introduce the three speakers in the pictures: Hiroki from Japan, Markus from Germany and Tanisha from the US. Then elicit a few predictions for how each speaker might answer the first question.
- Play the audio once or twice as needed, and ask students to write their notes in the table. Remind them that they should not write every word. They should write only key words that answer the question. For lower-level classes, you may want to play each speaker one at a time, stopping in-between to go over the answers.
- Ask students to compare their tables with a partner. Then go over the answers with the whole class.

Answers
(Answers will vary. The following are sample responses.)

Hiroki

a Mount Fuji, cherry blossoms, kimono, samurai, high-tech games and electronics, quiet, polite, hard-working

b some true (Mt Fuji, cherry blossoms,) but not everyone quiet, polite, don't all work so hard

c no, image of US different from what I thought

Markus

a efficient, punctual, good at manufacturing and engineering, drink beer, eat sausages

b no, except being punctual (always in a hurry, never want to be late)

c no, everyone different, dangerous

Tanisha

a Statue of Liberty, Grand Canyon, friendly, talk a lot

b yes, but Americans all different

c maybe (as starting point), important to keep an open mind

4

- Ask students to form groups of four or five. Read the instructions aloud. Then ask students to read the discussion questions aloud.
- Give students about ten minutes for their discussions. To facilitate independent discussion, tell groups to assign the following roles to each member:

  Facilitator: asks the questions, and makes sure all group members participate

  Time-keeper: makes sure the group spends equal time on each question, and that the discussion finishes on time

  Secretary: takes notes on the main points of the group's discussion

  Reporter: Reports the main points of the group's discussion to the class.
- Walk around the class as students work, listening in and encouraging students as necessary.
- When students finish, ask the reporter from each group to share the group's ideas with the class.
- To finish, ask the class question **c** from the table in Exercise 3, *Do you think stereotypes are useful?*, and elicit responses from several students.

In business:
An orientation for foreign students p17

- Before you begin this lesson, read the two sets of In business task activity instructions, so that you can be prepared to answer students' questions.

Scenario

- Ask a student to read the *Scenario* aloud for the class. Explain or elicit the meaning of *orientation* (a meeting designed to help new students [in this case] get to know their new school and surroundings).

Task 1

- Divide the class into two groups. If your class is large, divide each group (A and B), so that there are no more than five or six students per group.
- Tell each group to look at the appropriate page in their Student's Books (Group A – page 85; Group B – page 94).
- Give groups time to read the student profiles. Tell students to pay attention to the majors, interests, and other information that might help determine what the new students would enjoy doing. Walk around the class as students work, helping to clarify the activity as necessary.

Task 2

- Read the instructions aloud. Give groups time to brainstorm some ideas for their orientation. Refer students back to the bulleted instructions in the *Scenario*, and remind them to choose places and activities they think would be most useful and interesting for the new students.
- If available, supply each group with a piece of poster paper and a marker, and ask them to choose one student to write the group's brainstorm ideas.

Task 3

- Ask students to form new groups of three to join with one member from each larger group (A or B).
- Ask students to take turns sharing their ideas. Walk around the class, listening in and making sure all students have a chance to participate.
- Tell students they are going to make a plan for their orientation. To help structure the activity, give groups a basic general schedule to follow for each day, for example:

  8:30am start

  12:30–1:30 lunch

  4:00 finish
- Give groups about 15 minutes to plan their orientations. Walk around the class as groups work, offering suggestions and ideas as necessary.

Follow-up

- When groups have finished planning their activities, ask for a volunteer from each group to share their plans with the class. Ask the class to discuss each plan, saying what they like about it, and what could be improved. Then ask the class to vote on the best plan.

What's on the agenda? 3

Unit aims

In Unit 3, students learn about:

- Running meetings
- Meetings and discussions: Opening a meeting, Stating a topic, Giving and explaining reasons, Closing a meeting
- Viewpoints: Decision making
- In business: Redecorating the office

The aims for each class can be written on the board to orient students to the unit content and objectives.

Getting started

Begin this unit by reviewing the strategies students learnt in Unit 2 for making and responding to suggestions.

- Before class, prepare sets of cards with various types of activities written on them. You will need one set of cards for each pair of students in the class, for example:

  see some art

  see a local theatre or dance performance

  try some local dishes

  shop for souvenirs

  enjoy the outdoors

  learn about local history and culture

- At the beginning of class, review the expressions students learnt in Unit 2 for making and responding to suggestions, for example:

  We could go to … *Sounds great!*

  How about going to …? *It's a nice idea, but …*

  Why don't we go to …? *I'd love that.*

- Put students with a partner and distribute one set of cards to each pair, placed face down. Pairs should choose one student to be the visitor and one to be the host. The visitor should choose a card from the pile. Then students should begin their conversations as follows (write on board):

  Host: *Is this your first visit to _________?*

  Visitor: *Yes, it is. I'm hoping to look around this weekend.*

  Host: *Would you like me to show you around?*

  Visitor: *Yes, that would be nice. I'd love to (activity on card).*

- The host offers suggestions and the visitor responds as appropriate.

Listen and practise: Running meetings p18

Vocabulary and expressions

agenda

Administrative Assistant

brochure

design firm

summarise

1

- Read the instructions aloud. Ask students to discuss the photo with a partner.
- Ask students to tell you what they think the people are doing and who is in charge.
- Elicit that they are preparing for a meeting. Ask students *Who is in charge? How do you know?* (The man in the centre is in charge. He is taking notes and may be working through an agenda)

2 1.12

- Read the instructions aloud and ask a student to read the answer choices aloud.
- Play the audio and ask students to circle their answers. Then elicit the answers, and ask for volunteers to share any words or phrases that helped them get the answers.
- Ask for a volunteer to tell you the main aim of the meeting – what the group is going to decide (which conferences to attend this year).

Answers

a on time

b are going to make

Culture note

Time in different cultures: Different parts of the world have different attitudes about punctuality. In one culture, arriving late to a meeting or starting a meeting late might be a great offence, while in another, it may be common to arrive 30 minutes to an hour late. It is important for business travellers to be aware of how time is perceived in cultures where they do business. Countries that expect absolute punctuality include Germany, the Netherlands, Finland and Japan. Being on time is also expected in North America, the UK, and other parts of Scandinavia, though being less than five minutes late is generally acceptable. In some areas, it is considered acceptable to arrive within half an hour from the expected arrival time, for example, France, Belgium and Southeast Asia. Latin America, Africa and the Middle East tend to have more relaxed attitudes towards time.

3 1.12

- Before you play the audio, ask students to read the passage silently and predict the missing words. Elicit ideas from several students.
- Read the instructions aloud. Then play the audio once or twice as needed, and ask students to complete the passage. (You should tell students that there are a few extra lines of text at the start of the audio that are not in their Student's Books, just to avoid confusion.)
- To check answers, ask students to read the sentences aloud, inserting the correct information.

> ***Answers***
> copy, decide, budget, main factors, hear from

- Put students with a partner or into groups to practise reading the passage. Walk around the class as students work, listening in and offering help as needed.
- Once students are familiar with the passage, ask them to work in groups, taking turns playing the role of Hervé Cornejo.

4

- Read the instructions aloud. Go over any unfamiliar vocabulary.
- If students worked with a partner in Exercise 3, ask them to form groups now, and ask them to take turns opening the meeting, inserting the new information. Ask students to sit in a circle, if possible, and remind them to make eye contact.

5 1.13

- Read the instructions. Ask for volunteers to read the answer choices aloud. Elicit a few guesses from the class.
- Make sure students understand that they can choose more than one answer.
- Play the audio and ask students to check their guesses. Then go over the answers with the class.

> ***Answers***
> **a** He will give his opinion.
> **b** He will ask someone else for an opinion.

- To finish, ask for volunteers to tell you what specific topic Hervé discussed (location) and what his opinions are. (They should attend conferences in Germany, Turkey, France, Japan.)

Meetings and discussions:
Opening a meeting p19

1 1.14

- Read the instructions aloud. Then ask for volunteers to read the phrases aloud.
- Play the audio once or twice as needed, and ask students to number the phrases.
- Ask students to compare answers with a partner. Then go over the answers with the whole class.

> ***Answers***
> **a** 1 **b** 3 **c** 4 **d** 2

Meetings and discussions:
Stating a topic p19

Vocabulary and expressions

afford
factors
issues
promote
sides

1

- Read the instructions aloud. Read each question aloud and ask a student to read the corresponding statement.
- Point out that in the question form, the verb (or the auxiliary verb) and the subject are inverted (*How much money will it cost?*). In the second clause of the statement, they return to subject–verb order (*We need to find out how much money it will cost*).
- Put students with a partner and ask them to practise restating the questions. Encourage them to combine the phrases in a variety of different ways to form their statements.
- When students are comfortable with the exercise, ask them to cover the right side of the table, so that they can see only the questions. Then ask them to write down as many ways as they can to restate each question.
- When students finish, elicit the statements from several volunteers.
- For additional practice, ask the class to brainstorm more business-related questions, and write the questions on the board, for example:

  Which candidate should we employ?
  Do we need to downsize?
  How many new Managers do we need?
  Do we have enough money in the budget?
  Where should we build the new plant?

- Then put students with a partner to change the questions into statements. Elicit responses from several volunteers.

2

- Read the instructions and the two statements aloud. Then put students with a partner to write the questions. Walk around the class as students work, offering help as necessary.
- Check answers by asking for volunteers to write the questions on the board. Ask the class to suggest any necessary corrections.

> ***Answers***
>
> Can we start at 8:00?
>
> Which printer should we buy?

3

- Read the instructions aloud. Give students time to silently read the questions and think about ways to restate them. Go over any unfamiliar vocabulary.
- Ask students to form pairs and assign Students A and B roles. Ask two of the more advanced students in the class to model the task.
- Ask the Student As to begin asking the questions. Walk around the class as students work, listening in and noting any common errors to address later.
- When students finish, ask them to change roles.
- You can also do this exercise as a whole-class game: Divide the class into two to four teams. Then read each question aloud to the class. The first student to raise his or her hand gets a chance to restate the question. If the answer is correct, the team gets one point. If the answer is incorrect, the team to the left gets a chance.

> ***Answers***
>
> (Answers will vary. Below are possible answers.)
>
> From left to right:
>
> We have to choose where we should go on holiday.
>
> We need to decide which computer we should buy.
>
> Let's discuss how we can improve our English test scores.
>
> We have to consider who we should promote to manager.
>
> Let's consider whether we should use a cleaning service.
>
> We need to decide if we can afford a new video camera.
>
> Let's talk about how many people we can invite.
>
> We have to choose which car we should rent.

4

- Before you begin this exercise, ask students to look back at Exercise 3 on page 18. Ask the class *How does Hervé introduce the topics he plans to talk about?* Elicit the sentence *As you can see here, we'll look at three main factors: location, size and cost.*
- Explain that when introducing a meeting, as in a presentation, it is helpful to give a general outline of the topics you plan to discuss. Tell students that they will learn more useful ways to introduce meeting topics in Exercise 4.
- Read the instructions aloud. Give students time to read the expressions in the table. Explain any unfamiliar vocabulary.
- Ask students to form pairs to practise the sentences. Remind them that they can mix and match the expressions to form various sentences.

5

- Ask students to work with their partners from Exercise 4, or ask them to change partners. Read the instructions and the example aloud.
- For lower-level classes, go through the issues in Exercise 3, and have the class brainstorm one or two related issues for each one, for example:

  How can we improve our English test scores? = computer software, classes

  How many people can we invite? = cost, space
- Walk around the class as students work, offering help with spelling and vocabulary as needed.
- To finish, ask pairs to combine to form groups of four. Then ask students to take turns roleplaying their meeting introductions. Finally, ask for volunteers to share their introductions with the class.

Culture note

Tips for effective meetings

- **Arrive early:** Arriving a little earlier than you are expected to a meeting will allow you to settle in and relax before the meeting starts.
- **Come prepared:** Always bring paper and something to write on, as well as any necessary materials for the meeting. If an agenda was distributed, be sure to read it before the meeting.
- **Pay attention:** Listen to the meeting leader's as well as others' ideas, so that you can add any useful points.
- **Don't interrupt:** Wait until an appropriate time to offer suggestions or ideas.
- **Stick to the agenda:** Save comments or questions that do not relate specifically to the meeting agenda. Ask the appropriate person after the meeting.
- **Speak up:** Be confident when offering your ideas and suggestions.

Meetings and discussions: Giving and explaining reasons p21

Vocabulary and expressions

cheaper

database

Teaching tip

Expressing opinions: Students from some cultures, particularly some parts of Asia, may feel shy or uncomfortable expressing direct opinions in a group. It will be important to stress that in most English-speaking cultures, people often offer ideas and opinions at business meetings. Explain that this type of interaction is not considered rude in any way, rather a sign that you are a member of the team who is enthusiastic about your work and company.

1 1.15

- Tell students they are going to hear examples of people giving their opinions at business meetings.
- For additional listening practice, play the audio once and ask students to listen for the main topic of each discussion (**a** designing a brochure; **b** hiring a new employee; **c** a company dinner; **d** computer training).
- Give students time to read the sentences and answer choices. Then play the audio and ask students to circle their answers.
- Ask students to read the sentences aloud, inserting the correct answers.

Answers

a I think; For one thing

b If you ask me; because

c I agree with Diane that; Another reason is that

d We think; The main reason is that

2

- Read the instructions aloud. Do sentence **1a** with the whole class as an example; introduce an opinion: *I think, In my opinion*; explain a reason: *First of all, For one thing*).
- Ask students to form pairs to sort the rest of the expressions.
- Make two columns on the board labelled *introduce an opinion* and *explain a reason*. When students finish, check answers by having them come up to the board and write the expressions in the correct columns. Ask students to copy the table into their notebooks.
- Before students practise reading the sentences, ask them to do some pronunciation work. Introduce the correct stress for each expression, and ask students to practise saying the expressions aloud. (The correct stress is indicated in the answer table.)

Answers

Introduce an opinion	Explain a reason
I think	**First** of all
In **my** opinion	For **one** thing
As **I** see it	**Another** reason is that
If you ask **me**	The **main** reason is that
I agree with **Diane** that	**One** issue is that
My point of view is that	
We think	
According to the group members	

- When students are comfortable with the stress patterns, ask them to take turns reading the sentences in Exercise 1. Walk around the class as students work, listening in and modelling the correct stress as necessary.

3

- Read the instructions aloud. Give students time to read the opinions and reasons silently.
- Ask students to work individually to match the opinions to the reasons. Then check answers with the whole class.

Answers

a 3

b 5

c 2

d 6

e 1

f 4

- Put students with a partner to practise saying the opinions and reasons. Remind them to use the expressions from Exercise 1.
- For higher-level classes, extend the practice by asking students to cover the reasons with a piece of paper, and then try giving the opinions followed by their own reasons.

Meetings and discussions: Closing a meeting p21

1 1.16

- Before you begin this activity, take an opportunity to review the expressions students have learnt for beginning a meeting (stating a topic). Elicit some phrases students learnt and write them on the board. Tell them that they can look back at page 19 if they need help.
- Now tell students they are going to learn some expressions for closing a meeting.
- Read the instructions aloud. Then play the audio once or twice and ask students to mark their answers.
- Go over the answers with the whole class.

Answers

a made a decision

b will decide later

c made a decision

d will decide later

2 1.16

- Read the instructions aloud. Then play the audio and ask students to write their answers.
- Go over the answers with the whole class.

Answers

OK, to sum up …

Let's review what we've agreed on so far.

Let me summarise our decisions.

Let's go over what we've decided so far.

3

- Tell students that they will now have a chance to practise having a meeting with their classmates.
- Read the instructions aloud, and ask for volunteers to read the meeting topics aloud.
- Ask students to form groups of three, and tell each group to choose a leader to open and close the first meeting.
- Tell groups to choose a topic to discuss first. Then give students two or three minutes to prepare on their own. The meeting leader should begin to prepare the meeting opening while other group members think of ideas to share at the meeting.
- When students are ready, tell them that they will have three minutes for their first meeting. Walk around the class as students work, listening in and making note of any areas to address later.
- Ask groups to repeat the steps above until everyone has had a chance to be the meeting leader.
- To finish, ask for volunteers to share their reaction to the experience. Ask *What was difficult or challenging for you? What did you do well? What would you like to do better in the future?*

Extension activity

To help students become comfortable giving opinions in a group, tell the class to imagine that you need their help making an important decision. Choose a topic that affects all students, so that they will be sure to have an opinion, for example, when to have the next test, etc.

- Review the language students learnt for giving opinions and explaining reasons.
- Put students into groups of four to six. Then distribute three counters (coins, small stones, etc.) to each student.
- Tell groups that they will have five minutes to discuss their opinions and to come up with a decision. Students should use the expressions they learnt in Exercise 1 for giving opinions and reasons.
- Each time a student gives an idea, he or she should put a counter in the middle of the table. The aim is for all students to have used all their counters (i.e., to have offered three opinions) by the end of the discussion.
- Groups can begin their discussions when you say, *Go!*. Stop the discussions after five minutes and check that all students have used their counters.
- To finish, have each group choose one member to close the 'meeting' using one of the phrases from Exercise 2. Then elicit each group's decision (or what they have decided so far) and reasons.

Viewpoints: Decision making p22

Vocabulary and expressions

argue
bills
compromising
electing
equal
method
reach a consensus
roommates

1

- Ask students to think about their previous experiences with making decisions. Ask for volunteers to share whether they enjoy making decisions, and whether they feel they are good at it. Ask them to explain why or why not.
- Give students time to read the passages silently. For lower-level classes, read the passages aloud and ask students to listen and read along. Alternatively, ask students to read the passages aloud.
- To help students process the information in the reading, ask them to go back through the passages again. This time ask them to circle the sentence that tells what each decision is. Then ask them to underline the sentence(s) that tell how each decision is made.
- Ask students to share the sentences they chose with a partner. Then ask for a few volunteers to say what the decisions and decision-making methods are (choosing a film to show – discussing, reaching a consensus; choosing a design for a new product – voting; choosing new paint, office furniture – one person decides).
- For higher-level classes, lead a brief class discussion on each of the situations in the reading. Ask for volunteers to share their overall reactions to the situations, and/or any similar experiences they may have had.

2

- Read the instructions aloud and ask a student to read the discussion question aloud.
- Ask students to form groups of three or four to discuss their ideas. For lower-level classes, give students time on their own to think about the advantages and disadvantages of each decision-making style. Walk around the class as students work, listening in and offering ideas as needed.
- When students finish their discussions, elicit students' ideas and write the advantages and disadvantages of each style on the board.

3

- Read the instructions aloud. Give students time to read the list of decisions aloud.
- Give students about three minutes to write their answers. Then ask them to form groups of three or four to compare answers.
- Review the language for giving opinions and explaining reasons by asking students to use the expressions they learnt when they shared their answers in groups, for example, *In my opinion, a vote is the best method for this situation. For one thing, it's the fastest method.*
- To finish, ask the class to discuss (or vote) to decide the best method for each decision.
- Ask students to complete the matching task on page 4 in respect of Juan Torres.

> ***Answer***
> Juan Torres: b

Photocopiable activity p96

A question of ethics

1. Prepare one copy of *A question of ethics* for each student.
2. Ask students to read the story by themselves, or ask a volunteer to read it to the class.
3. Ask students individually to rank the characters from best (1) to worst (5) in the *My ranking* chart. Ask them to write some notes about their reasons.
4. Then ask students to work in a group of 4–5 students and share their rankings and reasons.
5. Explain that each group must agree on a final group ranking. Give students a time limit (15–20 minutes).
6. Ask each group to share their final ranking with the class, and also discuss how they made their decision. What was easy about the decision-making? What was challenging? What decision-making style did they use?
7. Variation: Ask each group to choose, or assign each group, a decision-making style to use.

In business: Redecorating the office p23

- Before you begin this lesson, read the five sets of In business task activity instructions, so that you can be prepared to answer students' questions.

Scenario

- Call on a student to read the *Scenario* aloud for the class.

Task 1

- Divide the class into five groups.
- Tell each group to look at the appropriate page in their Student's Books. (Group A – page 86; Group B – page 95; Group C – page 96; Group D – page 104; Group E – page 109.)
- Give groups time to read the roleplay instructions. Remind students as they prepare that they will need to use the expressions they have learnt for introducing and closing meetings and for giving and explaining opinions. Walk around the class as students work, helping to clarify instructions as necessary.

Task 2

- Ask students to form new groups of five with one member from each larger group (A, B, C, D or E).
- Tell them to imagine that they are a group of company managers who are having a meeting about redecorating the office.
- For lower-level classes, give students additional time to prepare notes to use during the meeting.
- Set a timer for 10–15 minutes, and ask Students A to begin the meeting. As this activity is designed as a fun roleplay, you may want to walk around and just listen in, but do not offer comments or suggestions during students' discussions.
- When the time is up, ask the Students A to summarise their group's discussion.

Follow-up

- Lead a whole-class discussion using the questions provided.
- To finish, review the expressions students learnt for giving and explaining opinions by asking students to say which method of decision-making they feel is most effective overall and why.

That's a great idea! 4

Unit aims

In Unit 4, students learn about:

- Discussing ideas
- Meetings and discussions: Agreeing and disagreeing, Moving through a meeting
- Viewpoints: Meeting styles
- In business: A French hypermarket

The aims for each class can be written on the board to orient students to the unit content and objectives.

Getting started

Begin this unit by reviewing the strategies students learnt in Unit 3 for participating in business meetings.

- Before class, write a list of five business-related questions on the board. For example:

  How can we save energy?

  How can we attract qualified employees?

  Should we build a fitness gym for employees?

  How can we reduce travel costs?

  What colour should we paint the new office?

  Where should we have our company party?

- At the beginning of class, review the expressions students learnt in Unit 3 for opening and closing meetings and for giving opinions and explaining reasons. For example:

We need to discuss …	*I think …*	*OK. To sum up …*
We have to talk about …	*In my opinion …*	*Let me summarise …*
Let's consider …	*As I see it …*	

- Put students into groups of four or five. Tell them to imagine that they are a group of managers at the same company. Groups should choose one question to discuss and one lead manager to open and close the meeting.
- Before groups begin their meetings, give students time to work individually to brainstorm some ideas about their group's chosen question. Remind them to support their opinions.
- Tell groups they will have ten minutes to try to reach a consensus.
- When the time limit is up, ask the lead managers to close the meetings. Then call on the group leaders to summarise the groups' decisions for the class.
- To finish, lead a brief class discussion to highlight students' experiences with the activity. Ask some guiding questions, for example:

  Do you think the meeting was successful? Why or why not?

  What was difficult or challenging?

  What did you do well?

  What could be improved?

Listen and practise: Discussing ideas p24

Vocabulary and expressions

charity run

off the top of my head

recruiting process

1

- Read the instructions aloud. Ask students to discuss the photo with a partner.
- Ask students to tell you what they think the people are doing. Elicit that they are having a brainstorming meeting to share ideas for the company.

2 1.17

- Read the instructions aloud and ask a student to read the questions aloud.
- Before you play the audio, ask students to predict some words or phrases they might hear in the audio that might help them answer the questions. For example, for question **a** *Are they discussing ideas from an earlier meeting?* students might hear *our last meeting, last week*, etc.
- Play the audio and ask students to circle their answers.
- Ask students to compare answers with a partner. Then go over the answers with the whole class.
- To finish, ask for a volunteer to tell you the two recruiting ideas the group discusses (a TV commercial, the company website).

> ***Answers***
>
> **a** No, they aren't.
>
> **b** Yes, they do.
>
> **c** Yes, she does.

3 1.17

- Before you play the audio, ask students to read the passage silently and predict the missing words. Elicit ideas from several students.

- Read the instructions aloud. Then play the audio once or twice as needed, and ask students to complete the passage.
- To check answers, ask students to read the conversation aloud, inserting the correct information.

> ***Answers***
>
> do you think, I'm not sure, come back to, maybe we could, What do you think

- Highlight the useful expressions in the conversation for making suggestions (*what do you think about; why don't we; [maybe] we could*). Ask students to underline these expressions in the conversation.
- Put students into groups of four to practise reading the conversation. Walk around the class as students work, listening in and offering help as needed. Remind students to take turns.
- When students are comfortable with the conversation, ask them to close their book and try the conversation in their own words. For lower-level classes, write the following prompts on the board to help students:

Sasha: *Suggest a TV commercial.*

Helena: *Disagree with Sasha's idea. Tell her why. Ask for the others' opinions.*

Ken: *Suggest the group discuss the idea later. Ask for other ideas.*

Joe: *Suggest the company website.*

Sasha: *Agree with Joe's idea. Suggest that people email them.*

Joe: *Agree with Sasha's idea.*

Helena: *Agree with Joe's idea. Ask for Ken's opinion.*

Ken: *Say that you agree.*

4

- Ask students to stay in their groups from Exercise 3. Read the instructions aloud. Go over any unfamiliar vocabulary.
- Ask students to practise the conversation, inserting the new information. Ask students to sit in a circle, if possible, and remind them to make eye contact.

5 **1.18**

- Read the instructions. Ask for volunteers to read the answer choices aloud. Elicit a few guesses from the class.
- Make sure students understand that they can choose more than one answer.
- Play the audio and ask students to check their guesses. Then go over the answers with the class.

> ***Answers***
>
> **b** Let's move on to the next topic.
>
> **c** Shall we have a break now?

- To finish, ask for volunteers to tell you what the group decides to do (continue working / take a break later).

Teaching tip

Brainstorming: The concept of brainstorming ideas with a group may be unfamiliar to students. Brainstorming is a useful skill to teach students as it is one they can use for making decisions and solving problems both in and outside of class. Here are some basic rules you can introduce for effective group brainstorming:

1 Choose a group member to write down ideas.

2 Begin sharing ideas.
Everyone should participate.
All ideas are written down.
There are no wrong or bad ideas.
Generate as many ideas as possible.

3 When the group finishes, read the list of ideas silently.

4 Select a short list of the best ideas to discuss further.

5 Discuss the short list and choose the best idea(s).

Meetings and discussions:
Agreeing and disagreeing p25

Vocabulary and expressions

cable
font size
overtime work

1 **1.19**

- To lead in, ask students to keep their Student's Books closed. Ask the class to brainstorm some ways that companies can reduce their costs, and write students' ideas on the board. For example, recycling, downsizing staff and office space, etc.
- Student's Books still closed, play the audio once and ask students to just listen for the staff's suggestions. Elicit responses from several students.
- Ask students to open their books. Read the instructions aloud. Explain or elicit an explanation for *intonation* (the way [or tone] in which you say something, which expresses how you feel). Make sure students understand that a strong response is more direct, while a weak response is more indirect.
- Ask students to read the staff suggestions aloud. Go over any unfamiliar vocabulary.
- Play the audio and ask students to complete Jim's responses.

2

- Play the audio again. Then ask students to decide whether each response is strong or weak.
- Ask students to compare answers with a partner before you go over the answers with the class.

Answers

a That's possible, I guess. (W)

b Um, no, we can't do that. (S)

c That's a good idea. (S)

d Mm, I'm not sure about that. (W)

e That's a great idea! (S)

- For additional practice with intonation, say Jim's responses aloud using the appropriate intonation, and ask students to repeat them after you. Alternatively, play the audio again, pausing after Jim's responses, and ask students to try to repeat with the same intonation.

3

- Read the instructions aloud. Explain that students should fill in the table with the expressions from Exercise 1. The left column is for positive expressions (agreeing), and the right column is for negative expressions (disagreeing). Pairs should discuss whether the expressions are strong or weak, and write their lists from strongest to weakest (top to bottom).
- To check answers, copy the table onto the board. Then ask for volunteers to come to the board and write the expressions in the correct columns / locations.

Answers

	Positive	Negative
Strong	I agree. Excellent!	No, that's a bad idea.
	That's a great idea!	**No, we can't do that.**
	I like that idea.	I don't think that's a good idea.
	That's a good idea.	I'm not sure that will work.
Weak	**That's possible, I guess.**	**I'm not sure about that.**
	We could do that, I guess.	

- For higher-level classes, introduce some other expressions for agreeing and disagreeing, and ask students to discuss where they would place them in the table. For example:

Agreeing	**Disagreeing**
I think so, too.	*I don't think so.*
Yes. That might work.	*No. That won't work.*
That's an excellent suggestion.	*Definitely not.*
That's a possibility.	*I'm not sure that's a good idea.*
That's not a bad idea.	*That's a bad idea.*

4 1.20

- Remind students about the expressions they learnt in Unit 2 for making suggestions (*Why don't we …; We could …; How about …*).
- Read the instructions aloud. Then play the audio once or twice and ask students to mark their answers. For lower-level classes, play the audio for each item one at a time, checking answers in-between.
- Ask students to compare answers with a partner. Then go over the answers with the whole class.

Answers

a strong **b** strong **c** weak **d** weak

5

- Elicit the expressions students learnt in Unit 2 for making suggestions, and write them on the board (*Why don't we …; We could …; How about …*).
- Read the instructions aloud. Then ask students to form pairs to practise the suggestions and responses from Exercise 2. Encourage them to use their own words, and remind them that they can change their responses. Walk around the class as students work, listening in and checking that students are using the appropriate intonation.
- For additional practice, ask pairs to combine to form groups of four. Tell students to roleplay the meeting with one student in the group playing the role of Jim, and the others playing the role of the employees. Ask them to change roles, so that everyone has a chance to play the role of Jim.

6

- Read the instructions aloud. Ask students to read the list of questions aloud.
- Do the first example with the whole class. Elicit suggestions from several volunteers and model a variety of responses from the previous exercises (*That's a great idea; I'm not sure about that,* etc.).
- Put students into groups of three to practise making and responding to suggestions. For lower-level classes, tell students they can use the pictures on page 25 if they need ideas for suggestions.

Photocopiable activity

p97

Who agrees?

1 Prepare one copy of *Who agrees?* for each student.
2 Explain to students that they will need to talk to every student in the class to see whether they agree or disagree with the ten ideas. Then they can judge whether the statements about the ideas are true or false. Point out that they can use the space under each idea to keep a tally of those who agree and those who disagree.
3 If necessary, ask students to brainstorm phrases for agreeing and disagreeing (or check page 25 in their books) and write those on the board.
4 Ask all of the students to stand up and circulate, asking their classmates if they agree or disagree with the ideas. They do not need to ask about each idea in order.
5 End the activity either after a certain time limit, such as 15 or 20 minutes, or after one student has answered T or F for all ten ideas. Check answers with the whole class by reading each idea and asking the whole class to raise their hand to show whether they agree or disagree.

Meetings and discussions:

Moving through a meeting p26

Vocabulary and expressions

running out of time
short of time

Culture note

Leading a group brainstorming meeting may seem daunting for students. Here are some useful group meeting-facilitation tips:

- **Be well prepared.**
  Make sure you have enough handouts for everyone.
  Arrive early and check that all audio-visual equipment works.
  Prepare an agenda and write it on a board or flip chart.
  Know the aims of the meeting well, so you can keep the discussion focused.
- **Stick to the agenda.**
  Keep the discussion focused on the meeting aims.
  Don't allow group members to interrupt each other.
  Allow group members to debate. Listen. You may hear some useful ideas.
- **Try to include everyone in the discussion.**
  At the beginning of the meeting, encourage everyone to offer their ideas.
- **Keep a record of ideas that everyone can see.**
  In addition to keeping regular meeting notes, write down people's ideas on the board or on a flip chart.
  Use the list to get the group to choose the best ideas. Type up final decisions and distribute them after the meeting.
- **Close the meeting with a summary and action points.**
  Summarise what the group has decided.
  Assign next steps and ask for volunteers to complete them by a certain date.

1

- Before you begin this exercise, review some of the language students have learnt in the course so far. Tell students to keep their Student's Books closed. Ask *What are some expressions you've learnt for beginning and closing meetings?* Ask for volunteers to write their ideas on the board. For example:

Beginning	**Ending**
Let's get started.	*OK. To sum up …*
My subject today is …	*Let's summarise our decisions so far.*
We need to discuss …	

- Tell students that now they are going to learn some useful expressions for leading that main part of a meeting.
- Read the instructions aloud. Explain that the information on the board shows Omar's brainstorm for expressions he can use when leading a meeting.
- Point out the example. Then put students with a partner and ask them to draw lines to connect the rest of the expressions to the situations. Make sure students understand that there is more than one expression for each situation.
- When students finish, check answers by reading each situation aloud and asking for volunteers to tell you the matching expressions.
- For lower-level classes, do some fluency and intonation work by asking students to repeat the phrases after you and then practise them with a partner.

Answers

... to start a meeting:
Is everybody here?; Let's get started.

... to focus the discussion:
Let's focus on ...
We need to decide ...; We have to discuss ...;

... to change the topic:
Let's move on to ...; Can we come back to this later?

... if the discussion is too slow or takes too much time:
We are running out of time here; We're short of time;

... to take a break:
Shall we take a short break?

... if someone hasn't spoken:
We haven't heard from (Peter) yet.

... to ask for opinions:
What do you think, (Amy)?;

... to ask if people agree:
Does everyone agree?

... to end a meeting:
OK. To sum up (we agreed ...); Let me summarise (today's meeting); I think that's everything. Thank you.

2 1.21

- Read the instructions aloud. Then give students time to write the phrases in the game board. Make sure they understand that they need to write the phrases in random order.
- When students finish, check that all students understand the instructions for the game. Ask a higher-level student to explain the instructions to the class in his or her own words. Some students may feel shy shouting *Bingo!*, so you may want to tell them that they can raise their hands instead.
- Play the audio and ask students to tick the phrases they hear.
- When a student wins, ask him or her to call out the phrases he or she has ticked and confirm that they are correct.

Answers

Is everybody here?
Let's get started.
As you know ...
We need to decide ...
Does anyone have any ideas?
What do you think, Taki?
Can I say something?
Let's focus on ...
We're short of time.
Let's move on to ...
We haven't heard from you yet, Martha.
Can we come back to this later?
I think we should talk about ...
That's a difficult question.
It's difficult to explain, but ...
We are running out of time here,
Let me summarise ...
Is there anything else?
Thank you for your time today.

3

- Tell students they are going to have a chance to practise leading meetings using the phrases from Exercises 1 and 2.
- Introduce the three meeting topics and give students time to think of some suggestions individually. Encourage lower-level classes to write down their ideas.
- Ask students to form groups of three, and tell groups to choose a leader for the first topic. Remind students of the leader's responsibilities, which are:
  - to start the meeting
  - to ask for and respond to people's opinions and suggestions
  - to keep the meeting moving and make sure all topics are discussed
  - to close the meeting.
- Give students a 10-minute time limit for their meetings. Walk around the class, listening in and making sure students are using the target phrases correctly.
- When the time is up, have the leader from each group summarise the group's decisions.
- Ask groups to change roles for each topic so that all students have a chance to lead a meeting.

Viewpoints:
Meeting styles p28

Vocabulary and expressions

advantages
ceremony
disadvantages
face-to-face communication
freely
in a higher position
punctuality
suitable

1

- Tell students they are going to discuss meeting styles in different cultures. Ask them to think about any situations when they have participated in a meeting, for example, a staff meeting for a part-time job, a planning meeting for a school event, etc. Elicit responses from a few volunteers.
- Ask students to form groups of three or four. Read the instructions and the discussion questions aloud.

- Give students about ten minutes for their discussions. Remind them to say whether they agree or disagree with their classmates' opinions.
- Volunteers share their responses. If you have a multicultural class, elicit some similarities and differences between meeting styles in students' home cultures.

2 1.22

- Read the instructions aloud. Students read the statements aloud. Go over any unfamiliar vocabulary.
- You can do the pre-listening as a whole-class activity. Volunteers say which speaker they think made the statement and why. Alternatively, students work individually and then compare answers with a partner. Tell students that they can use any background information they may have learnt (or heard) about Korean or American business culture.
- Play the audio once or twice as needed.
- Ask students to compare answers with a partner. Then go over the answers with the whole class.

Answers

a Stefan	**c** Stefan	**e** Stefan	**g** Jun-ha
b Jun-ha	**d** Jun-ha	**f** Stefan	**h** Jun-ha

3

- Read the instructions aloud. Give students time to read the discussion questions.
- Ask students to work individually or form groups of three or four to write their answers to the questions.
- When groups finish, volunteers share their responses and lead a brief class discussion about each topic.
- Ask students to complete the matching task on page 4 in respect of Jun-ha Kim.

Answers

Jun-ha Kim = f

In business:
A French hypermarket p29

Vocabulary and expressions

campaign
hypermarket
luxury
multiplex
units

- Before you begin this lesson, read the two sets of In business task activity instructions, so that you can be prepared to answer students' questions.

Scenario

- Ask a student to read the *Scenario* aloud for the class. Make sure students understand the concept of a *hypermarket* (a very large shopping complex that combines a supermarket and a department store).

Task 1

- Divide the class in half. Tell each group to look at the appropriate page in their Student's Books (Group A – page 86; Group B – page 95).
- Give groups time to read the instructions. Remind students that they will need to use the expressions they have learnt for leading and participating in meetings, as well as for giving and responding to suggestions and opinions. Walk around the class as students work, helping to clarify instructions as necessary.

Task 2

- Ask students to form groups of three or four, staying within their planning groups (A and B).
- Tell them to imagine that they are attending an important planning meeting. Ask each group to choose a leader.
- For lower-level classes, give students additional time to prepare notes to use during the meeting.
- Set a timer for 10 minutes. Ask the leaders to begin the meeting. If supplies are available, give each group a piece of poster paper and markers, so that the leader can list the group's brainstorming ideas. As this activity is designed as a fun roleplay, you may want to walk around and just listen in, but do not offer comments or suggestions during students' discussions.

Task 3

- Read the instructions aloud.
- Ask students to form new groups of three of four, still within their same planning group (A or B). Tell each group to choose two leaders.
- Give students 15 minutes to complete both meetings. Remind them that the aim of the first meeting is to share ideas, and the aim of the second is to make final decisions. You may want to give groups a limit as to how many 'best' ideas they can choose.

Task 4

- Read the instructions aloud.
- Ask students to form groups of four. Groups should have two members from Group A (who worked together in Task 3), and two members from Group B (who worked together in Task 3). Tell each group to choose a leader, and to choose one or two of Group A's and Group B's ideas to present to the class.
- Give groups about ten minutes for their discussions.

Follow-up

- Read the instructions aloud.
- Ask groups to take turns presenting their ideas. Ask for a volunteer to be the 'meeting secretary' and to come to the board and list each group's ideas.
- When all groups have finished, ask the class to decide whether they should make their decision by consensus or vote. Ask them to use the chosen method to decide on the best three ideas from Groups A and B.
- Ask students to complete the Review of Units 1–4 on pages 30 and 31 of the Student's Book.

I'll call you back

5

Unit aims

In Unit 5, students learn about:

- Leaving messages
- Telephoning: Using voicemail, Taking / leaving a message
- Viewpoints: Automated voicemail
- In business: Teleconference guidelines

The aims for each class can be written on the board to orient students to the unit content and objectives.

Getting started

Begin this unit by reviewing the expressions students learnt in Unit 4 for leading business meetings.

- Before class, write ten to twelve of the phrases on the board with the words scrambled in random order. For example:

  running here are out time we of
  (*We are running out of time here.*)

  today for you coming thank
  (*Thank you for coming today.*)
- As students enter the room, tell them to work individually to write the correct expressions.
- Ask students to compare answers with a partner. Then ask for volunteers to say the correct expressions while you write them on the board.

Listen and practise:
Leaving messages p32

Vocabulary and expressions

sales figures

1

- Read the instructions aloud. Ask students to discuss the photos with a partner.
- Ask students to tell you what they think is happening.
- To preview the unit language and check students' background knowledge of the topic of telephoning, ask the class to guess what the caller is saying. Try to elicit some phrases students know for telephoning and write them on the board, for example, *May I speak to …*, *This is …*, etc.

2 1.25

- Read the instructions aloud and ask a student to read the answer choices aloud.
- Before you play the audio, ask students to predict what they might hear in the audio that might help them answer the questions. For example, for answer choice **a**, *Melike answers the phone*, students might hear, *Hello, this is Melike. Can I help you?* For answer choice **b**, *Melike will call Linda back*, they might hear an answering machine's message *please leave a message*, etc.
- Play the audio and ask students to write T for true or F for false.
- Ask students to compare answers with a partner. Then go over the answers with the whole class.
- To finish, ask for a volunteer to tell you what message Linda leaves for Melike. (Linda will be in Istanbul next month.)

> ***Answers***
> **a** F **b** F

3 1.25

- Before you play the audio, ask students to work with a partner to predict the missing words. Ask pairs to read the conversation aloud, inserting their own words in the blanks.
- Read the instructions aloud. Then play the audio once or twice as needed, and ask students to complete the conversation.
- To check answers, ask students to read the conversation aloud, inserting the correct information.

> ***Answers***
> Thank you for calling, as soon as I can, I'm calling, Can you call me

- Put students with a partner to practise reading the conversation. To better simulate a telephone conversation, ask them to sit back-to-back. Encourage them to roleplay the scenario, including Linda's dialling the telephone. To start students off, ask the *Linda* students to dial the telephone and then say *Ring, ring!* Walk around the class as students work, listening in and offering help as needed. Remind students to take turns.
- When students are comfortable with the conversation, ask them to try the conversation without looking at their Student's Books. Encourage them to use the look-remember-speak technique. (Students look in their books, try to remember as much as they can of the text [one or two sentences], and then speak without looking at their books.)
- Ask students to change partners several times to maximise the practice.

4

- Ask students to form pairs. Read the instructions aloud. Go over any unfamiliar vocabulary.
- Ask pairs to practise the conversation in Exercise 3, inserting the first set of new information in Exercise 4. Then ask them to change roles.
- To maximise students' practice, set up two rows of chairs back-to-back (if possible), and ask students to sit back-to-back with their partner. Assign one row the role of Linda, and the other row the role of Melike. Then ask them to practise the conversation.
- When students finish the first conversation, have the students in the *Linda* row stand and move down one seat to the right, so that they are seated back-to-back with a new partner. The student at the end of the row walks up to sit in the first seat.
- Ask students to practise the conversation again, inserting the second set of new information. Continue until students have completed the conversation with all four sets of information. Then ask students to change roles, and repeat the steps above.

5 1.26

- Ask a student to read the instructions and the answer choices aloud. Elicit a few guesses from the class.
- Make sure students understand that they can choose more than one answer.
- Play the audio and ask students to check their guesses. Then go over the answers with the class.

Answers

a I'll be in the office until five o'clock.

c My number is ...

Telephoning:
Using voicemail p33

Vocabulary and expressions

beep
finance
give me a ring
publishing
sales data
tone
urgent

1 1.27

- Tell students they are going to hear some of Melike's other messages.
- Go over the message notes, and ask for volunteers to predict the content of some of the messages based on the notes.
- Play the audio once or twice and ask students to tick the correct box and add notes, if needed.
- Ask students to compare answers with a partner. Then go over the answers with the whole class.

Answers

a Pls call back; note: before lunch
b Pls call back; note: number is 206-555-7324
c Will call you back
d Pls call back; note: returning your call, cell phone: 070-5732-4565
e Will call you back; note: will call tomorrow morning, free for lunch next week?
f Other: will send email; not urgent

- For higher-level classes, extend the practice by asking students to try to reconstruct the messages from their notes (in their own words). Ask for volunteers to roleplay leaving the messages.

2 1.28

- Before you begin this exercise, ask students to look back at the conversation in Exercise 3 on page 32. Ask them to look for the expression each speaker uses that refers to returning a call (Melike: *I'll call you back;* Linda: *Can you call me back?*).
- Ask students to read the expressions in the table aloud. For lower-level students, ask the class to repeat the expressions after you.
- Play the audio once or twice, and ask students to tick their answers.

Answers

a caller **b** receiver **c** receiver **d** receiver

- For additional listening practice, play the audio again, and ask students to listen for the expressions each speaker uses to either offer or request a return call.

3 1.29

- Read the instructions aloud. For lower-level classes, do the first item with the class first. Write the first line on the board *Hi, this is* ______. Then ask for volunteers to complete the conversation. For example:

  *Hi, Steve, this is*_____. *I'm calling about the sales meeting. Can you call me back before lunch?*

- Ask students to work with a partner. Play the audio one item at a time, and ask students to take turns saying their messages. For lower-level classes, play the audio one item at a time, pausing for students to write their messages. Then ask them to form pairs, play the audio again, and ask them to say their messages.
- To finish, play the audio one more time. Pause after each item and ask a student to say his or her message.

Answers

(Answers will vary. Below are possible answers.)

a *Hi, Yoshi, this is* student's name. *I'm calling about the sales meeting. Can you call me back before lunch?*

b *Hi, Tom, this is* student's name. *I'm calling to check your schedule. I'll call you back tomorrow.*

c *Hi, Michelle, this is* student's name. *I'm calling about my trip to Hong Kong. Please call me back. My number is 0965-443-2278.*

d *Hi, Jamir, this is* student's name. *I'm calling to confirm my flight reservation. Can I call you back tomorrow?*

- For additional practice, ask students to work with a partner to create and roleplay the follow-up phone call (when the caller speaks to the receiver) for each of the messages in Exercise 3.

Language notes

- The number zero (0) in phone numbers is often read as *oh*.
- When saying telephone numbers in English, the hyphen is not pronounced. Instead, the speaker usually pauses between strings of numbers.

4

- To lead in, tell students to think about their own voicemail or answering machine recordings (or ones they have heard). Ask *What information does the message usually include?* (the receiver's name, phone number, the reason he or she is not available, etc.). *What does the message ask the caller to do?* (leave a name, message, telephone number, etc.). Elicit responses from several students.
- Read the instructions aloud.
- Ask students to form pairs, and give them about ten minutes to create their conversations. Walk around the class as students work, offering help as needed.
- When students finish, ask them to sit back-to-back to practise their conversations. Remind them to change roles.
- Ask students to change partners several times to maximise their practice.
- To finish, ask for volunteer pairs to present their conversations to the class.

Telephoning:
Taking / leaving a message
p34

1

- Read the instructions aloud. Ask students to read the phrases aloud.
- Make sure students understand that they should match the phrases that have similar meanings.
- Ask students to work individually to match the phrases. Walk around the class as students work, offering help as needed.
- Ask students to compare answers with a partner before you go over the answers with the whole class.

Answers

a 4
b 6
c 2
d 8
e 1
f 3
g 5
h 7

Extension activity

Concentration: Prepare several sets of 16 cards (one for every four students in the class) with the matching phrases from Exercise 1 written on them. Alternatively, ask students to make their own cards, divide the class into groups of four first. Then hand out 16 blank cards to each group and ask each student to complete four cards with phrases from Exercise 1 to make a full set.

- Tell groups to put their cards face down in random order. Students take turns choosing two cards. If they find a match (two phrases with similar meanings) they keep the cards and get another turn. If they don't make a match, it is the next player's turn.
- The player with the most matched cards in the end wins.
- Additional uses for the cards include the following:
  - Ask students to sort the phrases according to whether they are used by the caller or the receiver.
  - Play 'Snap'. One half of the card set is placed face-up. One student reads a phrase from the matching set aloud while the other students listen and try to be the first to put the correct matching card on the table.
  - Ask students to take turns reading the phrases aloud. Group members listen and try to say the matching phrase from memory.

2 1.30

- Ask students to look at the picture. Elicit some ideas about who the man is, what he is doing, and how he feels.
- Read the instructions aloud. Make sure students understand that they need to listen for and circle specific phrases in Exercise 1.
- Play the audio once or twice as necessary.
- To check answers, ask students to tell you the phrases they circled.

Answers

Can I speak to ... please?

Can I take a message?

Can you give her a message?

Please ask (her) to call me back.

Let me repeat that. That's ..., right?

I'll give (him) your message.

Can you tell me your name?

- For additional practice, hand out a copy of the audio script for Exercise 2 (see Teacher's Guide pages 115–116), and ask students to practise the conversation with a partner, changing partners several times. Highlight additional useful language for telephoning presented in the conversation. (*Just a moment, please.; I'm afraid ... is not here right now.; Please tell her ... called.; Can you repeat your number?; Thank you for your call.*)

3

- Read the instructions aloud. Explain that students are now going to learn some more useful phrases for leaving telephone messages. Ask for volunteers to read the phrases in the table aloud. For lower-level classes, ask students to repeat the phrases after you.
- Model the task by reading the example conversation with a student, inserting your own name and message. Alternatively, ask two students to model the conversation.
- Ask students to form pairs and sit back-to-back to practise the conversation. Remind them to change roles.
- When students finish, check their grasp of the new language: ask them to close their books, and then walk around the room, beginning the conversation and prompting students to complete the B role. If students need more practice, ask them to form new pairs and practise the conversation several more times.

4

- Read the instructions aloud. Give students time to read the prompts in the conversation map. Encourage lower-level students to make some notes if necessary.
- Make sure students understand the task. Model the first few lines with a student.
- Put students with a partner to practise. Ask them to decide who will be the caller and who will be the receptionist first. Give the callers time to write down a fake name and phone number to use. For lower-level classes, ask students to write out the dialogue before they practise it.
- Walk around the class as students work, listening in and offering help as needed.
- To finish, ask several pairs of students to stand back-to-back and perform the conversation for the class.

5

- Read the instructions aloud.
- Ask students to form pairs and practise their own telephone conversations.
- For additional practice, do this activity with the whole class. Assign half the class the role of caller, and the other half the role of receiver.
- Ask students to stand, walk around the class, and find a partner. The caller should begin the conversation by saying *Ring, ring*. When a pair finishes the conversation, they should walk around and find new partners.
- Ask students to change partners several times. Then have the groups change roles, and continue the process several more times.

Photocopiable activity

p98

Telephone conversations

1. Prepare enough copies of *Telephone conversations* so that each student can have one card. If you have more than 20 students in your class, it's OK for some pairs of students to have the same cards. (Note: If you have an odd number of students, one student will have a card that has no match. In that case, take the corresponding card yourself.)
2. Give each student a card. Explain that they have one side of the beginning of a telephone conversation. They will circulate about the class to find the person who has the other side of their conversation. Student A will read a line first, and then Student B will read the first line of his or her conversation. If it makes sense, A will read the next line, and B will read the next line. Then together they should continue the conversation by inventing information. If B's first or second line does not logically follow A's, then the pair should split and circulate again to find the correct match. (Note: There are two first B lines that will match each first A line, but only one correct match for each conversation.)
3. After students have all found their match, ask pairs or volunteers to perform their extended conversations for the class.
4. Higher-level classes can memorise the lines on their cards.

Viewpoints: Automated voicemail p36

Vocabulary and expressions

instant messaging
teleconference
web-conference

1

- Explain or elicit the meaning of *automated* (operated by machines, rather than by humans). Ask the class for some examples of automated services that they use, for example, cash machines, checkouts at some supermarkets, telephone information lines, etc. Tell students they are going to discuss the advantages and disadvantages of automated voicemail and other modern methods of communication.
- Read the instructions and the discussion questions aloud.
- Ask students to form groups of three or four to discuss the questions. Elicit responses from several students. Alternatively, have the discussion with the whole class.

2 1.31

- Read the instructions aloud. Make sure students understand that they should draw lines to show the route where Andrew's call is directed.
- Play the audio once or twice and ask students to mark their answers.
- Ask students to compare answers with a partner. Then go over the answers with the whole class.

> ***Answers***
> Main menu, Reservations (Make), International, Main menu, Reservations (Change), Today, Operator.

- To finish, ask the class *How do you think Andrew feels?* (frustrated, angry, etc.). To review the language students have learnt in this course for making suggestions, lead a brief class discussion and ask students to suggest what they think Andrew should do.

3

- Ask pairs to combine to form groups of four.
- Read the instructions and the discussion questions aloud.
- Give groups about ten minutes for their discussions. Then lead a brief class discussion and ask for volunteers to share their responses to each of the questions.

Extension activity

Board meeting: Tell students to imagine that they are the board of directors of a large company. Currently their customer service is operated by a staff of over 200 telephone operators. The company needs to make some budget cuts, so the board needs to decide whether to continue the customer service in this way, or cut staff and move to an automated voicemail system.

- Divide the class into groups of six to eight students for their meetings, and tell groups to choose a chairperson. Remind students to use the meeting strategies they learnt in Unit 4.
- When groups finish their discussions, ask the board chairs to summarise the groups' decisions.

4

- Ask students to form pairs.
- Read the instructions aloud. Elicit a description or an explanation for each method of communication. Ask students which methods they have used. Ask a student to read the questions aloud.
- Give the pairs about ten minutes for their discussions. Walk around the class as students work, listening in and offering help as needed.
- When students finish, ask them to join another pair and share their ideas. Tell students to explain the reasons for their decisions and how they reached them.
- To finish, hold a class poll to decide the best method(s) for global business communication.

In business: Teleconference guidelines p37

Vocabulary and expressions

the bottom line
confidential
internal
technical problems

- Before you begin this lesson, read the three sets of In business task activity instructions, so that you can be prepared to answer students' questions.

Scenario

- Ask a student to read the *Scenario* aloud for the class.

Task 1

- Divide the class into three groups (A, B and C).
- Tell each group to look at the appropriate page in their Student's Books (Group A – page 96; Group B – page 104; Group C – page 109).
- Give groups time to read the comments. Walk around the class as students work, helping to clarify instructions as necessary.

Task 2

- Ask students to form groups of three or four, staying within their planning groups (A, B and C).
- Tell them to imagine that they are attending an important planning meeting. Ask each group to choose a leader.
- For lower-level classes, give students additional time to prepare notes to use during the meeting.
- Set a timer for ten minutes, and have the leaders begin the meeting. If supplies are available, give each group a piece of poster paper and markers, so that the leader can write a summary of the issues, and the group's suggestions for improvements.

Task 3

- Read the instructions aloud.
- Ask students to form new groups of three or four. Groups should include one member from each group (A, B and C). Tell each group to choose a leader to start the meeting, summarise the issues, make sure that all members have a chance to participate, and summarise the meeting at the end.
- Give students about 15 minutes to share their ideas. Encourage students to offer additional suggestions to other groups. If supplies are available, hand out poster paper and markers and have groups make a summary poster to present to the class in the *Follow-up*.

Follow-up

- Ask groups to take turns presenting their ideas. Ask for a volunteer to be the 'meeting secretary' and to come to the board and list each group's ideas.
- When all groups have finished, ask the class to decide whether they should make their decision by consensus or vote. Then ask them to use the chosen method to decide on the best five ideas.

Can I get there on foot? 6

Unit aims

In Unit 6, students learn about:

- Checking in
- Asking for information
- Giving directions
- Non-verbal communication: Understanding gestures
- Viewpoints: Non-verbal communication
- In business: Explaining body language

The aims for each class can be written on the board to orient students to the unit content and objectives.

Getting started

Begin this unit by reviewing the expressions students learnt in Unit 5 for taking and leaving telephone messages.

On the board, write several partial telephone conversations for students to practise with a partner. Leave blanks for the key phrases students learnt. For example:

Receptionist: *Hello. Smith Construction.* ___________?

Caller: *Hello,* ______________ *Fred Wesson, please?*

Receptionist: _____________. *Mr Wesson is out of the office. Would you* _________________?

Caller: *Yes, please.* ____________________.

Receptionist: ____________________.

Caller: ____________________.

Give students time to look over the conversation and think about the missing words and phrases. Then put students with a partner and ask them to practise the conversations, inserting their own words. To finish, ask for volunteer pairs to perform the conversations for the class.

Listen and practise: Checking in p38

Vocabulary and expressions

deluxe suite

dormitory room

Is it walking distance?

on foot

single room

1

- Read the instructions aloud.
- To lead in, put students with a partner. Ask pairs to look at the photos. Explain that pairs should discuss what they think is happening in each of the photos. Then choose one photo and create a mini-dialogue between the two people. Give pairs time to complete the task. Walk around the class as students work, offering help as needed. Tell pairs to practise their dialogues, roleplaying the two characters.
- When students finish, ask pairs to stand and perform their dialogue roleplays for the class.

2 1.32

- Read the instructions aloud.
- Before you play the audio, ask students to predict what they might hear in the audio that might help them choose the correct picture. For example, for picture **a**, students might hear *Please could you fill in this form, Sir?* For picture **b**, they might hear *This is your room*, etc.
- Play the audio and ask students to mark their answers.
- Ask pairs to compare answers with a partner. Then elicit the answer from the class.

Answer

a

3 1.32

- Before you play the audio, ask students to work with a partner to predict the missing words. Ask pairs to read the conversation aloud, inserting their own words in the blanks.
- Read the instructions aloud. Then play the audio once or twice as needed, and ask students to complete the conversation.
- To check answers, ask students to read the conversation aloud, inserting the correct information.

Answers

reservation, under, confirmation number, someone else, company, five nights, credit card, anything else, Could you

- Put students with a partner to practise reading the conversation. Ask them to change roles a few times.
- When students are comfortable with the conversation, ask them to try the conversation without looking at their Student's Books. Encourage them to use the look-remember-speak technique. (Students look in their books, try to remember as much as they can of the text [one or two sentences], and then speak without looking at their books.)
- Ask students to change partners several times to maximise the practice.

4

- Ask students to stay with a partner. Read the instructions aloud. Go over the pronunciation of the names and explain any unfamiliar vocabulary.
- Ask pairs to practise the conversation in Exercise 3, inserting the first set of new information in Exercise 4. Ask pairs to change roles once. Then ask them to change partners and practise the conversation, inserting the second set of information.
- Repeat until students have completed the conversation with all four sets of information.

5 1.33

- Ask a student to read the instructions and the questions aloud. Elicit a few guesses from the class as to who might ask each question.
- Play the audio and ask students to check their guesses. Then go over the answers with the class.

Answers

	Receptionist	John
How much money do you want to spend?		
Can you drive me there?		
Where do you usually eat?		
What kind of food do you like?	✓	
Is it within walking distance?		✓
Are you going to go by yourself?		

Asking for information p39

1 1.34

- Before you begin this exercise, ask students to imagine that they are visiting an English-speaking city and they need to exchange some money at the bank. Ask *How will you find out how to get to the bank?* Try to elicit some language students already know for asking for directions, for example, (*Excuse me.*) *Where is the bank?; Where can I find a bank?; Can / Could you tell me where the bank is?*, etc.
- Tell students they are going to learn some useful phrases for asking for information politely.
- Read the instructions aloud. Then ask a student to read the questions aloud.
- Explain that indirect questions – those beginning with *Can / Could you tell me …*, or *Do you know …* – have a more polite tone than direct questions. Ask students for examples of situations when it would be better to use an indirect question, for example, when asking a stranger for information, when speaking to someone to whom you want to show respect (someone older or in a higher professional position), etc.
- Go over the first two examples. Be sure to point out that in the direct questions, the subject and verb are inverted. However, indirect questions follow subject-verb order.
- Give students time to write their indirect questions. Walk around the class as students work, offering help as necessary.
- Play the audio and ask students to check their answers. Then ask for volunteers to write the answers on the board. Ask the class to make any necessary corrections to the answers on the board.

Answers

a Do you know where the bank is?
b Can you tell me what time it is?
c Could you tell me who that man is?
d Do you know what building this is?
e Do you know how much tickets are?
f Can you tell me where the nearest bus stop is?

Language note

Polite requests: For higher-level classes, you can expand students' language skills by introducing the following additional phrases for making polite requests:

I was wondering if you could tell me where …?
Could you please direct me to …?
Excuse me. Where can I find …?
Would you happen to know where …?

Extension activity

Intonation practice: Go over the up-down-up intonation pattern of indirect questions with students. Write the following sentences on the board (with the arrows) and ask students to repeat them after you until they are comfortable with the pattern.

Do you know ↗ where the bank ↘ is ↗?
Could you ↗ tell me what time ↘ it is ↗?

Then ask them to practise with the questions below.

Can you tell me who the Manager is?
Do you know where the sales office is?
Could you tell me how much the tickets are?
Can you show me where the women's department is?
Do you know how many offices the company has?

2

- Read the instructions aloud.
- Ask students to look at the cartoon. Ask for volunteers to describe what is happening in the cartoon.
- Put students with a partner to write their conversation. Remind students to use indirect questions. For lower-level classes, ask the class to brainstorm some possible words or phrases to include in the conversation, and write them on the board for students' reference.
- Walk around the class as students work, helping with grammar, vocabulary and ideas as needed.
- When pairs finish, ask them to practise their conversation a few times. Then ask pairs to form groups of four to perform their conversation.
- To finish, ask for volunteer pairs to perform their conversation for the class.

Giving directions p40

Vocabulary and expressions

corner

1

- Read the instructions aloud. Explain – or elicit an explanation for – *location* (a description of a place) and *direction* (instructions for how to get to a place).
- Ask students to read the list of locations / directions aloud. Then ask students to work alone or with a partner to match them to the pictures.
- Ask students to compare answers with a partner. Then go over the answers with the whole class.

Answers

a 3, location
b 4, location
c 2, location
d 9, direction
e 6, direction
f 5, location
g 1, location
h 8, direction
i 10, direction
j 7, direction

2 1.35

- Before you begin this exercise, ask students to look at the map. To review the phrases for describing location from Exercise 1, ask several students to describe the location of various places on the map. For example, ask *Where is the aquarium?*
- Read the instructions aloud. Ask students to use a pen or pencil to point to the corner on the map where Sandra is standing. Make sure students understand that they will not hear the names of the places on the map, so they must listen carefully to the directions.
- Play the audio once or twice as needed. Encourage students to follow the directions with their pen or pencil as they listen.
- Ask students to compare answers with a partner. Then go over the answers with the whole class.

Answers

1 Pike Place Market
2 Nordstrom
3 Wild Ginger restaurant
4 Pharmacy

- For additional practice, play the audio again, and ask students to write down the phrases Sandra uses to ask for information:

  Could you tell me how to get to …?

  Excuse me, do you know where … is?

  I'm trying to find the … Do you know where it is?

  Is there a … near here?

  Hand out a copy of the audio script (see Teacher's Book, page 117) to each student. Ask students to practise the conversations with a partner.

3

- Read the instructions aloud. Ask students to point to Macy's on the map.
- Model the task with a student, beginning the conversation with the prompts provided. Continue the conversation to model the full exchange.
- Ask students to form pairs to practise asking for and giving directions. Alternatively, ask the whole class to stand with their Student's Books, and ask them to walk around the class and ask at least three people for directions to different places on the map.

Photocopiable activity pp99–100

Dinner at the Golden Pagoda

1 Divide students into pairs, A and B. Prepare enough photocopies so that each student A has a copy of the A sheet and each student B has a copy of the B sheet.

2 Explain to the whole class that A and B each have some places to go and things to do. They will take turns telling their partner what they want to do, where they want to go, and how to get there. Every student starts at the train station.

3 Each student will trace the route that they 'walk' on the map, and write in the names of the buildings their partner guides them to. At the end, they should arrive together at the Golden Pagoda restaurant to have dinner together.

4 Make sure that each student has a pencil or pen to mark the walking route and label the buildings. Ask student A to go first. Model or call on two students to model the first exchange, e.g.,

A: *I need to post a letter. Let's go to the post office.*

B: *Where is the post office?*

A: *Walk up one block, and then turn right …*

5 When pairs have finished, ask them to compare their maps and check to see that they arrived at the same place, having followed the same route. Ask them to discuss any directions that didn't work.

Non-verbal communication:
Understanding gestures p41

1 1.36

- To introduce the topic of body language and gestures, write a list of words, phrases and expressions on the board that are commonly expressed with gestures. For example:

  good

  bad

  Come here.

  Go away.

  money

  I don't know.

  I'm angry.

  I'm happy.

  Well done!

- Ask students *What gestures in your country have these meanings?*
- Elicit ideas from several pairs. You can do this as a whole-class game by asking for volunteers to stand and perform one of their gestures (without speaking). The rest of the class tries to guess the word or phrase from the board.
- Ask the class if anyone knows how British people use gestures to show the things on the board. Ask for volunteers to demonstrate any gestures they know.
- Read the instructions aloud. To preview the listening, elicit a few guesses for what the people in each picture are saying.
- Play the audio once or twice and ask students to number the pictures.
- Ask students to compare answers with a partner. Then go over the answers with the whole class.

Answers

a 4 **b** 1 **c** 6 **d** 3 **e** 5 **f** 2

Extension activity

Body language vocabulary: Students may not be familiar with the vocabulary for different types of gestures and body language. Here are some useful words and expressions for this unit:

shrug

nod

shake (hands, head)

raise (eyebrows, hands)

point

tilt (head)

wink

Viewpoints:
Non-verbal communication p42

1

- Explain or elicit the meaning of *non-verbal communication* (communicating without using words, for example, through body language, gestures, eye contact, etc.). Ask students to give some examples of common forms of non-verbal communication in their culture.
- Read the instructions aloud. Give students time to read the passages silently. Alternatively, ask students to read the passages aloud. For lower-level classes, you may want to read the passages aloud for the class after students read on their own.
- While students read, write the following comprehension sentences on the board:

  In China …

  it's polite to _________ to someone older. (bow)

  businessmen usually _______ when they meet. (shake hands)

  in cities, people usually don't ________ when they bump into someone. (apologise)

  young women sometimes __________ in public. (hold hands)

  men and women do not usually hold hands __________. (in public)

  In France …

  people stand _____ when they are talking. (close together)

  it's common to _________ when you meet friends and family. (kiss)

  business acquaintances shake hands _________ they see one another. (every time)

  shrugging your shoulders can mean ________. (several things)

- When students finish reading, ask them to close their books and complete the missing information on the board. Allow lower-level classes to refer to the reading passage if necessary.

- Go over the answers. Then lead a brief discussion about the reading. Ask students which practices described in the reading are common in their cultures.

Culture note

Students may wonder why standing close together is included as an example of non-verbal communication. Explain that different cultures have different perceptions about personal space. For example, in Latin American countries, it is common for people to stand close to each other when they are speaking, while in Scandinavia, people tend to stand quite far apart. Personal space is part of the way people in different cultures communicate.

2

- Read the instructions aloud. Then ask students to read the quiz statements aloud.
- Ask students to work with a partner to complete the quiz. Encourage them to make guesses when they don't know the answers.
- When pairs have finished the quiz, ask students to join another pair to compare answers.
- Go over the answers with the whole class.

Answers

a France	**d** Norway
b Egypt	**e** Turkey
c Thailand	

- To finish, lead a class discussion about how students arrived at their answers, and anything else they may know about non-verbal communication in the countries and cultures in the quiz. If you have a multicultural class, students share any examples of non-verbal communication from their cultures.

3

- Read the instructions aloud.
- Ask students to form groups of three or four to discuss the behaviours. Have groups assign a leader to keep the conversation moving and make sure all group members participate.
- When groups finish their discussions, ask for a volunteer from each group to share any interesting points from the group's discussion.

4

- Ask students to stay in their groups from Exercise 3.
- Read the instructions aloud. Then ask a student to read the list of words and phrases aloud.
- Give students time to think of gestures on their own. Then ask them to share their ideas. Encourage them to physically do the gestures as well as try to describe them verbally, e.g., *To say good, we give the thumbs up, like this.* Walk around the class offering help and ideas as needed.
- To finish, ask for volunteers to demonstrate and describe the gestures for the class.

Extension activity

Non-verbal communication rules: This activity is designed to help raise students' awareness of non-verbal communication practices in their own culture. Ask the class to brainstorm examples of non-verbal communication behaviours and write them on the board, for example, making eye-contact, shaking hands, bowing, standing close together, etc.

- Write the following on the board:

  People should / shouldn't …

  It's OK / It's not OK to …

  It's important / not important to …

  When people ______ , it means …

- Ask students to work with a partner to create a list of five non-verbal communication 'rules' for their culture.
- Ask pairs to combine to form groups of four. Pairs take turns acting out their rules one at a time, while the other pair watches and tries to guess the rule. For example, for *People should make eye contact.*, the pair could stand and act as though they are having a conversation, while making solid eye contact.

In business:
Explaining body language p43

Vocabulary and expressions

intercultural communication

- Before you begin this lesson, read the three sets of In business task activity instructions, so that you can be prepared to answer students' questions.

Scenario

- Ask a student to read the *Scenario* aloud for the class.

Task 1

- Divide the class into three groups (A, B and C).
- Tell each group to look at the appropriate page in their Student's Books (Group A – page 87; Group B – page 97; Group C – page 105).
- Give groups time to read the information. Walk around the class as students work, helping to clarify instructions as necessary.

Task 2

- Ask students to form groups of three or four, staying within their planning groups (A, B and C).
- Tell them to imagine that they are attending an important presentation-planning meeting. Explain that each group will become 'experts' on body language in their assigned country. Remind students that they will not be able to read the information, so in this meeting, they should do the following:
  - go through each bullet point in the body language and make sure they understand it

- make visual aids or notes to help them present the information
- review the presentation language on page 13 in their Student's Books.

- Encourage students to physically try out the gestures themselves, so that they have a better understanding of each one, and can demonstrate them during the presentation. If supplies are available, hand out poster paper and markers, so students can create drawings and/or notes to help them during the presentation.

Task 3

- Read the instructions aloud.
- Ask students to form new groups of three. Groups should include one member from each group (A, B and C).
- Allow about 20 minutes (about seven minutes per presenter) for the presentations. Encourage group members to ask each other questions. Walk around the class and listen to the presentations, noting any grammar or pronunciation issues to address later.

Follow-up

- Read the instructions aloud. Lead a whole-class discussion using the discussion questions provided.
- To finish, discuss the importance of learning about the customs of another culture before visiting, especially on business.

Best wishes, Thomas Kale 7

Unit aims

In Unit 7, students learn about:

- Understanding emails
- Writing emails
- Email expressions
- Email vocabulary
- Viewpoints: Email
- In business: Planning a meeting

The aims for each class can be written on the board to orient students to the unit content and objectives.

Getting started

Begin this unit by reviewing the expressions students learnt in Unit 6 for describing locations and giving directions. Draw a simple map on the board, for example:

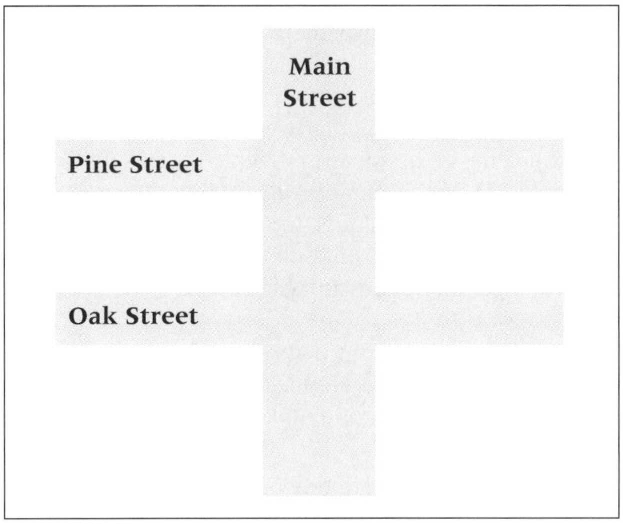

- When students come to class, tell them to draw *two copies* of the map in their notebook. On one map, they should draw the following buildings in any location they like: bank, post office, city library, Cream and Sugar café, police station, Don's Dry Cleaning, Miller's Market, Rick's Restaurant.
- When students finish creating their maps, put them with a partner. Explain that one student is on a business trip. He or she needs to ask the other student for directions to the places above, using the expressions they learnt in Unit 6 for asking for information.
- Students should listen to their partner's directions, asking for clarification when necessary, and draw the places on their *blank map*.
- When the first student has finished asking for directions and has drawn all of the buildings on the map, ask students to change roles.
- To finish, ask students to compare their maps, note any places where they are different, and discuss any misunderstandings they may have had with the directions.

Read and practise: Understanding emails p44

Vocabulary and expressions

abbreviation
attachments
Bcc
BTW
Cc
closing (of an email)
copy (someone on an email)
forward (an email)
jet lag
productive
update meeting

1

- Ask students to look at the reading text. Elicit that it is an email. Then ask them to scan quickly and tell you whether it is a business or a personal email (business), and ask for volunteers to tell you the words or phrases that gave them the clues (*met with the design team, Sales and Marketing, report,* etc.).
- Read the instructions aloud. Then ask a student to read the questions aloud.
- Give students time to scan the text for the answers. Ask them to underline or circle any information in the text that gives them the answers. Make sure students understand that the aim is to find the information as quickly as possible. For higher-level classes, give students a 20- or 30-second time limit to find the information.
- Go over the answers with the whole class.

Answers

a Thomas Kale
b Alfredo Giarchi
c yes
d formal

2

- Read the instructions aloud. Then ask students to

complete the email text. Remind students that one word will not be used.

- When students finish, check answers by asking students to read each line of the email, inserting the missing words. Correct pronunciation and intonation as necessary, and go over any unfamiliar vocabulary.

> ***Answers***
> office, Attached, forward, copy, meeting

- Put students with a partner to take turns reading the email aloud.

Teaching tip

Improving reading skills: Students at this level may benefit from additional practice with specific reading strategies such as skimming and scanning. The topic of email and the activities in this unit provide an excellent opportunity for reading skills practice. Explain the concepts of skimming (reading quickly to get the general idea) and scanning (reading quickly to find specific information). Encourage students to practise these skills when they do the exercises in this unit.

3

- Ask students to change partners. Read the instructions aloud.
- Ask pairs to practise reading the email in Exercise 1, inserting the new information in Exercise 3.
- To finish, ask for volunteers to read the email aloud for the class, inserting their own words.

4

- Read the instructions aloud. Explain that students should think about what makes a business email different from an email that one might send to a friend.
- Ask students to form pairs and give them about five minutes to discuss the questions. Walk around the class as students work, checking that students understand the task, and helping as needed.
- When the time limit is up, ask students to share their responses with the class.

> ***Answers***
> (Answers will vary. Below are possible answers.)
>
> Similar information: information about flight and jet lag, productive trip
>
> Different information included: information about Barcelona, what he did there

5

- Before you begin this exercise, ask students to scan the email message and check their guesses to the questions in Exercise 4. Ask for volunteers to tell you what is similar and what is different between the two messages in Exercises 1 and 5, for example, the message in Exercise 5 is very informal: the sentences are very short, and Tomasz includes lots of non-work-related information.
- Read the instructions aloud, and give students time to read the email silently. Answer any general questions students may have about the email or about specific vocabulary. For lower-level classes, ask for volunteers to read the email aloud to allow for more solid comprehension.
- Ask students to read the discussion questions below the email silently, and give them some time to think about their answers.
- Put students with a partner or in groups to discuss the questions. Walk around the class as students work, listening in and offering ideas as needed.
- To finish, elicit responses from several students.

> ***Answers***
> (Answers will vary. Below are possible answers.)
>
> **a** He wanted to be professional and polite and didn't want to complain to his boss.
>
> **b** His friend might not be interested in the information about his meetings or co-workers.

- In many cultures, particularly in Asia, it is common practice to build business relationships through social events, such as parties, meals at restaurants, etc. Introduce the popular western saying 'Never mix business with pleasure.', which warns that one should not be too friendly or casual with people with whom one does business, for example, colleagues, clients, etc., and ask students to discuss the potential advantages and disadvantages of both customs.

6

- Read the instructions aloud. Then ask students to read the list of features aloud. Go over any unfamiliar vocabulary.
- Ask students to work alone or with a partner to find the features in Thomas's email in Exercise 5. Walk around the class as students work, offering help as needed. For lower-level classes, do the first two or three items with the whole class.
- When students finish, go over the answers with the whole class. If possible, provide a larger visual of the email from Exercise 5, such as an overhead transparency or presentation software projection on the board. Ask students to come up and circle the answers in the email.

> ***Answers***
>
> **a** Hi Em
>
> **b** Really tired; Had tons of meetings; Weather wasn't so good; Much cheaper than here!; Next time!
>
> **c** Really tired – my flight was delayed; Weather wasn't so good – it rained almost every day.
>
> **d** (in the sunshine, of course!)
>
> **e** … hard to stay awake today!; (in the rain, of course!); Much cheaper than here!; Next time!
>
> **f** ☺☹
>
> **g** BTW
>
> **h** Thomas

- To finish, lead a brief class discussion about students' experiences using email. Ask them to share their opinions on the advantages and disadvantages of sending an email vs. writing a letter, and any additional abbreviations, emoticons, etc. that they may know.

Writing emails p45

1

- Read the instructions aloud.
- Put students with a partner to discuss the email and find any problems with it.
- Elicit ideas from the class. Then ask students to work individually and use pencil to correct any mistakes they find in the email.
- Ask students to compare their corrections with their partners. If possible, provide a larger visual of the email, such as an overhead transparency or presentation software projection on the board. Ask for volunteers to come up and make their corrections.

> ***Answers***
>
> There is no subject. Add subject: *Istanbul conference sales report*
>
> *Dear Marketing Department* should be addressed to a specific person, and greeting should be followed by a comma
>
> *Conference* is misspelled in the second sentence.
>
> *Bye* is a casual closing – Change to *Best, Best wishes* or *Best regards*, etc.

2 1.37

- Tell students they are going to hear Jasmine, the person who wrote the email on page 45, asking for some advice about how to improve her email writing skills.
- Read the instructions aloud, and give students time to read the prompts.
- Play the audio once or twice, and ask students to complete the sentences.
- To check answers, ask for volunteers to write the problems on the board. Ask the class to correct any mistakes on the board as necessary.

> ***Answers***
>
> **a** There's no subject.
>
> **b** She should use a name in the greeting.
>
> **c** She needs a comma after the name.
>
> **d** She should explain why she is writing.
>
> **e** There's a spelling mistake.
>
> **f** The closing is too informal.
>
> **g** She didn't write her name.

3 1.37

- Read the instructions aloud.
- Play the audio once or twice as needed, pausing after each item to give students time to correct the mistakes in the email.
- Ask students to compare answers with a partner. Then go over the answers with the whole class.

> ***Answers***
>
> To: Lisa Ruben
>
> From: Jasmine King
>
> Subject: **Istanbul conference sales report**
>
> Cc:
>
> Bcc:
>
> Attachments: A
>
> Dear **Ms Ruben**,
>
> **I'm writing to send you a copy of the sales report from the Istanbul conference, as you requested**. I'm sending this year's report and also a memo about our plans for next year's **conference** as attachments.
>
> **Best wishes**,
>
> **Jasmine**

Email expressions p46

Vocabulary and expressions

brochure
delete
having trouble
inbox
password
reception
regards
reset
server
show up
user name

1

- Read the instructions aloud. Then ask students to read the greetings and closings aloud. Point out that all of the phrases are followed by a comma.
- Put students with a partner to complete the table. Tell them to work together and discuss each greeting and closing, and remind them that some phrases may fit in more than one place.
- Walk around the class as students work, making sure they are working together.
- To check answers, copy the table onto the board and ask for volunteers to come up and write their answers.

Formal greetings	Informal greetings
Dear Susan, Dear Ms Kim,	Hey there, Jennifer,
Formal closings	**Informal closings**
Best wishes, Best regards,	Love, Take care,

- To finish, call on a student to read the note below the chart.

Language note

Tips for professional email etiquette: Here are some useful tips you can share with students.

- **It's OK to be informal, but not careless or sloppy**. Be sure to follow grammar, punctuation and spelling rules.
- **Keep messages clear and brief**. An unnecessarily long email can be confusing and frustrating for the reader.
- **Don't use all upper case (or lower case) letters**. All upper case letters give the impression of shouting, and all lower case looks sloppy and lazy.
- **Don't send inappropriate jokes, chain letters or other junk email**. Keep email content professional and pertinent.
- **Use email for appropriate situations**. More serious issues or emotional communication should be dealt with face-to-face.
- **Remember that email is not private**. Keep email messages professional, and don't write anything you wouldn't want seen by others.

2

- Read the instructions aloud.
- Give students time to read the phrases in the table. For lower-level classes, ask students to repeat the phrases after you.
- Before students create their own emails, do a model with the whole class on the board. Tell them to imagine they need to send you (their teacher) an email to let you know that they will be late to class on Friday. Elicit a greeting, purpose, conclusion and closing from several volunteers and write the email on the board. Then ask students to tell you which parts of the email constitute the greeting, purpose, etc.
- Give students time to create their own emails. Encourage students to be creative and to include additional appropriate information in their emails. Walk around the class as students work, helping with spelling, vocabulary and email format as needed.
- When students finish, ask them to form groups of three or four and pass their Student's Books around, so that they can read one another's messages.

Answers

(Answers will vary. Below are possible answers.)

a

Hey there Laura,

I'm writing to invite you to lunch. Are you free anytime next week?

I'll call you this weekend.

See ya,

Student's name

b

Dear Sir or Madam,

I'm writing to complain about a missing order. I ordered a set of dishes over a month ago. Could you please tell me the status of my order?

I look forward to hearing from you.

Sincerely,

Student's name

c

Dear Mr Bailey,

Hello. I'm writing in response to your recent job application. Attached, please find details about the position.

Let me know if you have any questions.

Best regards,

Student's name

d

Dear Masa,

Hi! I'm writing to wish you a happy birthday. I hope you have a great day. Here is a picture of us in high school!

I'll see you next summer, when I come to Japan to visit.

Love,

Student's name

3

- Read the instructions aloud. Remind students that they will be writing two emails – one to a friend, and one to a teacher. Students will need to choose the appropriate level of formality / informality for each email.
- Give students time to write their email messages. Walk around the class as students work, offering help as needed.
- When students finish, ask them to compare their message with a partner. Then give each student a piece of tape to post his or her email on the wall in the classroom. Ask the whole class to stand and walk around the class to read their classmates' emails.

Photocopiable activity

p101

I bet that's a mistake!

1 Ask students to work in groups of 3–4. Prepare one copy of *I bet that's a mistake!* for each group.

2 Explain that the email has 12 mistakes, including grammar, punctuation, spelling, email conventions and level of formality. In groups, students should find the mistakes and correct them.

3 For each mistake, groups have from one to five points that they can use to 'bet,' depending on how confident they are that they have correctly identified and fixed the mistake; i.e., a bet of one point indicates low confidence, and a bet of five points indicates high confidence.

4 Draw a quick scoring grid on the board, such as

	Group 1	Group 2	Group 3
1			
2			
3			
4			
etc.			

5 Go over the mistakes one by one. (You can use the number assigned to each mistake in the answer key below.) Have each group tell you how many points they bet. Then give or elicit corrections for each mistake. If a group is correct, they win the number of points that they bet. If they are incorrect, they lose that number of points. Where more than one correction is possible, you are the final judge!

6 At the end of the activity, the group with the most points 'wins'.

Answers (mistakes are listed in the order in which they appear)

1 There is no subject line. Possible correction: *Party invitation; This weekend; A party.*

2 The greeting uses both the first name and the last name. It should just say, *Hi Annie,*

3 In the first line of the 2nd paragraph, delete *in response.*

4 In the first line of the 2nd paragraph, *request* should be *invite.*

5 In the second sentence of the 2nd paragraph, there should be a full stop instead of a question mark at the end of the sentence.

6 In the second sentence in the 3rd paragraph, there shouldn't be a dash after *OK.*

7 In the second sentence in the 3rd paragraph, *friend* is misspelled.

8 In the 4th paragraph, there shouldn't be any parentheses.

9 The 4th paragraph says that a map is attached; however, there isn't any attachment.

10 In the 5th paragraph, it should say *call me on my mobile phone.*

11 In the 6th paragraph, the emoticon is wrong. It should be a happy face.

12 The closing is too formal. Possible correction: *Bye, See you later, Your friend,*

Email vocabulary p47

1 1.38

- Tell students they are going to learn some useful vocabulary related to email.
- Read the instructions aloud.
- Before you play the audio, give students time to read the dialogue – either alone or with a partner – and try to predict the missing words. Elicit some of the students' predictions.
- Play the audio and ask students to complete the dialogue. For lower-level classes, write the missing words in random order on the board for students.
- To check answers, ask students to read the lines of the dialogue, inserting the missing words.

Answers

send, receive, inbox, username, password, reset, mailbox, delete, attachments, server

- Ask students to take turns reading the dialogue with a partner.
- For additional practice, write the following prompts from the conversation on the board. Ask students to close their books and complete the sentences with the correct vocabulary words from the listening.

I can _____ messages, but I can't _____ any!
My _____ was empty this morning.
What's your _____?
I have to ask you for your _____.
You can _____ it later.
Your _____ is full.
You're going to need to _____ some old messages.
You have a lot of really big _____. Do you need all of them?
They're still on the _____.

2

- Read the instructions aloud. Then ask students to read the discussion questions aloud.
- Ask students to form groups of three or four to discuss the questions.
- When groups finish their discussions, ask the questions to the whole class and elicit responses from several students.

Viewpoints: Email p48

1

- Read the instructions aloud. Students may or may not be familiar with Japanese and British email behaviour. Encourage them to make guesses.
- When students finish, elicit some ideas from the class. Do not tell students the correct answers at this stage. Tell them that they will check their guesses when they do the reading in Exercise 2.

2

- Read the instructions aloud. To help develop students' scanning skills, you can first ask them to scan both emails and check their guesses about the behaviours in Exercise 1. Then give them time to read the passages silently. Alternatively, ask students to read the passages aloud. For lower-level classes, you may want to read the passages aloud for the class after students read on their own.
- When students finish reading, ask whether students were able to correctly guess which nationality has the email behaviours in Exercise 1.
- Go over the correct answers with the class. Ask students to tell you the words or phrases from the reading that gave them the answers. Then lead a brief discussion about the reading. Ask students whether they share the opinions expressed.

3

- Read the instructions aloud. This exercise provides an opportunity for students to review the language they learnt in Units 3 and 4 for giving opinions and reacting to ideas. Ask the class to brainstorm some phrases they can use and write them on the board, for example, *As I see it …, In my opinion …, I think …, That's a great idea., I'm not sure about that.*, etc.
- Ask students to form groups of three or four to discuss their ideas. Remind them to react to one another's opinions. Tell groups to decide on two or three pieces of advice for each office.
- When groups finish, have a whole-class business meeting roleplay. Each group takes a turn playing the role of the Consultants while the rest of the class plays the Company Managers. Ask for a volunteer to open the meeting, and state the topic, and another volunteer to keep the meeting moving using the expressions students have learnt in previous units in this course.

In business: Planning a meeting p49

- Before you begin this lesson, read the three sets of In business task activity instructions, so that you can be prepared to answer students' questions.

Scenario

- Ask a student to read the *Scenario* aloud for the class.

Task 1

- Divide the class into three groups (A, B and C).
- Tell each group to look at the appropriate page in their Student's Books (Group A – page 88; Group B – page 98; Group C – page 106).
- Give groups time to read the information and to create a name and email address. Ask for a member of each group to write the name and email address on the board for other groups to copy. Walk around the class as students work, helping to clarify instructions as necessary.

Task 2

- Explain that students will now write emails to their colleagues to set up the meeting. They will write and deliver their emails by hand, but should imagine they are sending and receiving the message on a computer.
- Ask students to form groups of three with one member from each original group (A, B and C).
- Give groups time to read their instructions. Then ask students to work individually to compose their emails. Tell them that they can look back at the expressions on page 46 for useful expressions to use in their emails.
- Walk around the class as students work, offering help as needed.

Follow-up

- Read the instructions aloud.
- Ask students to stay in their groups from Task 2. Groups should pass the messages around, so that all members have read all of the emails. Then ask them to discuss the experience, including any misunderstandings that arose and how / whether they were resolved.
- When groups have finished reading and discussing their emails, ask students to go back to their original larger groups (A, B and C) from Task 1. Ask groups to report on how their email experience went, whether their group was successful at setting up a meeting time, and what challenges they had.
- To finish, ask for volunteers to share what was easy / difficult for them about the email-writing task.

That's a good question! 8

Unit aims

In Unit 8, students learn about:

- Giving a presentation
- Presenting information: Giving and receiving feedback, Delivery (eye contact/voice), Endings/ conclusions, Dealing with questions
- Viewpoints: Presentations
- In business: On-the-job use of English

The aims for each class can be written on the board to orient students to the unit content and objectives.

Getting started

Begin this unit by reviewing the skills students learnt in Unit 7 for writing email messages.

- Before class, write several topic prompts on the board for students to choose from, for example:

  Write an email to …

  – *your boss asking to take a week off for a holiday*

  – *your HR manager inviting him or her to a lunch meeting to discuss recruiting strategies*

  – *a colleague to start planning the company holiday party*

  – *your manager describing a conference you attended and attaching a report from one of your meetings.*
- Ask students to form groups of three or four. Each group needs a blank piece of paper.
- Explain that students are going to work together to write the email. First the group chooses a topic from the board and decides on an appropriate opening for the email.
- The first student then begins the body of the email. Each student has one minute to write as much as they can. Then they pass the paper to the right. The next student reads what has been written and has 30 seconds to add to it.
- Give about six or eight rotations (so that each student writes twice). Then ask the group to decide on an appropriate closing.
- To finish, ask for volunteers from the groups to read their emails to the class.

Listen and practise:
Giving a presentation p50

Vocabulary and expressions

data
slide
pointer
wave around

1

- Read the instructions aloud. Ask students to discuss the photos with a partner.
- Ask students to tell you what they think is happening. Elicit that in all the photos, people are giving presentations, and that photos b and c show bad presentation style (not making eye contact, standing in front of visuals). Photos a and d show good presentation style (clear visuals, making eye contact).

2 1.39

- Read the instructions aloud and ask a student to read the answer choices aloud.
- Before you play the audio, ask students to predict what they might hear in the audio that might help them answer the questions. For example, for answer choice **a**, *They think Katy was perfect*, students might hear *That was great.* or *Well done, Katy.*
- Play the audio and ask students to write T for true or F for false.
- Ask students to compare answers with a partner. Then go over the answers with the whole class. Ask students to share the words or phrases they heard that gave them the answers.
- To finish, ask for a volunteer to tell you the specific feedback Katy's colleagues give to her (*slow down when you speak; look at people; don't wave the pointer around; try to relax*).

> ***Answers***
> **1** F **2** T **3** T

3 1.39

- Before you play the audio, put students into groups of three and ask them to try to predict the missing words. Ask groups to read the conversation aloud, inserting their own words in the blanks.
- Read the instructions aloud. Then play the audio once or twice as needed, and ask students to complete the conversation.
- To check answers, ask students to read the conversation aloud, inserting the correct information.

> ***Answers***
> Can you give me some, remember to, anything else I should do, You're welcome

- Ask students to stay in their groups to practise the conversation. Walk around the class as students work, listening in and offering help as needed. Remind students to change roles.
- When students are comfortable with the conversation, ask them to try the conversation without looking at their Student's Books. Encourage them to use the look-remember-speak technique. (Students look in their books, try to remember as much as they can of the text [one or two sentences], and then speak without looking at their books.)
- Ask students to change groups several times to maximise the practice.

4

- Ask students to form new groups of three. Read the instructions aloud. Go over any unfamiliar vocabulary.
- Ask pairs to practise the conversation in Exercise 3, inserting the first set of new information in Exercise 4. Then ask them to change roles.
- Ask students to practise the conversation again, inserting the second set of new information. Continue until students have completed the conversation with all three sets of information. Then ask students to change groups, and repeat the steps above.

5 1.40

- Before you begin this exercise, ask students to look back at the conversation in Exercise 3. Ask students to work in groups of three to write four or five more lines to continue the conversation. Ask for volunteers to read their continuations aloud for the class.
- Read the instructions aloud, and ask a student to read the answer choices aloud. Give students time to mark their guesses. Make sure students understand that they can mark more than one answer.
- Play the audio once or twice as needed and ask students to check their guesses.

> ***Answers***
>
> **d** Don't worry, you'll do a great job!
>
> **b** Do you want to try again?

Presenting information:
Giving and receiving feedback
p51

> ### Teaching tip
>
> **Preparing students for feedback:** Students in some cultures may be unaccustomed to giving feedback on their peers' work or receiving peer feedback. Plan to spend some time orienting students to the next exercise. Tell students that the aim of peer feedback is to allow students to observe and learn from one another, so that all students can improve their presentation skills. Remind students that they can learn a lot from one another, and point out that giving feedback means pointing out positive points (strengths) as well as suggesting areas for improvement (not simply pointing out weaknesses). Finally, explain that giving and receiving feedback are useful skills for the business environment, which students will practise more in Unit 12.

1 1.41

- Before you begin this exercise, review the expressions students learnt in Unit 2 for introducing a presentation. For example:

  Opening: *Good morning. My name is …*

  Subject: *Today I'm going to talk about …*

  Message: *My main point is that …*

  Outline: *My presentation is divided into three parts. First, …*

- To lead in, tell students that now they are going to build skills for the *delivery* of a presentation. Write a word map on the board with *presentation delivery* in the middle, for example:

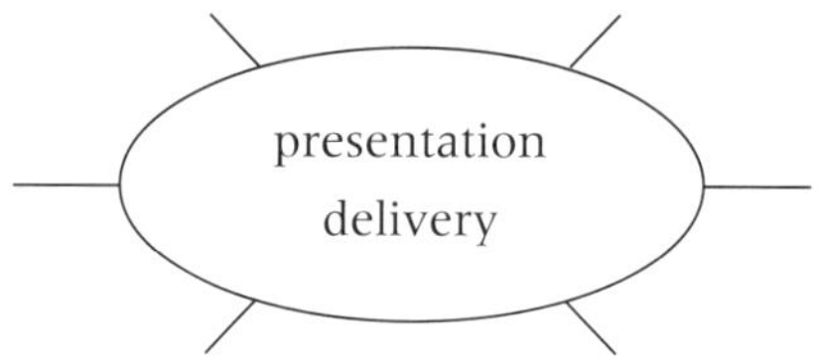

- Elicit some aspects of delivery, for example, eye contact, voice, posture, use of visual aids, etc., and add them to the spokes in the word map. Then tell students to think about what a good presentation looks like, and what a good presenter does (and does not do), for example, looks at audience, doesn't read directly from notes, speaks clearly, doesn't speak too fast, etc. Add students' ideas next to the appropriate categories on the word map.
- Read the instructions aloud. Explain *strong point* (something the presenter did well), and *improvement area* (a suggestion of something the presenter could do better).
- Play the audio once or twice. Ask students to take notes on each introduction on a separate piece of paper.
- Put students with a partner to discuss the introductions. Ask them to share their reactions to the delivery, and then decide on one strong point and one improvement area to comment on. Write some useful phrases on the board for students' reference, for example:

  Strong point:

  You … very well.

  Your … was excellent.

  One thing you did well was …

  Improvement area:

You need to …	*It would be a good idea to …*
Try to …	*You may want to …*
You should …	*Remember to …*

- Ask pairs to combine to form groups of four and compare their answers.

- To check answers, play the introductions one at a time again, pausing in-between to elicit students' feedback.

> ***Answers***
> (Answers will vary. Below are possible answers.)
> **1** Strong point: You sounded very confident.
> Improvement area: You need to speak a little faster.
> **2** Strong point: Your intonation was excellent.
> Improvement area: Remember to speak more slowly.
> **3** Strong point: You prepared very well.
> Improvement area: Don't tell the audience you're nervous.

2

- Before you begin this exercise, make sure that students have all written an introduction for Unit 2 (page 14). If some students do not have an introduction, you may want to have the whole class go back and do the exercise again.
- Read the instructions aloud and give students time to look over the table. Go over each of the criteria for feedback (content, subject, etc.), and make sure students understand them. You may want to provide some additional guidelines for what students should look / listen for. For example:

  1 *Content: Is the presentation clear and organised?*
  Subject: Is the subject interesting to the audience?
  Message: Is the message clear?

  2 *Delivery: Is the presenter confident? well prepared? organised?*
  Eye contact: Does the presenter look at the audience members? Does he or she avoid reading directly from the notes?
  Voice: Does the presenter speak too quickly? Slowly? Is he or she easy to understand?
- Put students with a partner, and ask them to take turns giving their presentations. The presenter should stand up and act as though he or she is presenting to an audience. The partner should just watch and listen first, and then write the feedback notes after – rather than during – the presentation.
- When both students have finished, ask them to share their feedback and discuss ways that they can improve their weaker areas.
- For additional practice, ask students to form groups of five or six and practise giving their presentations and feedback in a larger group.

Presenting information:
Delivery (eye contact / voice)
p51

1 1.42

- Before you begin this exercise, ask students to look at the first sentence. Ask for several volunteers to read the first sentence aloud for the class, inserting the pause where they feel it should go. Try to elicit a few different readings.
- Read the instructions aloud. Then play the audio and ask students to mark the pause in each sentence.
- Ask for volunteers to read the sentences as they were read on the audio. Then ask the class to discuss the various meanings of the sentence.

> ***Answers***
> **a** I'm busy this evening//around seven friends are coming for dinner.
> (I will be busy this evening. Seven friends are coming to dinner.)
> **b** I'm busy//this evening around seven friends are coming for dinner.
> (I'm busy now. Some friends are coming for dinner around 7:00.)
> **c** I'm busy this evening around seven//friends are coming for dinner.
> (I will be busy around 7:00 this evening. Some friends are coming for dinner.)

- To finish, emphasise the importance of speaking with correct stress, intonation and pauses, especially in a presentation.

Language note

Sentence stress: There are generally two types of words in all sentences:

1 structure words (smaller, less important words that give a sentence its grammatical structure, for example, articles, conjunctions, pronouns and prepositions)

2 content words (words such as nouns and verbs that carry the main meaning of the sentence).

Explain to students that it is the *content* words that carry the main stress in English sentences. For example:

Today, I'm going to TALK about the FUTURE of this COMPANY.

We're planning to BUILD a PLANT in RUSSIA next year.

2 1.43

- If necessary, go over the meaning of sentence stress. Give students a few example sentences on the board, and ask them to tell you which word(s) have the main stress. For example:

  I'm going to talk about our NEW RECRUITING plan.
  We need to discuss which CONFERENCES to attend this year.
- To lead in, ask for several volunteers to read the conclusion with natural stress and intonation. As this is just to raise students' awareness of the intonation patterns, do not correct students' pronunciation or intonation at this stage.

- Read the instructions aloud. Then play the audio once or twice as needed, and ask students to mark the pauses and stress. For lower-level classes, play the audio once and ask students to insert just the pauses. Then play it a second time and ask them to mark the primary stress.
- Ask students to compare answers with a partner. Then go over the answers with the whole class. If possible, use an overhead transparency to show where the marks go.

✓ ✓
In **conclusion**, // I've talked about our **new plans** for the Asia-Pacific region. //

✓ ✓
My **main point** was that we need to **improve** the way

✓
we **operate** in this market. //

✓ ✓
I talked about **changes** in our **organisation**, // changes

✓
in our **management style**, // and also changes in our

✓
recruiting process. //

✓ ✓
Finally, // I want to ask for your **support**. // With your

✓
help // I know we can be **successful** as we make these changes. //

✓ ✓
Thank you for your attention. Are there any **questions**?

3

- Read the instructions aloud. If necessary, play the audio again, and ask students just to listen before they begin practising the conclusion. For lower-level classes, play the audio one line at a time, pausing in-between for students to repeat before they practise on their own.
- Walk around the class as students practise, helping with intonation and stress as needed.

Presenting information:
Endings / conclusions p52

1

- Tell students they are going to learn some useful phrases for ending a presentation.
- Read the instructions and the chart categories aloud. Then ask for volunteers to read the phrases aloud.
- Put students with a partner to do the exercise.
- Ask pairs to combine to form groups of four to compare answers. Then, to check answers, write the four category headings on the board, and ask students to come up and write the phrases under the correct heading.

Answers

Summary: In summary, I've talked about two things …; Let me summarise my presentation. I've shown you …

Message: The main thing I wanted to say was this, …; My main point was …

Closing: Thank you for your attention.; Thank you for listening.; That's all the time I have. Thank you.

Asking for questions: Do you have any questions?; Are there any questions or comments?

2 1.44

- Read the instructions aloud.
- Play the audio once or twice as necessary. For higher-level classes, challenge students by having them listen with books closed. Pause the audio just when Katy begins to say one of the phrases from Exercise 1 (after she says the first couple of words), and ask students to write the full phrase.
- Ask students to compare answers with a partner. Then go over the answers with the whole class.

Answers

Let me summarise my presentation …

… I've talked about two things.

My main point was …

Thank you for listening.

Are there any questions or comments?

Photocopiable activity
pp102–103
3-minute presentations

1 Ask students to work in groups of about five students. Prepare one set of cards (both sheets) for each group. Cut out the cards and place them face-down in the middle of the group.

2 With the entire class, brainstorm and write on the board some phrases to introduce a *short* presentation and its main points; e.g.:

My topic today is …; I've been asked to talk today about …; Today I'd like to tell you about …

I will cover three main points: X, Y and Z.

First, / Second, / Finally, …

Today, we examined / looked at X, Y and Z.; In conclusion …

3 Explain to students that the topics they will get are not serious, and that they are only practising the structure of a presentation, and do not need to worry about content. They will speak for three minutes or less, so the information for each main point can be very brief – even just two or three sentences.

4 Give them an example or two to show how they can choose 2 or 3 main points for similar topics:

Shopping: how often I go, what I usually buy, what I usually spend

Conclusion: Shopping is one of my favourite ways to relax, but it is expensive!

The moon: in pictures; in songs

Conclusion: The moon inspires different kinds of artists

Homework: easy assignments; difficult assignments

Conclusion: I prefer easy assignments, but I learn more from difficult ones.

5 Ask each student to take one card. They can make notes about their main points on the card. Give students a time limit of five minutes.

6 Ask students to take turns giving their presentations. The presenter should stand, while the listeners sit.

7 Ask one student in each group to keep strict time (3 minutes per presentation!), or set a timer that the entire class can hear.

8 If students seem relaxed and confident, have listeners ask questions.

9 Ask each student to try at least two topics.

10 Remind the class when their presentations are finished that this structure and language can also be used for more formal, serious presentations.

3

- Read the instructions aloud. Give students time to choose a presentation topic. Encourage them to choose a topic they already know something about or that is of interest to them.
- Give students about ten minutes to write their introductions and conclusions. Walk around the class as students work, helping with vocabulary, grammar and spelling, and making sure students are using the phrases they've learnt for introductions and conclusions.
- Ask students to exchange papers with a partner and read one another's work. Encourage them to give one another feedback on the content of their introductions and conclusions.

4

- Before you do this exercise, give students time on their own to practise giving their presentations.
- Ask students to form groups of three to practise their presentations.
- Remind groups that presenters should stand up and imagine that they are making a professional presentation.
- Encourage students to write their feedback notes after each presentation – rather than during. Students can use the same feedback form that they used in Exercise 2 on page 51. Tell groups that they will have three minutes to give feedback after each presentation.
- For additional practice when groups finish, ask students to form new groups and give their presentations again, making changes or improvements based on their classmates' feedback.

Presenting information: Dealing with questions p53

1 1.45

- Read the instructions aloud. Go over the three ways of dealing with questions: react (acknowledge the speaker), respond (answer the question), reflect (check to see if your answer was OK).
- Play the audio once or twice as needed and ask students to complete the phrases.
- Ask students to compare answers with a partner. Then go over the answers with the whole class.

Answers

Speaker 1	That's a good question! Thank you for asking …
Speaker 2	I'm sorry, can you repeat your question?
Speaker 3	Thank you for asking that.
Speaker 4	I don't have that information with me, I'm afraid. Let me check and get back to you.
Speaker 5	Does that answer your question?

- For additional practice, hand out the audioscript for this exercise (see Teacher's Book, page 119), and ask students to practise the dialogues with a partner.

2

- Read the instructions aloud.
- Ask students to form groups of three or four to practise giving their presentations again.
- Explain that after each presentation, each member of the group should ask at least one question. Remind students to use the strategies and phrases they learnt in Exercise 1. For lower-level classes, write the phrases on the board for students' reference.

Viewpoints: Presentations p54

1

- Read the instructions and the discussion questions aloud.
- Ask students to form groups of three or four to discuss the questions. Elicit responses from several students. Alternatively, have the discussion with the whole class.

2 1.46

- Read the instructions aloud. Ask students to work with a partner to read the questions below the pictures, and to try to predict the answers.
- Play the audio once or twice as needed.
- To check answers, ask students to read the answers aloud in complete sentences.

> ***Answers***
> **a** 2 **b** 1 **c** 2 **d** 3 **e** 2 **f** 3

- To finish, ask students to discuss the speakers' opinions, and say whether they agree or disagree.

3

- Ask students to form groups of three or four.
- Ask a student to read the instructions aloud. Then ask for volunteers to read the statements.
- This exercise provides an excellent opportunity to review the language students learnt in Unit 3 for giving opinions, agreeing and disagreeing. Elicit some useful phrases for students' discussions and write the phrases on the board.
- Give groups about ten minutes for their discussions. Encourage students to explain their reasons for agreeing or disagreeing with the statements, and to react to one another's opinions.
- To finish, ask the class to come up with five tips for successful presentations.
- Ask students to complete the matching task on page 4 in respect of Leila.

> ***Answer***
> Leila = d

In business:
On-the-job use of English p55

Vocabulary and expressions

key findings

top management

- Before you begin this lesson, read the three sets of In business task activity instructions, so that you can be prepared to answer students' questions.

Scenario

- Ask a student to read the *Scenario* aloud for the class.

Task 1

- Divide the class into three groups (A, B and C).
- Tell each group to look at the appropriate page in their Student's Books (Group A – page 89; Group B – page 99; Group C – page 107).
- Give groups time to read the information in the Task files. Walk around the class as students work, helping to clarify instructions as necessary. You may want to go over the bar graph format with the class, to make sure all students know how to read it.

Task 2

- Explain that students will now meet with their colleagues to plan their presentations.
- Divide the larger groups into groups of three or four students. Each group should select a meeting leader. If art supplies are available, hand out poster paper and markers, so that students can create posters and / or mock PowerPoint® slides to use during their presentations.
- Give students 15 or 20 minutes to prepare their presentations. Remind them to use the expressions and skills they have learnt for giving presentations in this as well as in previous units. Walk around the class as students work, listening in and offering help as needed.

Task 3

- Ask students to practise giving the presentation, and give their group members feedback.
- If time allows, ask them to practise the presentation one more time, incorporating the feedback they received.

Task 4

- Ask students to form new groups of three with one member from each planning group (A, B or C).
- Give groups about 15 minutes to complete all presentations. Ask groups to assign a timekeeper to give each presenter a signal when two minutes are remaining.

Follow-up

a

- Ask students to stay in their groups from Task 4.
- Read the instructions aloud. Tell groups to assign tasks to each member of the group for during the presentation. For example:
  - Student A: introduction and first part of body
  - Student B: second part of body
  - Student C: summary, asking for questions (all group members can respond to questions)
  - Student A: conclusion
- Give groups a time limit of about five minutes for their presentations. If you have a large class, combine groups to form larger groups of nine students to give their presentations.

b

- When students finish, ask the class to discuss the presentations, giving feedback on strong points and areas for improvement. Then ask them to decide on the most effective presentation, and ask them to explain their choices.
- Ask students to complete the Review of Units 5–8 on pages 56 and 57 of the Student's book.

What was his major? 9

Unit aims

In Unit 9, students learn about:

- Discussing job applications
- Reading and writing a CV: Supporting opinions, Describing experience
- Viewpoints: CVs
- In business: Writing a CV

The aims for each class can be written on the board to orient students to the unit content and objectives.

Getting started

Begin this unit by reviewing the skills students learnt in Unit 8 for giving presentations. Ask students to work on their own to create a list of *Dos* and *Don'ts* for giving presentations. For example:

Do	*Don't*
make eye contact	*read from notes / slides*
speak loudly and clearly	*speak too fast*
practise a lot	*stand in front of posters / projections*
relax	

- Explain that students will give a two-minute mini-presentation on *Presentation Dos and Don'ts*. Their presentation should include an introduction, a body and a conclusion.
- Ask students to create small posters of their lists and give them time to make notes for and to practise their presentations.
- Ask students to give their presentations in groups of three. Remind them to use the phrases and expressions they learnt in Unit 8, and to follow the presentation *Dos and Don'ts* on their lists.
- When students finish, ask them to reflect on the experience of giving their presentations. Give them some time to write about how they felt before, during and after the presentation, what they thought they did well, and what was challenging about the exercise. Ask for volunteers to tell you what they felt their strong points were, and what areas they feel they still need to improve.

Listen and practise:
Discussing job applications p58

Vocabulary and expressions

BA
cash register
concentrated in
coordinated
correspondence
intern
inventory
multicultural environments
qualified

1

- Before you begin this lesson, ask students to keep their Student's Books closed. Tell them that in this unit, they are going to focus on CVs and job applications. Ask for volunteers to tell you what types of information are usually included on a CV (name, address, education, work experience, etc.).
- Ask students to open their books to page 58.
- Read the instructions aloud, and give students time to read the CV. Go over any unfamiliar vocabulary. Ask students to note any information included on the CV that they did not suggest above, as well as any additional information they think should be included.
- Ask students to form pairs to discuss what type of job the person is applying for, for example, a job in the Marketing Department at an international company. Encourage students to make guesses based on the person's education, work experience and skills.
- Elicit responses from several students, accepting all answers. Ask students to tell you how they arrived at their guesses.

Cultural note

Academic degrees: Students may not be familiar with the British system of abbreviations for academic degrees. Here are some of the most common ones:

Undergraduate degrees

BA – Bachelor of Arts
BSc – Bachelor of Science
BFA – Bachelor of Fine Arts

Post-graduate degrees

MA – Master of Arts
MSc – Master of Science
MFA – Master of Fine Arts

PhD – Doctor of Philosophy (research doctorate)
EdD – Doctor of Education (professional doctorate)

2 1.50

- Read the instructions aloud and ask a student to read the answer choices aloud.

- Before you play the audio, ask students to predict what they might hear in the audio that might help them answer the questions.
- Play the audio and ask students to mark their answers.
- Ask pairs to compare answers with a partner. Then go over the answers with the whole class. Ask students to share the words or phrases they heard that gave them the answers.
- To finish, ask for volunteers to tell you which qualifications they liked in particular (education, internship at trading company, sales experience, language skills).

> ***Answer***
> **b** They aren't sure if he will be good enough.

3 1.50

- Before you play the audio again, put students into groups of three and ask them to predict the missing words on the CV. Elicit some guesses from the class.
- Read the instructions aloud. Then play the audio once or twice as needed, and ask students to complete the CV.
- To check answers, ask the class questions about the CV to elicit the correct information, for example, *What were Jason's main subjects in college?*

> ***Answers***
> international, market, customers, Spanish, Spanish, computer

4

- Read the instructions aloud. Ask three pairs of students to read the model conversations.
- Put students with a partner (or ask them to change partners if they worked in pairs to come up with the questions) and ask them to practise the conversations again, changing roles once.
- Ask students to change partners and ask and answer the questions again, inserting the new information from the CV.
- For additional practice, give students time to think of three more original questions about the CV. Then ask them to ask and answer their questions with a partner.

5 1.51

- Ask a student to read the instructions and the answer choices aloud.
- Give students time to mark their guesses.
- Play the audio once or twice as needed and ask students to check their guesses.
- Go over the answers with the whole class.

> ***Answer***
> **d** They will make a decision later.

- To finish, ask for volunteers to tell you what Frances and Mr Keen decide to do with the CV (put it in the 'maybe' pile).

Reading and writing a CV: Supporting opinions p59

Vocabulary and expressions

fields of study
marital status
relevant

1 1.52

- Read the instructions aloud. Then give students time to read the information silently.
- Play the audio, and ask students to repeat the sentences. Point out that *For example* is stressed at the beginning of a sentence, and ask students to practise the correct stress pattern: *For exAMple*. Point out that the expression *such as* is unstressed in the sentence.
- Go around the class and ask individual students to say the sentences aloud. Work on intonation and stress as needed.
- For additional practice, ask students to look back at the CV on page 58, and try to come up with one or two more sentences using *For example* or *such as*. Elicit ideas from the class.

2

- Read the instructions aloud.
- Ask students to work alone or with a partner to match the statements to the examples. For lower-level classes, go through the right-hand column, and ask students to identify which are complete sentences. Walk around the class as students work, offering help as needed.
- To check answers, ask for volunteers to read the full statements aloud, inserting *For example* or *such as*.

> ***Answers***
> **a 3** The position has some good benefits, such as a high salary, long holidays and a comfortable office.
> **b 4** I have some experience with people from other cultures. For example, my family hosted an exchange student from Brazil.
> **c 5** I'm interested in several different fields of study, such as engineering and computer science.
> **d 1** She doesn't have some very important office skills. For example, she can't use Excel™ or PowerPoint.
> **e 2** British people don't include personal information on their CVs, such as age, race, and marital status.

3 1.53

- Read the instructions aloud. Then ask students what kinds of qualifications they think would be good ones for an applicant to have (international experience, language skills, computer skills, etc.).
- Play the audio and ask students to complete the table. Tell them that they should just write brief notes, and not full sentences in the *Reason* and *Examples* columns. For lower-level classes, play the audio and ask students just to listen the first time. Then play it again and ask them to fill in the table.
- Ask students to compare answers with a partner. Then go over the answers with the whole class. Copy the table onto the board, and ask volunteers to come up and complete it with their notes.

Answers

a like; good experience; works for company similar to that company

b dislike; not professional; pink paper, font, email address

c dislike; job experience not relevant; video shop assistant, swimming coach, coffee shop

d like; education; double major: Business / German, classes in International Law, Contracts

e dislike; overqualified; General Manager, might want high salary

Extension activity

CVs in the UK: Exploit the useful cultural information on the Exercise 3 audio about British-style CVs. Ask students to copy the following table into their notebooks:

British people do	British people don't

- Play the audio for Exercise 3 again and ask students to listen and complete the table with the three pieces of information the speakers give about British CVs.

Answers

British people do	British people don't
list their most recent jobs first	include photos include their age

- To finish, lead a brief class discussion about how British CVs differ from CVs in students' own cultures.

4

- Read the instructions aloud. Then ask students to read the prompts aloud.
- Give students time to complete the information about themselves. Remind students to use the correct punctuation for the sentences: when they are using *such as*, they will need a comma, and when they use *For example*, they will need to add a full stop and begin a new sentence. Walk around the class as students work, offering help as needed.
- When students finish, ask them to form pairs to share their answers. Remind students to use the correct stress and intonation.

Answers

(Answers will vary. Below are sample answers.)

a I have some interesting hobbies and interests. For example, I enjoy rock climbing and sailing.

b I know some people with good jobs, such as a Market Researcher and Financial Analyst.

c I took some useful classes in college, such as Chinese, International Law and Economics.

d There are some jobs I wouldn't like. For example, I wouldn't like to be an Office Assistant, a Bank Clerk or a Receptionist.

e I have some plans for the future. For example, I'd like to travel the world and open my own hotel.

Photocopiable activity

p104

A hiring puzzle

1 Ask students to work with a partner, A and B. Prepare enough photocopies so that each student A has a copy of the A sheet and each student B has a copy of the B sheet.

2 Go over the instructions with the whole class. If students are not familiar with this type of puzzle, read A's first clue aloud (The 50-year-old person is a woman) and explain that therefore students know that Mr Marks and Mr Levitz cannot be 50.

3 Ask students to work with a partner to read their clues aloud and solve the puzzle.

4 After ten minutes, if any pair is having trouble, let them ask another pair (or you) for one answer or hint.

5 You may give the class a time limit of 15–20 minutes and then see which students have the most squares filled in correctly. Or wait until one or more pairs have completely finished and then check their answers by calling on a volunteer to write the answer grid on the board.

6 To finish, ask students to discuss in their groups or as a whole class which applicant they would hire.

Answers:

name	Mr Marks	Ms Singh	Mr Levitz	Ms Salazar
age	30	40	20	50
years of exp	6	3	1	9
languages	1	3	4	2
salary	£40,000	£45,000	£50,000	£55,000

Reading and writing a CV: Describing experience p61

1

- Read the instructions aloud. Then ask for volunteers to read the information and the examples aloud for the class.
- Ask students to look back at the *Experience* and *Skills* sections of the CV on page 58. Ask them to work with a partner to find and underline examples of the two styles presented, (*Worked as an intern …*, *Assisted with sales …*, *Fluent French …*, etc.).

2

- Tell students they are going to have a chance to practise their CV-writing skills.
- Read the instructions aloud. Then give students time to read the paragraph and the CV silently.
- Ask students to work alone or with a partner to complete the CV. For lower-level classes, do the first one or two examples with the class to help students get started.
- When students finish, go over the answers with the whole class.

Answers

Experience with/in

Familiar with

Responsible for

patient, organised, energetic

Photocopiable activity p105

A CV

1 Prepare one copy of *A CV* for every student.

2 Ask students to work individually to fill in true information about themselves to create their own CV. Allow them to use dictionaries if necessary.

3 Circulate while students are working, to answer questions and help out. You can also direct them to check pages 58 and 61 in their books for examples.

4 Collect the finished CV to go over later, or ask students to share them with a partner or in small groups.

5 As a variation, ask students to work alone or with a partner to create CVs from their imaginations. They can imagine a completely fictional character or can write a mock CV for a celebrity.

Language note

CV phrases: To help students develop their CV-writing skills, introduce the following useful CV-writing phrases:

… years' successful experience in / as …

Gained hands-on experience in …

Motivated and enthusiastic (about) …

Participated in …

Assisted in / with …

Worked on / as / with …

Developed …

Organised …

Served as …

Managed / Handled / Supervised / Trained / Instructed …

Represented the company at …

Developed expertise in …

Received … award

Viewpoints: CVs p62

1

- Read the instructions and the three statements aloud. Make sure students understand the concept of *scanning*. They should not try to read and understand every word. They should look for specific information related to the statements.
- Give students about one or two minutes to scan the passage. Then ask them to discuss the statements with a partner, saying whether they think they are true or false.
- Elicit the answers from the class, and have volunteers explain how they arrived at their conclusions.

Answers

a T **b** T **c** F

2

- Ask students to form groups of three or four.
- Ask a student to read the instructions aloud. Then elicit some responses from the class.
- Give groups five or ten minutes to discuss the similarities and differences between CVs in France and in their own countries.
- When students finish their discussion, ask for a volunteer from each group to summarise the group's discussion.

- To finish, ask the class to list the important features of CVs in their own cultures. Give students prompts to help them, for example:

  It's important to include …

  When we describe education, we …

  A good CV has …

  You shouldn't include …

3

- Ask students to stay in their groups from Exercise 2, or ask them to form new groups.
- Ask for volunteers to read the instructions and the list of items aloud. Do an example with the class before groups begin their discussion. Ask the whole class to discuss the advantages and disadvantages of including a photo on a CV. Guide students to support their opinions with reasons and examples, and remind them to use the phrases they have used in this course for doing so, for example, *As I see it, including a photograph isn't a good idea. For one thing, your appearance shouldn't matter.*
- To finish, lead a brief class discussion about each of the items on the list. Try to elicit advantages and disadvantages for each.
- Ask students to complete the matching task on page 4 in respect of Sabine Belanger.

> ***Answer***
>
> Sabine Belanger = e

In business:
Writing a CV p63

Vocabulary and expressions

graduate (n)

Graphic Designer

- Before you begin this lesson, read the three sets of In business task activity instructions, so that you can be prepared to answer students' questions.

Scenario

- Ask a student to read the *Scenario* aloud for the class.

Task 1

- Ask students to form pairs or groups of three or four.
- Ask for volunteers to read the instructions and the list of features aloud.
- Give students time to tick the features of a British CV. Encourage students to go back and look through the unit tasks if they need help remembering.
- When students finish, go over the answers with the whole class.

> ***Answers***
>
> **a** ✗ **b** ✗ **c** ✓ **d** ✗ **e** ✗ **f** ✗ **g** ✓

Task 2

- Divide the class into three groups (A, B and C).
- Tell each group to look at the appropriate page in their Student's Books (Group A – page 90; Group B – page 100; Group C – page 108).
- Give groups time to read the information in the Task files. Walk around the class as students work, helping to clarify instructions as necessary.
- Tell students that they can look back at the examples of CVs on pages 58 and 61 in their Student's Books if they need ideas.

Task 3

- Ask students to form new groups of three with one member from each original group (A, B or C).
- Give groups about fifteen minutes to compile their CV. Encourage them to give one another feedback on the strong points and areas for improvement on the CV, and to make changes based on that feedback.
- Remind groups to think of one additional piece of information to include on the CV. Tell them to think about something they feel would be helpful to include for a Graphic Designer position. Walk around the class as students work, helping with ideas as needed.
- Ask groups to write the final draft of their CV on one piece of paper. (If time allows, you may want to ask them to type and print a copy and submit it for homework.)

Follow-up

- Before you begin this activity, ask students to share their CVs from Task 3 with the class. You can have groups post their CV on the wall around the classroom. Then ask students to stand and walk around looking at the CVs.
- Read the instructions and the discussion questions aloud.
- Lead a class discussion with the questions provided. Ask what information they think would help or hinder the person's chances of getting a job as a Graphic Designer, and elicit students' feedback about their classmates' CVs.

10 Tell me about yourself

Unit aims

In Unit 10, students learn about:

- Giving key information
- Being interviewed: Describing your background, Talking about your future, Talking about your strengths
- Viewpoints: Interviews
- In business: Who should we hire?

The aims for each class can be written on the board to orient students to the unit content and objectives.

Getting started

Begin this unit by reviewing the skills students learnt in Unit 9 for writing CVs. Before class, find a sample CV (use your own, or one printed from the Internet). Use correction liquid to blank out some key words on the CV, for example, the section headings *Work experience and skills*, as well as verbs and adjectives commonly used on CVs (*responsible for, managed, worked as*, etc.). Make one copy of the CV for every pair of students in the class.

- When students come to class, ask them to form pairs. Hand out the partial CV and ask pairs to work together to complete the missing information.
- For an additional challenge, before handing out the CV to students, cut the sections up into 10 to 12 strips, and ask students to put the strips in the correct order before completing the missing information.

Listen and practise:
Giving key information **p64**

Vocabulary and expressions

manufacturing

industries

1

- Read the instructions aloud. Ask students to discuss the photo with a partner.
- Ask students to tell you where the people are and what they think is happening.
- To preview the unit language and check students' background knowledge of the topic of job interviews, ask for volunteers to guess some of the questions Alexandra might be asking the candidate in the photo, for example, *What kinds of work experience do you have? Do you have any computer skills? Do you speak any foreign languages?*

2 2.01

- Read the instructions aloud and ask a student to read the answer choices aloud.
- Before you play the audio, ask students to predict some words or phrases they might hear in the audio that might help them answer the questions.
- Play the audio and ask students to mark their answers.
- Ask students to compare answers with a partner. Then go over the answers with the whole class. Ask students to share the words or phrases they heard that gave them the answers.

> ***Answers***
>
> **a** T **b** F (she hasn't yet graduated) **c** F

- To finish, ask for volunteers to tell you why Jessica says she wants to join the company (wants to work in manufacturing, use her English, looks like an exciting place to work).

3 2.01

- Before you play the audio, ask students to work with a partner to predict the missing words. Ask pairs to read the conversation aloud, inserting their own words in the blanks.
- Read the instructions aloud. Then play the audio once or twice as needed, and ask students to complete the conversation.
- To check answers, ask students to read the conversation aloud, inserting the correct information.

> ***Answers***
>
> Does that sound OK?, I was born in, I grew up in, my major is, I want to work in, it seems

- Put students with a partner to practise reading the conversation. Ask them to change roles a few times.
- When students are comfortable with the conversation, ask them to try the conversation without looking at their Student's Books. Encourage them to use the look-remember-speak technique. (Students look in their books, try to remember as much as they can of the text [one or two sentences], and then speak without looking at their books.)
- Ask students to change partners several times to maximise the practice.
- To finish, lead a brief class discussion about students' own experiences with job interviews. Ask for

volunteers to share what kinds of jobs they have had interviews for, what questions they were asked, challenges they had, and recommendations for how to prepare for an interview.

4

- Ask students to form new pairs.
- Read the instructions aloud. If necessary, go over the pronunciation of the place names in the table.
- Ask pairs to practise the conversation in Exercise 3, inserting the new information in Exercise 4.
- When pairs finish, ask them to change roles and repeat the exercise.
- To finish, ask for volunteer pairs to perform the conversation for the class, roleplaying the two characters and inserting the information of their choice.

5 2.02

- Before you begin this exercise, ask the class to brainstorm some interview questions they think Alexandra should ask Jessica. Elicit responses from the class and write the questions on the board, for example, *What kind of job experience do you have? Do you have any international experience?*, etc.
- Ask a student to read the instructions and the answer choices aloud.
- Give students time to tick their guesses. Make sure students understand that they can choose more than one answer.
- Play the audio once or twice as needed, and ask students to check their guesses.
- Go over the answers with the whole class.

Answers

a c d

- For additional listening practice, play the audio again and ask students to listen for Jessica's answers to the questions (**a** wants to work for a company that makes things, not finance or service industries; **c** likes travel, likes English, father worked overseas; **d** March of next year).

Being interviewed:

Describing your background

p65

Vocabulary and expressions

biochemistry

Construction Engineer

mathematics

medical research

1 2.03

- Ask students to look at the pictures. Ask what they can guess about each person's background and interests from the pictures. For example, person number 1 is probably studying mathematics, and enjoys snowboarding in his free time.
- Read the instructions aloud. Then give students time to read the information silently.
- Play the audio and ask students to match the information to the pictures. If necessary, play the audio again for students to complete the missing information.
- Ask students to compare answers with a partner. Then go over the answers with the whole class.

Answers

Speaker a, picture 3: Bruce; Toronto; Stanford 2008; biochemistry; researcher for a pharmaceutical company, plays cello

Speaker b, picture 2: Larry, Manchester; Sheffield 2013; teacher in future?

Speaker c, picture 1: Chris; San Francisco, Colorado 2014; mathematics, snowboarding

2

- Read the instructions aloud.
- Ask students to work alone or with a partner to come up with questions about the people in Exercise 1, based on the answers provided. For lower-level classes, do the first example with the whole class. Walk around the class as students work, offering help as needed.
- To check answers, ask pairs of students to read the questions and the answers aloud for the class. Write the correct questions on the board for students' reference.

Answers

(Answers may vary. Below are sample answers.)

a What was Bruce's major?

b When did Bruce graduate?

c Does Larry go to college in San Francisco?

d Who majors in mathematics?

3

- Read the instructions aloud.
- Ask students to work alone or with a partner to write additional questions based on the information in Exercise 1. Ask lower-level students to work with a partner. Walk around the class as students work, offering help as needed.
- Ask students to form groups of three or four to ask and answer their questions. Encourage them to try to answer the questions without looking at the information in Exercise 1.
- To finish, ask for volunteers to share some of their questions and answers with the class.

> ***Answers***
> (Answers may vary. Below are possible answers.)
> **a** When will Larry graduate?; This year.
> **b** Does Bruce play the cello?; Yes, he does.
> **c** Who enjoys making model aeroplanes?; Larry does.

4

- Tell students that they will now have a chance to practise describing the backgrounds of the people in Exercise 1.
- Read the instructions aloud. Then ask a pair of students to read the conversation prompt aloud. Encourage Student B to continue the second line of the conversation based on the information in Exercise 1.
- Give students time to prepare on their own. Tell them to choose one person from Exercise 1, look at the information, and think about how to best describe the person's background. Remind students that they should imagine that they are the person from Exercise 1 (so they will need to use the first person, *I was born …*). Encourage lower-level students to make some notes to help them during the exercise.
- When students are ready, ask them to form pairs and assign Student A and B roles. Give pairs about three minutes to practise, and ask them to switch roles once. Walk around the class as students work, listening in and helping as needed.
- To finish, call on several pairs to perform the conversations for the class.

> ***Answers***
> (Answers will vary. Below are sample answers.)
> **A:** Can you tell me something about yourself?
> **B:** Sure, I was born in Toronto, Canada. I'm a graduate of Stanford University. My major was biochemistry. In my free time, I enjoy playing the cello.

5

- Explain that students will now practise giving background information about themselves.
- Review the types of information students should include when describing their background (hometown, college or university, major, interests). To help students prepare, give a brief description of your own background first.
- Give students time to prepare on their own. Allow lower-level students to make some notes.
- Ask students to form pairs and take turns describing their backgrounds.
- To finish, ask for volunteers to roleplay a job interview scenario with you. Ask students to imagine that you are interviewing candidates for a position at your company, and ask volunteers to describe their backgrounds for you.

Being interviewed:
Talking about your future p66

1 2.04

- To lead in, elicit the professions of the three people in the pictures (Scientist / Medical Researcher, Engineer, Advertising Executive). Ask students to read the partial information below the pictures and try to predict the missing information. Elicit one or two predictions for each picture.
- Read the instructions aloud.
- Play the audio once or twice as needed, and ask students to complete the missing information. For lower-level classes, play the audio once first, and ask students just to listen.
- Ask students to compare answers with a partner. Then go over the answers with the whole class.

> ***Answers***
> **a** I'd like to be researching
> **b** I want to be
> **c** I want to be working for

- For additional listening practice, write the following questions on the board. Then play the audio again and ask students to listen for the answers.

  When will Cindy graduate?

  What kinds of projects does Dimitri want to work on?

  Why does Max like his job in advertising?

2

- Read the instructions aloud and give students time to think about their hopes for their future careers. Tell them to think about their skills and background, and encourage them to be creative and think about their true goals and dreams.
- Give students a few minutes to make some notes in the table. Walk around the class as students work, helping with ideas as needed.

3

- Read the instructions aloud. Then ask students to read the example language in the tables aloud. For lower-level classes, ask students to repeat the example sentences after you.
- Ask students to form pairs to practise asking and answering the questions about their future goals. For higher-level classes, ask students to think of one or two follow-up questions to extend the conversation. For example:

  A: *What do you want to be doing three years from now?*

  B: *I hope to be working overseas.*

  A: *Oh, really? Where would you like to go?*
- Ask students to change partners and repeat the exercise.
- When students are comfortable with the conversation, ask them to close their Student's Books, stand and walk around the classroom, and ask three different people about their future goals.

Being interviewed:
Talking about your strengths
p67

Vocabulary and expressions

candidates
attentive to detail
hardworking
creative

1

- Read the instructions and the strengths aloud. Elicit explanations or examples for each strength, for example, *someone who is good with people enjoys talking and working with others.*
- Ask for volunteers to tell you which phrases best describe their own strengths and to give examples to explain why.
- Ask the class to brainstorm a list of additional strengths and write them on the board, for example, *responsible, reliable, good at managing projects / working in a team.* If students in the class know each other well, ask them to discuss which phrases they think describe their classmates' strengths, for example, *Jun is responsible. He always comes to class on time.*
- Ask students to work alone to match the strengths to the jobs. Walk around the class as students work, offering help as needed.
- To check answers, ask students to tell you the matching strength for each job, and ask them to give examples. Note that there may be more than one answer possible for some of the jobs.
- To finish, elicit additional important strengths needed for each job.

Answers
(Additional possible answers shown in parentheses.)
a 4 (or 3) **b** 3 (or 1) **c** 2 (or 3/1) **d** 1

2 2.05

- Read the instructions aloud. Before you play the audio, ask students to think about any words and phrases they might hear that would help them get the answers, for example, for *strengths,* they might hear characteristics such as *good with people* or *creative.*
- Play the audio and ask students to complete the table. Remind them that they should write brief notes in the table, not full sentences.
- Ask students to compare their tables with a partner. Then copy the table onto the board and ask for volunteers to come up and write their answers.

Answers

	Strengths	Work experience
May	working with people, well organised, on time, able to motivate students	tutor for two years
Yohei	hardworking, good at management	ran own business (import) for about three years
Zofia	language skills, computer skills, manage office, talk to customers	translator for six months; travel agency for one year

3

- Read the instructions aloud. Then ask two students to read the example conversation aloud. Ask Student B to continue the conversation with information from the table in Exercise 2. Write some useful phrases on the board for students' reference, for example:

  One of my strengths is that ...
  I'm attentive to ...
  I can ...
  I'm good at ...
- Ask students to form pairs. Before they talk about their own strengths, ask them to practise the conversation, inserting information from the chart in Exercise 2.
- Give students time to think about their own strengths and personal characteristics. Allow lower-level students to make some notes to help them.
- Ask students to take turns describing their strengths. For higher-level classes, encourage students to give examples to illustrate their strengths, for example, *I'm very creative. I'm good at coming up with new ideas.*
- To finish, ask students to describe their partner's strengths for the class. Then have the class think of some jobs their classmates might be good at, based on their strengths.

4

- Tell students to imagine that they are applying for a job, and they have an interview today.
- Read the instructions and the interview questions aloud. Give students time to think about their responses to the questions. Allow lower-level students to make notes to help them.
- Tell students to decide who will be the interviewer and who will be the candidate first. To help make the roleplay more realistic, ask the candidates to choose a specific job or company they want to apply to.
- Teach students some useful closing phrases for the candidate, for example:

  Thank you very much for your time.
  I look forward to hearing from you.

- Give students about five minutes for their interviews. Then ask them to switch roles. Remind the interviewers to ask follow-up questions when possible, and remind the candidates to add examples to illustrate their strengths and experience. Walk around the room as students work, listening in and noting any areas to address later.
- When students finish, ask the interviewers to say whether they think the person's background and strengths make them a good candidate for their chosen job or company.
- For additional practice, ask students to change partners several times and repeat the interview. Then ask for several volunteer pairs to perform their roleplays for the class.
- To finish, lead a brief class discussion and ask students to reflect on the experience of being interviewed. Ask *How did you feel being interviewed? What was challenging about the experience? What would you do differently the next time?*

Photocopiable activity pp106–107

Interview roleplay

1 Prepare enough copies of *Interview roleplay* so that each student can have one card. If you have more than 16 students in your class, it's OK for some pairs of students to have the same cards. If you have an odd number of students, take one of the cards yourself.

2 Tell students they are going to roleplay either a person hiring a new employee, or an applicant interviewing for a job. They have some information on their card. However, they may invent other details. Explain that some of the applicants might be qualified for more than one of the possible jobs. Employers should write down the names of any applicants they'd like to hire.

3 Ask those students who are employers to sit at one side of the classroom, with a chair in front of them for the applicant. Give students time to read their role cards and prepare any additional notes they would like.

4 Ask the whole class to brainstorm questions the interviewers might ask and write them on the board, or refer back to Unit 10 in their books (*Can you tell me a little bit about yourself? What is your major? When did you graduate? What do you want to do in the future?* etc.), as well as questions the applicant can ask (*Can you tell me a little bit about the job? What kind of experience are you looking for? Is it a full-time or a part-time job?* etc.).

5 Ask the applicants to choose an interviewer at random and sit down in front of them for the interview. Time the interviews (about five minutes). When the time is up, the applicants should stand up and move to another interviewer.

6 When applicants have interviewed with every employer, or when you decide to end the activity, bring the class back together to discuss the activity. Ask the employers if they interviewed anyone they would like to hire. Ask all students to reflect on what was easy and what was challenging for them about the interviews.

Viewpoints: Interviews p68

Vocabulary and expressions

achievements
conservatively
flexibility
leadership
passion
reliability
speak out
teamwork

1

- Read the instructions and the discussion questions aloud.
- Give students time on their own to think about their responses to the questions. For lower-level classes, encourage students to write their responses. Ask students to form groups of three or four to discuss the questions. Elicit responses from several students. Alternatively, have the discussion with the whole class.

2 2.06

- Read the instructions aloud. To make sure students have checked any unfamiliar vocabulary in the list, elicit examples for some of the challenging terms. For example, ask *What are some examples of reliability? (Coming to work every day, being on time, being willing to work hard for the company.)*
- Play the audio once or twice as needed, and ask students to tick their answers.
- To check answers, ask for volunteers to tell you what qualities each speaker is looking for. Write the qualities on the board.

Answers

Fiona: communication skills, work experience, leadership, flexibility, teamwork

Brian: reliability, technical skills, communication skills, work experience

- For additional practice, play the audio again, and ask students to listen for the reasons the speakers give for why the qualities are important.

3

- Read the instructions aloud. Then ask for volunteers to read the advice aloud.
- Give students time on their own to tick the advice that applies to their culture. Walk around the class as students work, offering help as needed.
- Ask students to compare answers with a partner. Then elicit some responses from the class. Ask students to share any advice that was surprising or interesting to them.

4

- Read the instructions aloud, and give students time to think of their advice. Encourage them to write down their ideas. For lower-level classes, ask students to work with a partner, so that they can help each other.

5

- Ask students to form groups of three or four.
- Read the instructions aloud. Elicit the main parts of a meeting students have learnt in this course, and write them on the board:
  - *opening*
  - *state the topic / purpose*
  - *discuss ideas / give opinions and reactions*
  - *summary / closing*
- Tell groups to choose a leader to open the meeting and a reporter to share the group's ideas with the class at the end. Give groups about ten minutes to discuss their ideas and choose the top five pieces of advice.
- After five minutes, tell the group leaders to summarise and close the meeting.
- Ask the reporters to share their advice with the class, and explain how they arrived at their decisions.

In business:
Who should we hire? p69

- Before you begin this lesson, read the two sets of In business task activity instructions, so that you can be prepared to answer students' questions.

Scenario

- Ask a student to read the *Scenario* aloud for the class.

Task 1

- Divide the class in half and assign students the roles of Student A or Student B.
- Tell each group to look at the appropriate page in their Student's Books (Group A – page 91; Group B – page 101). Give students time to read the information on their own and to think about their responses to the interview questions. Remind them that the aim is to present the background and skills that will help them get employed for the company and position described on the Task file.

Task 2

- Ask students to form groups of three or four. All students should be from the same original group (A or B).
- Explain that groups should go through the company descriptions and interview questions, and brainstorm ideas for how to best answer the questions. Encourage students to write notes to help them remember the group's ideas.
- Give groups about ten minutes for their brainstorms.

Task 3

- Ask students to stay in their groups from Task 2. Ask them to read the information for Exercise 2 on their Task file page.
- Explain that students will now interview a member of the other group, using the suggested questions on their Task file. Remind students to try to follow the appropriate advice from the *Viewpoints* lesson on page 68 of their Student's Book.
- Ask one member from each A group to go and join a B group. Then have one member from each B group go and join an A group.
- Ask groups to conduct their interviews. Allow lower-level students to use their notes. Remind students to follow the interview format they practised in Exercise 4 on page 67.
- When groups have finished their first interviews, ask the interviewees to rejoin their original groups. Then have the next A and B students switch groups, and repeat the interview process. Interviewers should take notes on each candidate's skills and background, as they will need it to help them decide which candidate to employ.
- Continue until all students have had a chance to be interviewed.

Task 4

- Ask students to return to the two larger groups from Task 1 (class divided in half, Group A and Group B). If you have a large class, divide the groups so that there are no more than five or six students per group.
- Ask students to talk about their experiences interviewing and being interviewed, discussing how they felt, what they thought went well, and any challenges they had.
- Ask groups to discuss the background and skills of candidates they interviewed, and choose one they want to employ. In a large class, have each group choose two or three qualified candidates.

Follow-up

- Read the instructions aloud.
- Ask groups to decide who will write the acceptance and rejection emails. Then ask them to work with a partner or in small groups to write the emails.
- When students finish, ask them to exchange emails with another group, and give feedback on strengths and areas for improvement.

11 They're too expensive

Unit aims

In Unit 11, students learn about:

- Discussing gifts
- Selecting gifts
- Explaining a problem / mistake: Giving and accepting apologies
- Viewpoints: Cultural mistakes
- In business: Choosing a wedding gift

The aims for each class can be written on the board to orient students to the unit content and objectives.

Getting started

Begin this unit by reviewing the skills students learnt in Unit 10 for preparing for and participating in job interviews.

- When students come to class, ask them to write a common job interview question on a small piece of paper. Tell them that they can refer back to Unit 10 if they need ideas, for example:

  Can you tell me a little about yourself?

  What do you hope to be doing in five years?

  What job skills would you like to learn in the future?

- When all students have written a question, ask students to stand up and walk around the class. They should find a partner and ask and answer their questions. Then partners should swap questions, go and find a new partner, and ask and answer their new questions.
- Tell students to speak to at least five partners, exchanging questions each time.

Listen and practise: Discussing gifts p70

Vocabulary and expressions

attractive
fragile
plenty of
vendor
personal

1

- Read the instructions aloud, and give students time to look at the photo. Elicit that the woman is choosing a gift from a website.
- Focus students on the question *Why?* Ask the class *Why do some companies give gifts to clients?* (To show their appreciation for the customers' business, and to build good relationships with them.)

Culture note

Explain to the class that in many western cultures, the Christmas / New Year's season in December and January is a popular time for companies to give gifts to their customers. However, this type of gift-giving is not customary for all companies. Some companies give gifts, and others do not. Ask students what times of year are common gift-giving seasons for businesses in their cultures, and what types of gifts are common.

2 2.07

- Read the instructions and the answer choices aloud.
- Play the audio and ask students to circle their answer.
- Ask students to compare answers with a partner. Then elicit the answer from the class. Ask students to share the words or phrases they heard that helped them get the answer.

> ***Answer***
>
> **b** calendars

- To finish, ask for volunteers to tell you why the two speakers decide not to send Christmas cards (because not everyone celebrates Christmas).

3 2.07

- Before you play the audio, put students with a partner and ask them to predict the missing information. Ask for volunteer pairs to read the conversation aloud, inserting their own information.
- Read the instructions aloud. Then play the audio once or twice as needed, and ask students to complete the conversation.
- To check answers, ask pairs to read the conversation aloud with the correct information.

> ***Answers***
>
> choose, not everyone, else, company, useful, mail, What about, fine

- Ask pairs to practise reading the conversation. For additional fluency practice, play the audio again line by line, and ask students to try repeating the lines with the same pace and intonation on the audio.

4

- Ask students to form new pairs. Read the instructions aloud.
- Ask pairs to practise the conversation in Exercise 3, inserting the first set of new information in Exercise 4. Ask pairs to change roles once. Then ask them to change partners and practise the conversation, inserting the second set of information.
- Repeat until students have completed the conversation with all four sets of information.

5 2.08

- Ask a student to read the instructions and the answer choices aloud.
- Give students time to mark their guesses. Make sure students understand that they can tick more than one answer.
- Play the audio once or twice as needed, and ask students to check their guesses.
- Go over the answers with the whole class.

> ***Answers***
>
> **b** It's not the custom for many British companies to send gifts.
>
> **c** Companies don't like to accept gifts.

- To finish, ask for volunteers to explain the cultural misunderstanding that Jake describes. (A vendor sent some expensive gifts. In Singapore, employees can't accept expensive gifts, so they returned them.)

Selecting gifts p71

Vocabulary and expressions

fancy
fiancée
funerals
greedy
Hindu religion
ordinary

1

- Read the instructions aloud. Then ask for volunteers to read the phrases in the table aloud. Go over any unfamiliar vocabulary. Highlight the gerund form used with *How about …?*

2

- Read the instructions aloud. Ask for two volunteers to read the model conversation aloud.
- To elicit some useful vocabulary and prepare students for the task, ask them to look at the pictures. Elicit some adjectives to describe each gift, for example, *small, inexpensive, short, stylish, fragile,* etc. Then write the following phrases (from Exercise 1) on the board:

  It's / They're too …

  It isn't / They aren't … enough.

  Go through the pictures of the gifts one by one, and ask students to make sentences about the pictures using the phrases on the board, for example, for *key ring* students could say *It's too small.* or *It isn't special enough.*
- Put students with a partner to practise the conversation, inserting the information below the pictures. Walk around the class as students work, listening in and offering help as needed.
- When students are comfortable with the conversation, ask them to cover the example conversation with a piece of paper, and then look at the pictures and try the conversations again in their own words.

> ***Answers***
>
> (Answers will vary. Below are sample answers.)
>
> **a** (key ring) A: It's isn't special enough.; B: How about a sweater?
>
> **b** (mini-skirt) A: It's too short.; B: How about a box of chocolates?
>
> **c** (vacuum cleaner) A: It's too ordinary.; B: How about a trip to Hawaii?
>
> **d** (video game system) A: It isn't special enough.; B: How about a picture of you together?
>
> **e** (skateboard) A: It's too dangerous.; B: How about a set of golf clubs?
>
> **f** (photo of yourself) A: It's too personal.; B: How about some local crafts?

3 2.09

- Read the instructions aloud.
- Give students time to read the sentences silently. Then ask them to discuss the sentences with a partner and try to guess the answers.
- Play the audio once or twice as needed, and ask students to circle the answers. Tell students they should write brief notes for the reasons, not full sentences. For lower-level classes, play the audio once and ask students to circle the correct words in the sentences. Then play it again, and ask them to listen for and write the reasons.
- To check answers, ask for volunteers to read the sentences aloud, inserting the correct information.

> ***Answers***
>
> **a** after the giver has left; looks greedy if opened while giver is still there
>
> **b** Chinese; looks like their food is not good enough
>
> **c** four; sounds like the word for death
>
> **d** odd; luckier than even numbers
>
> **e** leather; cows special in Hindu religion
>
> **f** white; means death

- For additional listening practice, play the audio again and ask students to listen for and write any other gift-giving customs the speakers mention.
- To finish, lead a brief class discussion about the gift-giving customs. Ask students to say which customs are similar to or different from their own cultures.

Photocopiable activity pp108–109

Intercultural quiz

1. Prepare one copy of the *Intercultural quiz* for every pair of students in the class.
2. Give half the class the Student A handout, and the other half the Student B handout.
3. Ask students to stand and walk around and ask one another the quiz questions to find out the answers.
4. When students find an answer, they should write it on the quiz sheet, and then go and ask another person the next question. If students don't have the answer, they can say, *I'm sorry. I don't know.*
5. When students finish the quiz, ask them to check their answers with a partner.
6. To finish, ask students to share any additional information they know about the countries or customs on the quiz.

Extension activity

Gift-giving advice: Ask students to discuss gift-giving customs for different occasions in their own culture. Ask the class to brainstorm occasions when gifts are typically given in their culture, for example, birthdays, anniversaries or specific holidays. Then tell students to think of gift-giving advice for a visitor to their culture. Write the following phrases on the board for students' reference.

... is / are always a good gift.

You should never give ...

If you give ..., it means ...

- Put students into groups to discuss their ideas. Ask them to choose a group member to write down the group's ideas. Tell them to create specific advice for the occasions on the board, for example, *For a birthday, sweets are always a nice gift.*
- When groups finish their lists, ask for a volunteer from each group to share the group's ideas with the class.

Explaining a problem / mistake p72

Vocabulary and expressions

Jewish

Muslims

romantic relationships

1 2.10

- Tell students they are going to learn some useful expressions for apologising or explaining when they make a mistake.
- Ask students to keep their Student's Books closed. Play the audio and ask them just to listen to the conversation.
- Ask for a volunteer to tell you what the two speakers are talking about, and what the problem is. (One person has given a gift that is inappropriate in the other person's culture: a *lei* made of flowers that are usually used at funerals.)
- Ask students to open their books. Then play the audio and ask students to listen and read along silently.
- Put students with a partner to practise the conversation. To help them focus on the correct intonation, ask them to repeat the line *Oh, no! I'm so sorry!* after you a few times.
- When students are comfortable with the conversation, ask them to stand and roleplay the situation using their own words.
- To finish, ask for a few volunteer pairs to perform the roleplay for the class.

Explaining a problem / mistake: Giving and accepting apologies p73

2

- Read the first sentence of the instructions aloud. Then give students time to read the expressions in the table silently.
- Read the expressions aloud, modelling the correct intonation, and ask students to repeat them. For lower-level classes, ask students to work with a partner and take turns reading the expressions aloud, until they are comfortable with the intonation.
- Read the rest of the instructions aloud. Then ask students to underline the expressions in the conversation on page 72.
- Go over the answers with the whole class.

> ***Answers***
> It's just that, I'm so sorry, That's perfectly OK.

- Ask students to practise the conversation, inserting the new expressions from Exercise 2. Ask them to change partners several times, to maximise the practice.
- To finish, ask students to close their books and continue practising the conversation in their own words.

3

- Read the instructions aloud. Then ask students to read the situations aloud. Go over any unfamiliar vocabulary.
- Put students with a partner and ask them to decide who will be the gift-giver / receiver first.
- Give students time on their own to look over the four issues and the conversation map and prepare for their role in the conversation. For lower-level classes, go through each step on the conversation map, and elicit phrases students can use. Write the phrases on the board for students' reference. Allow lower-level students to make some notes to help them.
- Ask students to practise the conversation several times. Encourage them to make eye contact with their partner, and to use the correct intonation. Then ask them to change roles and practise several more times.
- For additional practice, ask students to brainstorm one or two more gift-giving situations that might occur in their own culture. Then ask them to practise the conversation with those situations.
- To finish, ask pairs to combine to form groups of four or six and take turns performing their roleplays.

Viewpoints: Cultural mistakes p74

1

- Read the instructions and the predictions aloud. Ask students to circle their predictions with a partner, and then compare them. Elicit a few predictions from the class.

2

- Give students about five minutes to read the passages. For lower-level classes, read the passage aloud and ask students to listen and read along.
- Ask students to tell you whether their predictions were correct, and to cite the correct information in the passages (In Thailand, it's rude to point at something with your foot; In Germany, the custom is to close the door whenever you leave a room).
- To finish, lead a brief class discussion about each reading passage. Ask the class the following questions:

  What was the cultural mistake?

  How did the person (from the host culture) react?

  How did the visitor feel?

  Have you ever had a similar experience?

3

- Ask students to form groups of three or four.
- Ask a student to read the discussion questions aloud.
- Give students about ten minutes for their discussions. To facilitate independent discussion, tell groups to assign the following roles to each member:

  Facilitator: asks the questions, and makes sure all group members participate

  Time-keeper: makes sure the group spends equal time on each question, and that the discussion finishes on time

  Secretary: takes notes on the main points of the group's discussion

  Reporter: reports the main points of the group's discussion to the class.
- Walk around the class as students work, listening in, and encouraging them as necessary.
- When students finish, ask the reporter from each group to share the group's ideas with the class.
- To finish, ask the class the last question *What are some ways a foreign visitor can learn about local customs?* and elicit responses from several students. Point out the importance of learning about local customs when working in an international setting, or with clients from other countries.
- Ask students to complete the matching task on page 4 in respect of Emily Olsen. In pairs, ask them to check all their answers on page 4.

> ***Answer***
>
> Emily Olsen = a

In business: Choosing a wedding gift p75

Vocabulary and expressions

acquaintances

appropriate

evaluate

- Before you begin this lesson, read the two sets of In business task activity instructions, so that you can be prepared to answer students' questions.

Scenario

- Ask a student to read the *Scenario* aloud for the class.

Task 1

- Divide the class into two groups (A and B).
- Tell each group to look at the appropriate page in their Student's Books (Group A – page 92; Group B – page 102).
- Give groups time to read the information in the Task files.
- Allow about 15 minutes for students' discussions. Walk around the class as students work, listening in and offering help as needed. Remind students

to discuss the reasons why they think a gift is appropriate or inappropriate.

Task 2

- Ask students to form new groups of four with two members from each original group (A and B).
- Give students time to read the model conversations silently. Then ask for volunteers to read the conversations aloud for the class, inserting the information from their Task files.
- Give groups about ten minutes to discuss the gifts and to share their final choices.
- To finish, ask groups to share their final decisions with the class. Ask them to explain how they arrived at their decisions.

Follow-up

- Ask students to stay in their groups from Task 2. Alternatively, do this activity with the whole class.
- Read the instructions and the discussion questions aloud. Give students about ten minutes for their discussions.
- Ask for volunteers to share any international or intercultural gift-giving experiences they may have had.

I need to work harder

12

Unit aims

In Unit 12, students learn about:

- Reviewing performance
- Responding to feedback and asking for clarification
- Checking understanding
- Self-evaluation
- Discussing performance plans
- Viewpoints: High- and low-context cultures
- In business: Evaluating and recommending

The aims for each class can be written on the board to orient students to the unit content and objectives.

Getting started

Begin this unit by reviewing the skills students learnt in Unit 11 for choosing appropriate gifts. Before class, prepare two sets of cards. You will need one set of occasion cards, with a common gift-giving occasion written on each card (a co-worker's birthday, a boss's wedding, thank you to a client). You will also need a set of gift cards, with a type of gift written on each (if possible, you can also use pictures printed from computer clip art, or cut from magazines). Make sure the types of gifts are varied and try to include some that may have cultural implications, for example, a box of chocolates, a new car, a set of four pens, a calendar, clothing, etc. Make enough sets of both the occasion and the gifts cards for each pair of students in the class.

- Ask students to form pairs, and give each group one set of occasion cards and one set of gift cards.
- Write the following conversation on the board:

  A: *I need to get a gift for (occasion).*

  B: *Why don't you get him / her a ____________? They're attractive / useful / easy to mail / personal.*

  A: *That's a great idea. Thanks. / Hmm. I'm not sure. It might be too expensive / personal / fragile. / In (country), that's not a good gift because …*
- Student A chooses an occasion card, and Student B chooses a gift card. Then they begin the conversation. Ask pairs to switch roles halfway through.
- To give students practice with offering and receiving gifts and apologising for inappropriate gifts, ask them to use only the gift cards. Student A offers the gift to Student B, and Student B responds accordingly.

Listen and practise:

Reviewing performance p76

Vocabulary and expressions

accurate
annual review
expectations
objectives
outstanding

1

- Before you begin this lesson, ask students to keep their Student's Books closed. Tell students that in this unit, they are going to focus on job skills and performance. Ask the class to brainstorm a list of qualities of a good employee, and write students' ideas on the board, for example, being organised / responsible / hardworking, working well with others, etc.
- Ask students to open their books to page 76.
- Read the instructions aloud, and give students time to read the performance review form. Go over any unfamiliar vocabulary.
- Point out any qualities written on the board that match the ones on the form. Ask students to note any information included on the form that they did not suggest above.
- Explain, or elicit an explanation for *Performance review* (an evaluation of an employee's work, usually done annually). Ask students to form pairs to discuss the purpose of the form and who will use it.
- Elicit responses from several students. Clarify the purpose of the form, if necessary. (PR forms are used by managers to evaluate employees' work performance. Generally, both the individual employee and his or her supervisor(s) see the form.)

2 **2.11**

- Before you play the audio, put students with a partner and ask them to predict the missing words on the performance review form. Elicit some guesses from the class.
- Read the instructions aloud.
- Play the audio once, and ask students to tick the ratings on the performance review form. Then ask students to compare answers with a partner.
- Play the audio again, and ask students to complete the supervisor's comments.
- To check answers, ask the class questions about the form to elicit the correct information, for example, *What rating did Erik give Zara for job knowledge? What was his comment?*

> *Answers*
>
> Job knowledge: above expectations; has worked hard
>
> Quality and quantity of work: above expectations; pays attention to; needs to ask
>
> Planning and organisational skills: meets expectations; to make sure
>
> Interpersonal skills: outstanding; always positive

- To finish, ask students to tell you how they think Zara feels about her performance review. To preview the phrases students will learn for responding to feedback, ask students to tell you any words or phrases in the audio that indicate her overall reaction, for example, *Good, thank you.* and *OK, that's true.*

3

- Read the instructions aloud.
- Ask students to form pairs and tell them to decide who will play Erik and who will play Zara in the conversation. Give students time on their own to review the form in Exercise 1 and prepare for the conversation. If students need additional support, play the audio again, and ask them to note any useful phrases. Alternatively, hand out a copy of the audioscript on pages 124–125 of this Teacher's Book, and ask students to practise the conversation a few times before they do so in their own words.
- Ask students to practise the roleplay several times. Remind them to change roles.
- To finish, ask for volunteers to perform the roleplay for the class.

4 2.12

- Before you begin this exercise, ask the class to think of advice they could give Zara on how she could improve her work performance. Elicit several ideas and write them on the board, for example, *When she has a question, she should ask a colleague right away.*
- Ask students to open their books to page 77. Ask a student to read the instructions and the answer choices aloud.
- Give students time to tick their guesses. Make sure they understand that they can choose more than one item.
- Ask students to compare answers with a partner. Then elicit a few guesses from the class.
- Play the audio and ask students to check their guesses.
- Go over the answers with the whole class. Ask students to share the words or phrases they heard that helped them get the answer.

> *Answers*
>
> **b** I can take some training courses.
>
> **d** I'm not sure. Do you have any suggestions?

- To finish, ask for volunteers to tell you what specific skills Zara would like to improve (time management and writing).

Responding to feedback and asking for clarification p77

1 2.13

- Read the instructions aloud. Ask students to work with a partner to try to remember Zara's reactions to Erik's feedback. Then ask for volunteers to read the sentences, inserting their guesses.
- Play the audio and ask students to complete the missing information.
- To check answers, ask students to write the sentences on the board.

> *Answers*
>
> that's true, for the feedback, I appreciate that

2

- Read the instructions aloud. Then ask for volunteers to read the phrases above the boxes aloud.
- Explain that the phrases indicate the person's reaction to the feedback.
- Give students time to complete the boxes. Walk around the class as students work, offering help as needed. If students need hints, read the phrases aloud with the proper intonation to indicate the person's reaction.
- Go over the answers with the whole class.

Answers

Agreement	Understanding	Disagreement
You're right, thank you. I think that's true. I agree with you.	I see. I understand what you're saying.	I don't agree. I'm not sure that's true. I don't think that's correct.

3 2.14

- Read the instructions aloud. Ask for volunteers to try to predict the missing information. Write students' ideas on the board.
- Play the audio and ask students to complete the sentences.
- To check answers, ask students to read the correct sentences aloud.

> *Answers*
>
> What do you mean by that, can you explain that, give me an example

4

- Read the instructions aloud. Ask for volunteers to try reading the sentences aloud using the same intonation as Zara used on the audio.
- If necessary, play the audio again, pausing after the phrases for students to repeat. Then ask students to continue the practice with a partner.

> **Teaching tip**
>
> **Review of peer feedback:** Before you do Exercise 5, students may need a review of the rationale behind having them give and receive peer feedback. Remind them that the aim of peer feedback is to allow students to observe and learn from one another so that they can help one another improve their skills. Point out that giving feedback means pointing out positive points (strengths) as well as suggesting areas for improvement (not simply pointing out weaknesses).

5

- Read the instructions aloud. Tell students they are going to have a chance to practise giving and receiving feedback about their work in this course.
- To model the task, tell the class that you would like to take the opportunity to get some feedback, so that in the future, you can continue to improve the course for your future students. Ask students to first think of a few strengths and areas for improvement for the course in general. Elicit feedback from the class, and respond or ask for clarification using the appropriate phrases from page 77.
- Ask students to form groups of three. Allow students to choose their groups, as it will be helpful for this activity if students are somewhat familiar with one another.
- Give students time to think of feedback and complete the table about their two classmates. Refer students to the examples above the table if they need ideas.
- When students finish their tables, ask them to take turns sharing and reacting to the feedback. Remind students to use the phrases they learnt on page 77. Walk around the class as students work, listening in and encouraging students as needed.
- To finish, lead a brief class discussion about students' experiences with the exercise. Ask for volunteers to share how they felt giving and receiving the feedback, and any challenges they had.

Checking understanding p78

1 2.15

- Tell students they are now going to learn some useful expressions for checking their understanding when they are listening to another person explaining something or giving information.
- Read the instructions aloud. Ask the class why they think it's important to check one's understanding, particularly in a business situation. Elicit several responses from the class, for example, *If people misunderstand important information, it could create problems for the company.*
- Play the audio once and ask students just to listen to the conversations. Then play the audio again, and ask them to complete the expressions.
- To check answers, ask students to read the expressions aloud.

> ***Answers***
>
> let me check that I understand, Let me confirm, Can I confirm

- For additional practice, ask for volunteers to play the role of the second speaker in each of the conversations. Play the audio again, stopping after the first speaker in each conversation. Then ask the volunteers to check understanding and repeat the information.

2

- Ask students to form pairs. Read the instructions and the list of tasks aloud. Model the activity by explaining one of the tasks to the class yourself. Explain that students should check their understanding when you are finished, using the phrases they learnt in Exercise 1.
- Give students time to choose one of the tasks and prepare their explanation. Encourage lower-level students to make notes to help them.
- When students are ready, give pairs about six minutes (three minutes per partner) to explain the information and check understanding. Walk around the class as students work, listening in and making note of any areas to address later.
- To finish, ask students to share their reactions to the exercise. Ask the class *Were the instructions successful? What was challenging? How could you improve the next time?*

Self-evaluation p79

1

- Before you begin this lesson, make some time to review what students have learnt in the course. You may even want to dedicate an entire class period to review. (See Review ideas in the Extension activity below.)

> **Extension activity**
>
> **Review ideas**
>
> - Create a review worksheet using the Performance language (Review) on pages 122–124 of the Student's Book. Make a copy of the lists and use correction fluid to blank out some words in the phrases. Make one copy of the worksheets

for each student in the class. Hand out the worksheets, and ask students to work together (looking through the Student's Book and their notes) to complete them.

- Ask students to work in groups of four or five to go through the textbook and create review quiz questions. Write some model question formats on the board for students to follow, for example, multiple choice, true / false, fill-in-the-blank, etc. Each group should write about ten to twelve questions. When groups finish, ask them to exchange papers with another group, and then work to complete the review quiz. Allow them to use their Student's Books to find the answers.
- Ask students to work in groups of three or four. Tell groups to look at the table of contents on pages 2 and 3 of their Student's Books. Groups should look together at the column labelled 'Contents'. Ask students to read the list of contents together, and brainstorm phrases and expressions they have learnt for each topic. Then ask them to refer to the Performance language (Review) on pages 122–124 of the Student's Book to compare their lists.
- Once students have had a chance to review the language and skills they have learnt in the course, ask them to look at the self-evaluation form on page 79 of the Student's Book.
- Read the instructions aloud, and give students time to read the self-evaluation form silently. Allow at least 15 to 20 minutes for students to complete the form. Encourage them to look back through their notes as well as the Student's Book units, and to add specific comments about their own performance and improvement. Walk around the class as students work, offering help and encouraging students as needed.

2

- Ask students to form pairs.
- Read the instructions aloud. Write some useful phrases on the board to help students, for example:

  One area I think I improved in is …

  I'm confident about my ability to …

  I think I'm good at …

  I worked hard on …

  Something I'd like to continue working on is …

  I'd like to develop my skills in …
- Give pairs about ten minutes to share their self-evaluations. Remind students to give one another feedback on their performance in the class, for example:

  I think you're really good at …; One thing you could do is …
- Walk around the class as students work, reminding them to check understanding and clarify information. Encourage students to share ideas on how to improve their skills, and to take notes on their partner's feedback.
- To finish, ask for volunteers to share one strength and one area for improvement. Ask the class to suggest ideas for how to improve.

Discussing performance plans p79

1 2.16

- Read the instructions aloud. Then give students time to read the answer choices silently.
- Before you play the audio, ask students to work with a partner to predict the answers. Elicit some guesses from the class.
- Play the audio once or twice as needed, and ask students to mark their answers.
- Ask students to compare answers with a partner. Then check answers by calling on students to read the correct statements aloud.

> ***Answers***
>
> **a** 2 **b** 4 **c** 3 **d** 2

- To finish, ask the class *Why does Erik want to send Zara overseas? Where does he plan to send her? How does she feel about it?*

Viewpoints:
High context – low context p80

Vocabulary and expressions

criticise

praise

task-focused

1

- Focus students' attention on the chart. Go through the words and phrases one by one, and try to elicit an explanation or example for each one, for example, *indirect*: preferring not to say things or give answers directly, for example, when giving feedback or saying *no* to a request. Explain that the words describe very general characteristics of communication styles.
- When students are familiar with the concept of high- / low-context cultures, read the instructions and the discussion questions aloud.
- Put students into groups of three or four to discuss the questions. Give them about ten minutes.
- When groups finish their discussions, ask for a volunteer from each group to share the highlights of their group's discussion. Ask students to give examples of ways their own or others' communication style is high-context or low-context.

2 2.17

- Read the instructions aloud.
- Before you play the audio, ask students to predict some information they might hear that would help them get the answers, for example, information about relationships, feelings, direct / indirectness, etc.
- Play the audio once, and ask students to mark *high context* or *low context*.
- Ask students to compare answers with a partner. Then play the audio again and ask students to take notes on each speaker's attitude about giving feedback.
- Ask students to compare notes and explain their answers.
- To finish, elicit the answers from the class, and ask students to give examples from the audio.

> ***Answers***
>
> **a** high context: don't think I need to tell them directly; need to work well together as a team and have a good relationship
>
> **b** low context: be clear, focused, and direct; give details and examples; focus on what the next steps are, and what changes they need to make

3

- Ask students to look at the iceberg picture. Explain that the aspects of culture that are above the water are those aspects that one can physically see examples of within a culture, for example, food, music, holidays, etc. The aspects below the water are the parts of a culture that are 'invisible': feelings, attitudes, emotions, etc.
- Give students time on their own to think about the items in the list and where they fit in the iceberg model of culture.
- Ask students to discuss their ideas in groups of three or four. Tell them to give reasons and examples to support their ideas. Walk around the class as students work, listening in and offering ideas as needed.
- When students finish, copy a large version of the iceberg onto the board. Then ask for volunteers to come up and write the items in the correct places.
- When students have written all of the items, lead a whole-class discussion about the picture on the board. Ask students to give examples for why they chose to place the items above or below the water. Confirm students' answers.

> ***Answers***
>
> Above the water: clothes, gestures, literature, history, music, food
>
> Below the water: religious beliefs, values, importance of time, respect for others, nature of friendship

4

- To finish, ask the class *Can you think of any examples of how items below the water affect the visible items?* Give one of two examples to help clarify the question, for example, *Religious beliefs may affect customs, such as holidays and food.* Lead a class discussion about the items, and ask students to give examples from their own and other cultures.

In business:
Evaluating and recommending
p81

Scenario

- Explain that students will now have a chance to use their skills for giving feedback to evaluate their textbook, and make valuable recommendations for how to improve it.
- Ask a student to read the *Scenario* aloud for the class.

Task 1

- Read the instructions and the questions aloud. Encourage students to look back through the units of the Student's Book, and make note of any units, sections, or activities that were particularly enjoyable / challenging / interesting (or uninteresting).
- Allow about ten minutes for students to complete the table with the feedback. For lower-level classes, ask students to work with a partner, so they can help each other. Walk around the class as students work, offering help as needed.

Task 2

- Ask students to form groups of three or four to share ideas. Ask groups to choose a group leader to open and close the meeting. You may want to set a limit for how many recommendations groups should make, for example, five. Remind students to take notes on the group's ideas and decisions.
- Allow about 10 to 15 minutes for their meeting. Walk around the class as students work, listening in and making sure all students are participating.

Task 3

- Ask students to form new groups of three or four.
- Give groups about 15 minutes to share their ideas (three to five minutes per student). Tell students to give reasons to support their opinions and recommendations.

Task 4

- Read the instructions aloud. Divide the class into groups of six to eight students. Alternatively, do the activity with the whole class.
- You can do this activity as a roleplay with half the class playing managers, and half the class playing consultants who have been asked to give feedback on the book. Have students change roles once. This way, students will also have a chance to practise the

language and skills they have learnt for responding to feedback.

- When students finish the meeting, ask them to give a brief presentation outlining the strengths and areas of improvement they have identified. Remind students to use the language and skills they have learnt in this course for giving presentations.
- Encourage students to ask one another questions about their decisions, so that they have a chance to practise responding to questions.

Follow-up

- Read the instructions and the questions aloud. Give students time to write their answers to the questions.
- Ask students to form pairs or small groups to share their answers to the questions. Tell them to share ideas and give recommendations for how to improve.
- To finish, ask for volunteers to share with the class their own strengths and areas for improvement, as well as ideas for how to improve.
- Ask students to complete the Review of Units 9–12 on pages 82 and 83 of the Student's Book.

Teaching tip

Written feedback: If time allows, you may want to collect students' written answers to the Follow-up task questions and respond to them in writing as part of your final feedback on students' work in the course. This will give you an idea of how students feel about their progress in the course, and students will enjoy receiving personalised feedback and suggestions for improvement.

Photocopiable activity

p110

Feedback form

1 Prepare one copy of *Feedback form* for every student.

2 Tell students NOT to write their names on the form. You will get more honest answers that way!

3 Ask students to complete the form individually, either in class or as homework.

4 Collect the forms from the students and go through them while the course is still fresh in your mind. If you learnt anything that would influence how you teach the course the next time, write it down so that you won't forget it.

Review unit answer key 1–4

1 What's the question?

(Sample answers. Answers will vary.)

What's your name?

Where are you from originally?

What do you do?

What kind of things do you like to do?

2 Who are they?

Lizzy **Brown**

Chicago, U.S.

Research Assistant

Scuba-diving

Peter Swain

Bath, England

Student (history)

Rock climbing, **Scuba-diving**

3 What's wrong?

Hi everyone, I'm Emil! I graduated ~~in~~ **from** UCLA last year. I'm **from** Hungary originally but I ~~live~~ **lived** in California when I was a student. I like swimming and ~~play~~ **playing** music. I'm excited **about** working here and getting to know everyone.

4 Mixed-up

A: Hi, Phil. Do you know Sofia?

B: No, we haven't met.

A: Oh, OK. Phil, this is Sofia – she's studying Japanese with me. Sofia, this is Phil.

C: Nice to meet you, Phil. Where are you from?

B: Nice to meet you, too. I'm from England originally. How about you?

C: Well, I was born in Italy, but I moved to the US when I was young.

5 Odd one out

a 3 (others are related to presentation openings)

b 2 (others are talking about presentation openings)

c 2 (others are related to presentation outline)

6 In my next slide …

Title: Process improvements – **reducing** cycle time

Message: **We can cut** costs by **17%**

Outline: 1 Current situation

2 Recommendations (Improvements)

3 Expected **cost savings**

7 Would you like me to show you around?

(Answers will vary. Below are sample expressions students could include.)

Why don't we …?	Sounds great!
How about …?	Absolutely.
We could …	I'd love that.
	That sounds great.
	We could do, but …
	It's a nice idea, but …

8 We need to talk …

(Sample answers. Answers will vary.)

Let's consider whether we have enough money.

We need to talk about how much time it will take.

We have to discuss when the project will start.

We need to consider how many people we need.

9 Connect two

a 3 **b** 4 **c** 5 **d** 2 **e** 1

10 What's the word?

Students' own answers.

5–8 Review unit answer key

1 I'm not here right now

a Please call back – after 5:00p.m. today

b Will call you back – about the soccer game this weekend

c Please call back – about the meeting tomorrow

2 Can I take a message?

Students' own answers.

3 Could you tell me where the bus stop is?

(Sample answers. Answers will vary.)

A: Can you tell me where the bank is?
B: I'm sorry, I don't know.

A: Excuse me, do you know what time it is?
B: Yes of course, it's two o'clock.

A: Do you know who that man is?
B: That's my brother.

A: Could you tell me where the nearest post office is?
B: There's one over there, around the corner.

4 Go straight for four blocks

5 Best regards

(Sample answer. Answers will vary.)

Dear Mr Richie,

Attached please find the report you requested. Let me know if you have any questions on this.

Regards,

Ruth Osborne

6 You need to look more confident

Students' own answers.

7 Thanks so much for your feedback!

Students' own answers.

8 What's the word?

Students' own answers.

Review unit answer key 9–12

1 I was born in 1986

(Sample answers. Answers will vary.)

Jill's name should be typed.

Jill's date of birth should not be included.

Jill's gender should not be included.

Jill's marital status should not be included.

Jill's hobbies should not be included.

Jill's photo should not be included. The font should be more professional, and should be black.

2 Can you give me an example?

Students' own answers.

3 I enjoy the work, but …

Paris, France

England

London 20**12**

Hotel management

Welcoming guests

accepting **reservations**

dealing with problems

hiking

5 years from now

helicopter pilot

4 It's a long story …

Students' own answers.

5 Tell me about yourself

Students' own answers.

6 It's perfect!

(Sample answers. Answers will vary.)

It's **too big.**

It isn't **small enough.**

It's **too easy.**

It isn't **difficult enough.**

7 Don't worry about it

(Sample answers. Answers will vary.)

a Please don't worry about it.

b That's perfectly OK.

c It's all right.

8 Can you explain that a little more?

Students' own answers.

9 What's the word?

Students' own answers.

1–12 Grammar reference answer key

Unit 1 – Verb tense review

1 1 didn't/did not study 2 met 3 started 4 have (never) tried 5 Have (you ever) been 6 have gone 7 're/are not going to finish 8 going to rent 9 'll/will go 10 won't/will not be

2 1 Have you heard of 2 have wanted 3 was 4 worked 5 am going to work 6 wanted 7 am going to 8 will be 9 am going to 10 will

Unit 2 – Suggestions – *Why don't /doesn't / We could / How about*

1

(Sample answers:)

1 How about a bouquet of flowers and some chocolates.

2 Why don't we go to the cinema?

3 We could organize a charity fun run.

4 Why don't we use low-energy light bulbs?

2

(Sample answers:)

1 I don't think so. I'd rather do some exercise.

2 I'd love that!

3 I don't think that's a good idea. We already have a lot of work.

4 That sounds great!

3

(Student's own answers)

Unit 3 – Modals

1 1 shouldn't 2 have to 3 Can I 4 should 5 should 6 need to 7 should we 8 Can you 9 shouldn't 10 don't have to

2 1 d 2 a 3 g 4 e 5 b 6 c 7 f

Unit 4 – *Can* and *could*

1 1 ability 2 possibility 3 ability 4 ability 5 possibility 6 possibility 7 possibility

2 1 can, can, can, couldn't, can, can/could, can/could, can/could, can/could, can, can

2 could, could, can't, can, could, could, could

Unit 5 – Subject and object pronouns

1 1 Please tell him to call me back.

2 Can you let him know I'll be late?

3 I will see them sometime next week.

4 Let her know we will see her tomorrow.

5 Tell him I'll call him back after lunch.

6 Can you ask her to call me back?

2 1 him, us 2 she 3 I 4 me 5 me 6 I 7 she and I 8 me, them

Unit 6 – Direct and indirect questions

1

(Sample answers:)

1 Can you tell me where the photocopier is?

2 Do you know how you pronounce this word?

3 Can I ask what time lunch is?

4 Could you tell me how long you have worked here?

5 Can you tell me whether you received my email?

6 Do you know how far it is from here to the hotel?

7 Can I ask when the meeting will finish?

8 Could you tell me who those people are?

9 Can you tell me whether you are going to the office tomorrow?

10 Do you know why they didn't tell us yesterday?

11 Can I ask how long it will take to get there?

12 Could you tell me whether you have sent them the report?

Unit 7 – Expressions with infinitives and gerunds

1/2 1 ✗ I'm calling to reschedule my appointment next week.

2 ✓

3 ✓

4 ✗ I look forward to doing business with you in the future.

5 ✓

6 ✗ I look forward to talking to Mr Park.

7 ✓

8 ✓

9 ✗ I'm writing to thank you for the lovely gift.

10 ✗ Thank you for editing my reports.

3 1 attachment 2 closing 3 Emoticons 4 copy in 5 forward 6 attached 7 reply

Unit 8 – Cleft sentences: *The main thing I want to say is …*

1 1 What we need is new software.

2 What I don't want to do is make any mistakes.

3 What they have to do is improve their English.

4 What you need to do is try harder.

5 What I like doing is walking in the mountains.

6 What you should do is stop smoking.

2

(Suggested answers:)

2 The time when it is best to study is …

3 The thing that I like about studying English is …

4 The thing that I don't like about studying English is …

5 The reason why we need to use a textbook is …

6 The best way to improve my vocabulary is …

7 The best way to improve my speaking ability is …

Unit 9 – Quantifiers: *a lot of, some, much, many*

1 1 many 2 many 3 much 4 much 5 many 6 much 7 many 8 many 9 many 10 much

2 1 many 2 a lot of 3 some 4 a lot of 5 a lot of 6 many 7 a lot of 8 some

Unit 10 – Adjective + preposition – *good at, interested in, famous for*

1 1 about 2 at 3 about 4 for 5 for 6 with 7 about

2

(Student's own answers)

Unit 11 – Quantifiers: *too / enough*

1 1 I have too many plants in my office.

2 We don't have enough time to finish.

3 The package is too expensive to send overnight.

4 These flowers aren't pretty enough for a gift.

2

(Suggested answers:)

2 It isn't cheap enough.

3 The room is too hot.

4 That shelf isn't low enough.

5 This film is too boring.

6 My boss isn't generous enough.

7 This cord is too short.

3 1 That's perfectly OK.

2 I'm really sorry.

3 I feel terrible!

4 Please don't worry about it.

Unit 12 – Agreement and understanding

1 1 A 2 U 3 A 4 U 5 A 6 U

2/3

(Student's own answers)

TOEIC® practice answer key 1–7

Unit 1

LISTENING: A Photographs

1 D 2 B

B Sentence – Response

3 A 5 A
4 C 6 B

READING: Sentence completion

7 D 10 B
8 A 11 D
9 C 12 B

Unit 2

LISTENING: Short conversations and talks

1 C 4 B
2 B 5 B
3 D 6 A

READING: Passage completion

7 A 10 A
8 D 11 C
9 B 12 C

Unit 3

LISTENING: A Photographs

1 D 2 B

B Sentence – Response

3 A 5 B
4 C 6 C

READING: Sentence completion

7 B 10 D
8 C 11 A
9 A 12 C

Unit 4

LISTENING: Short conversations and talks

1 B 4 B
2 C 5 D
3 A 6 C

READING: Reading comprehension

7 B 9 C
8 D 10 A

Unit 5

LISTENING: A Photographs

1 A 2 C

B Sentence – Response

3 B 5 B
4 C 6 A

READING: Sentence completion

7 B 10 C
8 D 11 B
9 A 12 C

Unit 6

LISTENING: Short conversations and talks

1 C 4 D
2 B 5 C
3 B 6 D

READING: Passage completion

7 D 9 A
8 C 10 B

Unit 7

LISTENING: A Photographs

1 D 2 A

B Sentence – Response

3 A 5 C
4 B 6 B

READING: Sentence completion

7 B 10 B
8 A 11 D
9 D 12 C

8–12 TOEIC® practice answer key

Unit 8

LISTENING: Short conversations and talks

1 A	4 C
2 C	5 B
3 A	6 C

READING: Paired Reading

7 D	9 D
8 C	10 B

Unit 9

LISTENING: A Photographs

1 C 2 B

B Sentence – Response

3 C	5 A
4 B	6 A

READING: Sentence completion

7 B	10 B
8 A	11 D
9 D	12 A

Unit 10

LISTENING: Short conversations and talks

1 C	4 B
2 D	5 A
3 A	6 D

READING: Passage Completion

7 D	9 A
8 C	10 C

Unit 11

LISTENING: A Photographs

1 C 2 A

B Sentence – Response

3 B	5 C
4 A	6 B

READING: Sentence completion

7 C	10 C
8 B	11 B
9 D	12 A

Unit 12

LISTENING: Short conversations and talks

1 B	4 A
2 D	5 C
3 C	6 D

READING: Passage completion

7 A	9 D
8 C	10 B

BEC practice answer key 1–12

Unit 1

Reading Part 1

1 B 2 A 3 A 4 A

Speaking Part 1

Answers should be appropriate responses to the questions, and brief. The first phase of the Speaking test is intended to put candidates at their ease.

Unit 2

Listening Part 2

1 Wilstead 2 01998 376 77 3 GK 57 4 PL 448
5 HT 31 6 409.35 7 June 15

Writing Part 1

Answers should deal appropriately with all three points and communicate effectively with the target reader. They should be within the word limits.

As in the whole of the Writing test, communicative competence is more important in the marking than accuracy. Candidates are assessed on their ability to communicate effectively in English in a business context, not on their knowledge of business.

Unit 3

Reading Part 2

1 G 2 B 3 F 4 E 5 H

Speaking Part 2

The mini-presentation should answer the question (*What is important when organizing visits to your company?*). The three bullet points (*Who the visitors are*, etc) are intended to help candidates, and it isn't essential to talk about any or all of them.

Answers to the questions should communicate effectively, and be appropriate responses. Candidates should aim to say one or two sentences in answer to each question.

As in the whole of the Speaking test, communicative competence is more important in the marking than accuracy. Candidates are assessed on their ability to communicate effectively in English in a business context, not on their knowledge of business.

Unit 4

Reading Part 4

1 B 2 A 3 B 4 C 5 A 6 B 7 C

Writing Part 2

Answers should deal with all four points and communicate effectively with the target reader (Rick Wilson). They should be within the word limits.

Unit 5

Listening Part 1

1 B 2 A 3 A 4 C 5 C 6 B 7 B 8 C

Speaking Part 1

Answers should be appropriate responses to the questions, and brief. Candidates should give a reason for their answer, if appropriate, e.g. for the first question, *'Yes, because I often visit factories in France.'*

Unit 6

Reading Part 5

1 C 2 B 3 C 4 A 5 A 6 C

Speaking Part 3B

Answers to the questions should communicate effectively, and be appropriate responses. Candidates should aim to say one or two sentences in answer to each question, and give a reason for their answer, if appropriate.

Unit 7

Speaking Part 3

In the Speaking test, the examiner tells the candidates the scenario, twice. The candidates are given a card showing the visual or written prompts (here 'Ideas for open day'). The two candidates should discuss the scenario together for about two minutes.

The examiner asks the questions.

Writing Part 1

See notes on Unit 2, Writing Part 1.

Unit 8

Reading Part 6

1 B 2 A 3 A 4 C 5 B 6 A 7 C 8 A 9 B 10 C
11 A 12 B

Writing Part 2

See notes on Unit 4, Writing Part 2.

Unit 9

Listening Part 3

1 corner room 2 information centre 3 HR officer
4 salaries 5 strategy 6 programmer 7 skills

Speaking Part 2

See notes on Unit 3, Speaking Part 2.

Unit 10

Reading Part 3

1 D 2 H 3 G 4 C 5 B

Writing Part 1

See notes on Unit 2, Writing Part 1.

Unit 11

Reading Part 7

1 CROFT 2 FREEZER 3 BEFORE 14 MAY
4 LARRY SMITH 5 GUARANTEE ON THE WORK

Speaking Part 3B

See notes on Unit 6, Speaking Part 3B.

Unit 12

Listening Part 4

1 A 2 B 3 A 4 C 5 C 6 B 7 C 8 B

Writing Part 2

See notes on Unit 4, Writing Part 2.

1–6 TEST 1

LISTENING section (24 points)

A Listen to the conversation (CD2:20). Tick true or false. (4 points)

1 Mark and Tina work for the same company.
☐ True ☐ False

2 Mark feels uncomfortable talking about his job.
☐ True ☐ False

3 Tina's husband is a business professor.
☐ True ☐ False

4 Mark is taking a class with Tina's husband.
☐ True ☐ False

B Listen to the talk (CD2:21). Circle the correct answers. (4 points)

1 Maria Hernandez is speaking to …
a her own company.
b a different company.
c people from many different companies.

2 She is going to focus on …
a expanding business into Mexico.
b relationships between Mexicans and Americans.
c training employees for international business trips.

3 She has ___ main points.
a two
b three
c four

4 She is going to start by …
a giving some background.
b asking a question.
c showing some slides.

C Listen to the conversation (CD2:22). Circle the correct information. (4 points)

1 The *man / woman* is in charge of the meeting.

2 The woman wants to talk about *time / space* and cost.

3 The man *agrees / doesn't agree* with the woman's opinion.

4 They will make a decision by *voting / consensus*.

D Listen to the talk (CD2:23). Circle the correct answers. (4 points)

1 The man says that one reason for his ___ is meetings.
a job
b budget
c travel

2 The man says that ___ is important.
a body language
b meeting new people
c being on time

3 Face-to-face meetings help the man make decisions …
a by himself.
b more quickly.
c later.

4 The man believes face-to-face meetings help his company …
a save money.
b make better decisions.
c get more business.

E Listen to the telephone call (CD2:24). Tick true or false. (4 points)

1 John Sandefer is off sick today.
☐ True ☐ False

2 If the caller needs help right away, he or she should email Mr Sandefer.
☐ True ☐ False

3 The caller wants to talk about a schedule.
☐ True ☐ False

4 The caller says she will call back next week.
☐ True ☐ False

F Listen to the conversation (CD2:25). Circle the correct answers. (4 points)

1 The concert hall is …
a around the corner.
b past the corner.
c across the street.

2 After 6:30, the tickets will be …
a sold out.
b cheaper.
c free.

3 Finally, the man wants to find a …
a bank.
b café.
c hotel.

4 The woman tells the man to go down the street and …
a turn right.
b turn left.
c cross the street.

LANGUAGE AND VOCABULARY section
(51 points)

A Put the words in the correct order to make the questions. (8 points)

1 of / Brazil / part / from / you / what / are

________________________________?

2 you / what / studying / are

________________________________?

3 don't / café / why / we / to / a / go

________________________________?

4 should / restaurant / go / to / which / we

________________________________?

5 to / this / later / can / we / back / come

________________________________?

6 back / in / I / you / call / minutes / ten / can

________________________________?

7 it / here / is / distance / from / walking

________________________________?

8 where / is / you / could / the / station / me / tell

________________________________?

B Match the questions from Part A above to these responses. Write the number of the question in the box. (8 points)

[ ] **a** I'm a business student.
[ ] **b** OK. Let's take a break now.
[ ] **c** Actually, I recommend taking a taxi.
[ ] **d** That's a great idea.
[ ] **e** Rio de Janeiro.
[ ] **f** Sure. It's right around the corner.
[ ] **g** How about going for pizza?
[ ] **h** No problem. I'll be here.

C Fill in the blank with the correct letter. (10 points)

1 Raj, would you like to _______ a few words?
a know **b** do **c** make **d** say

2 My _______ today is that we need to work harder.
a speech **b** vision **c** message **d** presentation

3 Let me start by giving you _______ background.
a a **b** some **c** much **d** every

4 How about _______ to the market?
a going **b** go **c** we go **d** to go

5 Let's consider _______ we have enough money to buy new phones.
a how **b** when **c** whether **d** what

6 We'll focus _______ two main factors.
a at **b** on **c** with **d** for

7 _______ the top of my head, why don't we set up a website?
a From **b** Over **c** Off **d** On

8 Let's _______ the next point.
a move on to **b** hear from **c** agree to **d** find out

9 We _______ from Hyun Jin yet.
a don't hear **b** won't hear **c** aren't hearing **d** haven't heard

10 Would you like to _______ a message?
a make **b** say **c** leave **d** give

D Fill in the blank with the correct word or phrase from the box. (There are six extra words.) (10 points)

anything	foot	recommend	turn
confirmation	intersection	reservation	twin
corner	nothing	straight	under
lift	over	tell	walking

A: Welcome to the Daisy Chain Hotel. Can I help you?
B: Yes, I have a (1) __________ for tonight.
A: OK … what is your family name?
B: Barker. Keith Barker.
A: Uh … I'm sorry, I don't seem to have (2) __________ here under that name. Do you have a (3) __________ number?
B: Yes, here it is …
A: Oh, Barker! I'm sorry, I was looking (4) __________ Parker. So, that's a (5) __________ room, for two nights?
B: Yes, that's right.
A: OK, here you go … Room 703. That's on the seventh floor, of course.
B: Right, and, uh … where's the (6) __________?
A: Oh, it's right around the (7) __________ there. Do you have any other questions?
B: Yes … can you (8) __________ a good café?
A: Oh, certainly. You should try the Supreme Bean.
B: Can I get there on (9) __________?
A: Yes, of course. When you leave the hotel, turn left, and then go (10) __________ for two blocks, and you'll see it on your right.
B: Thank you.

E Match the vocabulary words to their meanings. (8 points)

1	major	a	hope or plan for the future
2	vision	b	asked for
3	hire	c	your main field of study at college or university
4	examine	d	where two streets cross
5	punctuality	e	not polite
6	requested	f	look or think over carefully
7	corner	g	give a job to
8	rude	h	being on time

F Correct the errors in the sentences. (7 points)

1 Where are you from, original?

____

2 I'm going to talking about three main points.

____

3 As I see, we should hire another assistant.

____

4 How about ask the sales staff in Hong Kong?

____

5 Let me summary last week's meeting.

____

6 Please leave your name and message for the beep.

____

7 Where is the near coffee shop or restaurant?

____

SPEAKING section (25 points)

* See Teacher's Book page 89 for *Speaking section* scoring guidelines.

A Interview questions

1 Imagine you are a new employee at a company. Give an introductory speech about yourself to the other people in your office.

2 Give the opening of a presentation, with two or three main points, about one of these topics:

- what you have learnt in this class so far
- your plans for an upcoming holiday
- an important issue for your school, neighbourhood or city
- important features of your mobile phone, computer, or other piece of favourite technology.

3 Give suggestions for these questions:

- 'What are some good restaurants near this school?'
- 'What is a good way to improve my listening ability in English?'
- 'What kind of decision-making style should the teacher use to decide about our final exam?'
- 'What are some good sites for online shopping?'

4 React to these questions and statements:

- 'How much money do you have?'
- 'Is everyone from your culture shy?'
- 'I think we should have English homework every day.'
- 'Voicemail systems are important for businesses to be successful.'

B Roleplay cards

1

A You are at a company party. You see a new employee.

- Start a conversation with Student B.
- Ask some questions to find out about Student B's personal interests and hobbies. Try to find some things in common.
- Answer Student B's questions.
- End the conversation.

1

B You are a new employee. You are at a company party.

- Greet Student A.
- Answer Student A's questions. Remember to add some information or ask questions back.
- Ask Student A some questions about the company.
- End the conversation.

2

A You are in charge of planning a class party for your English class.

- Start a conversation with Student B. Tell him or her about the party.
- Answer Student B's questions about when the party is.
- Ask Student B what kinds of activities he or she thinks the class should do, and what kinds of food and drink there should be. Agree or disagree (politely) with Student B's suggestions.
- End the conversation.

2

B You and Student A are in the same English class.

- Greet Student A.
- Ask questions about the event. Find out what day and time it is.
- Give Student A your opinions on the topics he or she asks about.
- End the conversation.

C Conversation map

CALLER	RECEIVER
Ring ring!	
	Give the company name. Offer to help.
Say your name. Ask to speak to Mr / Ms . . . Say why you are calling.	
	Ask the caller to wait. Tell the caller that Mr / Ms … is not there – give the reason.
Ask for Mr / Ms … to call you today.	
	Explain that Mr / Ms … will probably not be able to call today. Offer to take a message.
Leave a message.	
	Ask the caller to spell his / her family name.
Respond.	
	Ask for the caller's telephone number.
Respond.	
	Thank the caller. End the call.

7–12 TEST 2

LISTENING section (24 points)

A Listen to the conversation (CD2:26). Tick true or false. (4 points)

1 Jack will have three different email accounts.
☐ True ☐ False

2 Now, Jack uses his university account for personal email.
☐ True ☐ False

3 Jack's new email account is free.
☐ True ☐ False

4 The woman likes Jack's name for his email account.
☐ True ☐ False

B Listen to the conversation (CD2:27). Circle the correct information. (4 points)

1 The woman is *beginning / ending* a presentation.

2 The man wants to *turn his light off / keep his light on.*

3 The man works in *an open / a private* office.

4 The woman *helps / can't help* the man find a solution.

C Listen to the conversation (CD2:28). Circle the correct answers. (4 points)

1 The people are …

a writing a job announcement.

b reading a CV.

c interviewing an applicant.

2 The people …

a don't care if the applicant is a man or a woman.

b would rather hire a woman.

c would rather hire a man.

3 Pat Morgan is now …

a not working.

b studying at the university.

c working at a company.

4 The people believe that Pat is ___ for the position.

a overqualified

b qualified

c not qualified

D Listen to the talk (CD2:29). Tick true or false. (4 points)

1 The woman is talking about her strengths.
☐ True ☐ False

2 She likes to work independently.
☐ True ☐ False

3 She believes that she is honest.
☐ True ☐ False

4 She is applying for a job in a restaurant.
☐ True ☐ False

E Listen to the conversation (CD2:30). Circle the correct information. (4 points)

1 The woman is buying a gift for her nephew's *birthday / graduation.*

2 She thinks Peter can help her because *he is a man / he knows her nephew.*

3 She thinks cash is too *ordinary / expensive.*

4 Her nephew can use her gift to get *films / music.*

F Listen to the conversation (CD2:31). Circle the correct answers. (4 points)

1 The woman is …

a giving a performance review.

b interviewing someone for a job.

c giving a presentation.

2 The man doesn't have enough …

a experience.

b confidence.

c information.

3 The man is going to …

a ask more questions.

b come to work earlier.

c move to another office.

4 The woman didn't know about the man's …

a complaints about his job.

b writing ability.

c language skills.

LANGUAGE AND VOCABULARY section (51 points)

A Put the words in the correct order to make the sentences. (8 points)

1 request / your products / some information / writing / I'm / to / about

____.

2 some / could / you give / feedback / me

____?

3 does / have / experience / how / she / much

____?

4 something / me / you / about / could / your background / tell

____?

5 doing in / hope / what / five years / you / do / be / to

____?

6 of / about / chocolates / what / box / a

____?

7 black cats / US / aren't / the / why / popular in

____?

8 you / year / English this / have / studying / enjoyed

____?

B Match the questions from Part A above to these responses. Write the number of the question in the box. (8 points)

[ ] **a** Well, I graduated with a degree in marketing.
[ ] **b** Yes. And I've learnt a lot.
[ ] **c** I want to be working as a teacher or a coach.
[ ] **d** Your slides were great, but you need to make the writing a little bigger.
[ ] **e** That sounds like a great idea.
[ ] **f** She worked as a sales clerk for two years.
[ ] **g** Attached please find a copy of our 2012 catalogue.
[ ] **h** Well, they're considered unlucky.

C Fill in the blank with the correct letter. (10 points)

1 I look ________ to hearing from you.
a soon **b** forward **c** next **d** often

2 My inbox was ________ this morning.
a empty **b** free **c** space **d** resolved

3 You should ________ some more slides.
a have **b** having **c** be having **d** has

4 I've had some interesting part-time jobs. ________ example, I worked at a zoo.
a By **b** One **c** As **d** For

5 Wanted: Receptionist. ________ for the front desk of a busy doctor's office.
a Reliable **b** Responsible **c** In charge **d** Experienced

6 I ________ in Hong Kong.
a born **b** raised **c** grew up **d** went

7 I'm not sure what I'm going to do after ________.
a major **b** graduation **c** career **d** future

8 How about ________ her a photograph?
a give **b** give to **c** giving **d** to give

9 Thank you for the CD. It was a lovely ________.
a think **b** thinking **c** thought **d** thoughtful

10 ________ you enjoyed working here?
a Do **b** Did **c** Would **d** Have

D Fill in the blank with the correct word or phrase from the box. (There are six extra words.) (10 points)

back	data	pointer	relax
bullet points	front	practise	screen
conclusion	introduction	presentation	slides
confident	nervous	quickly	summary

A: Well … how was it?

B: Your (1) __________ was really good. And you started very well – your (2) __________ was interesting and clear.

A: Oh, thank you! I felt a little (3) __________, you know.

B: Yes, I know. I think that's why you spoke so (4) __________. I think you should speak a bit more slowly.

A: Yes, you're right. I'll work on that. How about my presentation (5) __________? Were they OK?

B: Well … yes, I think so. But you were standing in (6) __________ of them, so it was hard to see them sometimes.

A: Oh, no, really? I won't do that again. I guess I should use the (7) __________.

B: Exactly. Use that to point to things on the (8) __________, and then you can stand to the side.

A: Good idea. Anything else?

B: Well, your (9) __________ was a bit short. It was good, but I think it's also important to include a (10) __________ all of your main points, so people don't forget what you said.

A: OK, thanks for the feedback. It was really helpful!

B: You're welcome. And again, well done.

E Match the vocabulary words to their meanings. (8 points)

1 parentheses — **a** be in charge of
2 feedback — **b** choose
3 responsible for — **c** happening once a year
4 qualified — **d** to cover with paper or cloth
5 strengths — **e** punctuation marks that look like ( )
6 select — **f** special abilities; things you are very good at
7 wrap — **g** having the appropriate education, skills and experience
8 annual — **h** comments, opinions and suggestions

TEST 2

F Correct the errors in the sentences. (7 points)

1 I'm writing in responding to your recent phone call.

____

2 You need to slow up when you speak. It's too fast for me to understand.

____

3 Let me summarise about my main points.

____

4 I'm not sure he's enough experienced for this position.

____

5 Do Europeans include personality information on their CVs?

____

6 You should avoid to give very expensive gifts.

____

7 You've really done good job this year.

____

SPEAKING section (25 points)

* See Teacher's Book page 89 for *Speaking section* scoring guidelines.

A Interview questions

1 Imagine you are giving a presentation about what you have learnt in this class with at least three main points. Give the introduction and the conclusion for this presentation.

2 What are these like in your country or culture? Talk about *two* of them.

- email
- presentations
- CVs
- job interviews

3 Respond to these interview questions:

- Can you tell me a little something about your background?
- What is your major, and why did you choose it?
- Why did you decide to take an English class?
- What do you hope to be doing in three years?

4 Is your culture a high-context or a low-context culture? What aspects of that culture are comfortable for you? Are there any aspects that are challenging for you? If so, why?

B Roleplay cards

1

A You work for the IT department of your company. Student B is having trouble with his or her email account.

- Greet Student B. Ask what the problem is.
- Ask what was in the email.
- Remind Student B that your company's server has trouble with large attachments. Ask if they are necessary.
- Advise Student B to ask the email sender to send each attachment in a separate email.
- Ask Student B to tell you later if this worked.

1

B You are an employee who is having trouble with your email account. Student A works for the IT department and will help you.

- Explain that someone sent you an email, but you never got it.
- The email had two large PowerPoint® presentations attached.
- Explain that the attachments are very important (say why).
- Agree to try Student A's suggestion.
- Thank Student A for the advice, and end the conversation.

2

A You are a manager at Global Enterprises giving Student B his or her annual review.

- Greet Student B and ask him / her to sit down.
- Ask Student B how he / she feels about his / her first year of work.
- Explain that the review form evaluates quality of work, job knowledge and interpersonal skills. Say that Student B's quality of work and job knowledge are rated as 'outstanding'.
- However, explain that Student B's interpersonal skills are rated as only 'meets expectations'.
- Explain that some people think Student B is a little difficult to work with because he / she seems shy or not friendly. You've noticed that Student B doesn't eat lunch with any co-workers or socialise during the break times.
- Accept at least one of Student B's ideas. Then thank him / her for coming.

2

B You joined Global Enterprises last year. Student A is your manager and is giving you your annual review.

- Greet Student A.
- Say that this year has been a little difficult, but that you have enjoyed the challenge.
- Thank Student A for the compliment.
- Ask Student A if there are any problems. Ask for an example.
- Suggest some ideas of your own that could help you improve in this area.
- Thank Student A for talking to you.

C Conversation map

CALLER	**RECEIVER**
Ring ring!	Give your name. Ask who is calling.
Say your name. Ask how he / she is.	Reply and reflect ('And you?').
Reply. Say you are calling to ask for some advice. Explain that you are travelling to another country and want to bring some small gifts. Ask for some ideas.	Make several suggestions. (It's OK to have some bad ideas!)
React to the ideas by saying whether you think the items are appropriate or not.	Make one more suggestion.
Decide which gifts you will buy.	Tell your friend that he / she made a good choice. Ask if he / she will wrap the gifts or not.
Answer your friend's question. Then thank your friend for the suggestions.	Respond to your friend's thanks. End the call.
End the call.	

1–6 TEST 1 and 2 – answer key

TEST 1

LISTENING section

A

1 False 2 True 3 True 4 False

B

1 b 2 b 3 c 4 a

C

1 woman 2 space
3 doesn't agree 4 voting

D

1 c 2 a 3 b 4 a

E

1 False 2 False 3 True 4 True

F

1 c 2 b 3 a 4 b

LANGUAGE AND VOCABULARY section

A

1 What part of Brazil are you from?
2 What are you studying?
3 Why don't we go to a café?
4 Which restaurant should we go to?
5 Can we come back to this later?
6 Can I call you back in ten minutes?
7 Is it walking distance from here?
8 Could you tell me where the station is?

B

a 2 b 5 c 7 d 3
e 1 f 8 g 4 h 6

C

1 d 2 c 3 b 4 a 5 c
6 b 7 c 8 a 9 d 10 c

D

1 reservation 2 anything 3 confirmation
4 under 5 twin 6 lift
7 corner 8 recommend 9 foot
10 straight

E

1 c 2 a 3 g 4 f
5 h 6 b 7 d 8 e

F

1 Where are you from, originally?
2 I'm going to talk about three main points.
3 As I see it, we should hire another assistant.
4 How about asking the sales staff in Hong Kong?
5 Let me summarise last week's meeting.
6 Please leave your name and message after the beep.
7 Where is the nearest coffee shop or restaurant?

TEST 2

LISTENING section

A

1 True 2 False 3 True 4 False

B

1 ending
2 keep his light on
3 an open
4 helps

C

1 b 2 a 3 c 4 b

D

1 True 2 False 3 True 4 False

E

1 graduation 2 he is a man 3 ordinary 4 music

F

1 a 2 b 3 a 4 c

LANGUAGE AND VOCABULARY section

A

1 I'm writing to request some information about your products.
2 Could you give me some feedback?
3 How much experience does she have?
4 Could you tell me something about your background?
5 What do you hope to be doing in five years?
6 What about a box of chocolates?
7 Why aren't black cats popular in the US?
8 Have you enjoyed studying English this year?

B

a 4 b 8 c 5 d 2
e 6 f 3 g 1 h 7

C

1 b 2 a 3 a 4 d 5 b
6 c 7 b 8 c 9 c 10 d

D

1 presentation 2 introduction 3 nervous
4 quickly 5 slides 6 front
7 pointer 8 screen 9 conclusion
10 summary

E

1 e 2 h 3 a 4 g
5 f 6 b 7 d 8 c

F

1 I'm writing in response to your recent phone call.
2 You need to slow down when you speak. It's too fast for me to understand.
3 Let me summarise my main points.
4 I'm not sure he's experienced enough for this position.
5 Do Europeans include personal information on their CVs?
6 You should avoid giving very expensive gifts.
7 You've really done a good job this year.

SPEAKING section See table below.

Speaking section assessment guide

	1	2	3	4	5
Communication	Unable to communicate concepts or ideas successfully	Unable to communicate most ideas and concepts without great difficulty	Able to communicate some ideas and concepts with some difficulty	Communicates most ideas and concepts with minimal difficulty; has slight difficulty with complex ideas and concepts	Consistently communicates all ideas and concepts without difficulty
Fluency	Unable to respond; or gives only one-word, or very short responses	Often unable to respond, or responds with frequent pauses and hesitation; often unable to produce specific words or structures	Able to respond with some pauses and hesitation; sometimes unable to produce specific words or structures	Responds to most tasks with minimal pauses or hesitation; has slight difficulty producing complex words or structures	Consistently responds without pauses or hesitation
Accuracy	Uses incorrect grammatical structures and syntax in most responses; difficult to understand	Often uses incorrect grammatical structures and syntax; errors interfere with communication	Uses incorrect grammatical structures in some tasks; some errors interfere with communication	Rarely uses incorrect grammatical structures and syntax; minor errors do not interfere with communication	Consistently uses correct grammatical structures and syntax
Language	Unable to use target vocabulary and structures from the unit	Often unable to use target vocabulary and structures from the unit	Able to use target vocabulary and structures from the unit in some tasks; has some difficulty producing the correct language	Uses target language and vocabulary from the unit in most tasks; rarely has difficulty producing the correct language	Consistently uses target vocabulary and structures from the unit
Interaction	Unable to understand or interact with teacher/partner, does not ask for repetition or clarification	Often unable to understand or interact with teacher/partner, does not ask for repetition or clarification	Able to understand and interact with a partner with some difficulty; rarely asks for repetition or clarification	Understands and interacts appropriately with teacher/partner in most tasks; asks for repetition or clarification when needed	Consistently understands and interacts appropriately with teacher/partner; asks for repetition or clarification when needed

Photocopiable activities
Classroom language

To talk to the instructor		
I'm sorry, I didn't catch that.		
Could you say that	again?	
	more slowly?	
	another way?	
Could you	spell	that?
	pronounce	that?
	explain	that?
	write that on the board?	
I don't know	the answer.	
	what to say.	
	what to do.	
I don't have	my book	today.
	my homework	today.
	a pencil / pen	today.
	any paper	today.
I'm sorry	I'm late.	
	I was absent.	
What	did I miss?	
	should I do?	
I'm going to be absent	tomorrow.	
	next week.	
	on Wednesday.	
I have to leave early today.		
Excuse me. I need to use the bathroom.		

To talk to a partner / group	
Do you want to	be my partner?
	work together?
	join our group?
May I	be your partner?
	join your group?
I'll be Student A. You can be Student B.	
OK, I'll go first.	
Let's switch roles and do it again.	
Let's try it again.	
Are you finished? Let's compare answers now.	
What's the answer to number (3)?	

Pair introductions 1b

Student A

Partner's name: ______________________

1 What's your favourite ______________________?

____

2 Do you like ______________________?

____

3 Do you have a ______________________?

____

4 How many ______________________ do you have?

____

5 Do you ever ______________________?

____

6 When you were a child, did you ______________________?

____

7 Have you ever been to ______________________?

____

8 Have you ever tried ______________________?

____

9 Are you going to ______________________ this weekend?

____

10 Would you like to ______________________?

____

Student B

Partner's name: ______________________

1 Do you know how to ______________________?

____

2 Who's your favourite ______________________?

____

3 What kind of ______________________ do you like?

____

4 How often do you ______________________?

____

5 Do you enjoy ______________________?

____

6 What's your ______________________'s name?

____

7 Have you ever ______________________?

____

8 Have you ever seen a ______________________?

____

9 Are you going to ______________________ this year?

____

10 Do you think you will ______________________ one day?

____

My family is hosting a visitor from the US for three days. They would like me to show him around. He's ten years older than I am, so I'm not sure what he would like. Can you help me think of some ideas?	I'd like to change or update my style. Maybe a new haircut? Or different clothes? I'm not really sure. I just want to try something different.	I can't relax! I have a busy life and a lot of stress. My shoulders and neck feel tight all the time, and it's hard to fall asleep at night. Everyone tells me to 'take it easy,' but I don't know how!
I'm mostly happy with my progress in English class. However, I'd like to learn more vocabulary. Also, it's hard for me to remember new vocabulary after I learn it. Do you have any advice?	My friend is depressed because of some family problems. I can't solve his problems, but I would like to cheer him up. What can I do to help him feel happy again?	I'd like to exercise more. I've heard that exercise will give me more energy and help me feel better. But I don't know where to start, or even what kind of exercise to try. I don't have a lot of money for expensive equipment or classes.

Suggestions roleplay 2

I always listen to the same music. I like my music, but I want to try something new. Can you recommend any great new music that I should try? I'd like to find something I've never heard before.

My aunt is coming to visit my family, and she is spending her birthday with us. My parents say I should buy her a gift, but I have no idea what kinds of things she likes. What's a good gift for someone I don't know?

I'd like to get a part-time job so I can earn some money. However, I'm also busy with schoolwork, so I don't want something that's too difficult or takes too much time. I'd like to do something fun, too!

I have a good friend who emails me too often. Also, her emails are very long. These days, I'm very busy, and I don't always have time to answer her – and then she gets annoyed with me! What should I do? She's a good friend, and I don't want to upset her.

I want to be a good singer. However, I feel very shy about my voice! How can I learn to sing well, without feeling embarrassed?

My cousin is graduating from high school, and asked my advice about the best university degree for someone who wants to make a lot of money without doing much work. I don't know what to tell him!

3 A question of ethics

Anne was a high school girl in love with Chris. Anne and Chris lived in different cities. Every weekend, Anne would travel by bus to see Chris. Although she had no money, the bus driver took her for free. One day, the bus driver said he wouldn't drive her anymore if she couldn't pay. Anne explained that she had no money. The bus driver said that he would still drive her if she would steal an expensive video game system for him.

Anne didn't know what to do, and went home to talk to her mother. Her mother said, 'You are almost an adult now. You need to make your own decisions.' So Anne stole the video game system and gave it to the bus driver.

When she met Chris, she told him what she had done. Chris was very angry, and said he didn't want a girlfriend who was a thief and didn't want to see her ever again.

Anne was heartbroken. She went back home and told her story to her friend Jake. Jake said, 'I will be your boyfriend, Anne.' Then Jake took Anne to see Chris, and Anne watched happily as Jake beat Chris up.

My ranking

	Name	Reasons
1		
2		
3		
4		
5		

My group's ranking

	Name	Name	Name	Name	Name	Final decision
1						
2						
3						
4						
5						

Who agrees?

1	Everyone agrees with this idea: *We should have no homework on weekends.*	T	F
2	More than half of the class agrees with this suggestion: *Why don't we have regular vocabulary tests?*	T	F
3	No one agrees with this idea: *Our class should take a test together, and then compare scores.*	T	F
4	At least five people agree with this suggestion: *How about having a class party?*	T	F
5	Almost everyone agrees with this idea: *Our class should always start on time.*	T	F
6	Less than half of the class agrees with this idea: *The instructor could lower a student's grade for three or more absences.*	T	F
7	At least three people agree with this idea: *Students should stop asking so many questions in class.*	T	F
8	No more than four people agree with this idea: *We could write out the questions and answers for several exercises in each unit.*	T	F
9	Fewer than seven people agree with this idea: *We should sit in a different seat each time we come to class.*	T	F
10	About half of the class agrees with this suggestion: *Each student could give a special presentation in class at the end of this course.* If yes … what should the presentation be about? ___________________	T	F

5 Telephone conversations

A: I'd like to make a reservation for dinner tonight. **A:** Um, for 7:00pm.	**B:** Certainly. For what time? **B:** We're a bit busy then … how about 7:30? Or 6:30?
A: I'd like to make a reservation for dinner tonight. **A:** Let's see … there will be six of us.	**B:** All right. For how many people? **B:** OK, a table for six … and for what time?
A: I'd like to speak to Ms Zilinski, please. **A:** No, thanks. I'll call back later.	**B:** She's not at her desk right now. Would you like to leave a message? **B:** All right. Can I tell her who called?
A: I'd like to speak to Ms Zilinski, please. **A:** Oh, yes, this is Chris Bowden.	**B:** One moment, please. May I ask who's calling? **B:** Oh, I'm sorry, she's in a meeting. Would you like her to call you back?
A: Could I speak to Mark Troye, please? **A:** I see. Could I leave a message?	**B:** I'm sorry, he's out of the office today. **B:** Sure. Let me get a pencil.
A: Could I speak to Mark Troye, please? **A:** Uh, sure. Could you ask him to call me back?	**B:** He's on another line right now. Would you like to leave a message? **B:** Of course. Could I have your name, please?
A: Hi, Kelly, this is Chen. I'm returning your call. **A:** Yes, I think so. What time?	**B:** Oh, hi, Chen. I wanted to ask you if you could meet on Friday morning. **B:** Well, is 10:30am OK?
A: Hi, Kelly, this is Chen. I'm returning your call. **A:** Well, I'm going to be out this afternoon. How long is your meeting?	**B:** Chen, I'm really sorry, but I'm just on my way to a meeting. Can I call you back? **B:** Oh, it goes on until 1:00. Can I call you tomorrow, then?
A: Hi, I'd like to speak to Haru Morita, please. **A:** Well, I'm calling about the English class for new staff.	**B:** This is Mr / Ms Morita. How can I help you? **B:** Oh, OK. What would you like to know?
A: Hi, I'd like to speak to Haru Morita, please. **A:** Oh, hi, Haru, this is Cory. I'm returning your call.	**B:** This is Haru. **B:** Oh, yes, I'm glad you called back. Listen, would you like to go to the basketball game with us on Saturday night?

Dinner at the Golden Pagoda

Student A

1 First, you need to post a letter. Give directions from the train station to the post office.

3 You need to pick up your jacket. Give directions from the bank to the dry cleaner's.

5 Oh, no! You forgot your phone, and you have to call your friend. Give directions from the coffee shop to a public telephone.

7 You need to buy a gift for your cousin. Give directions from the book shop to the gift shop.

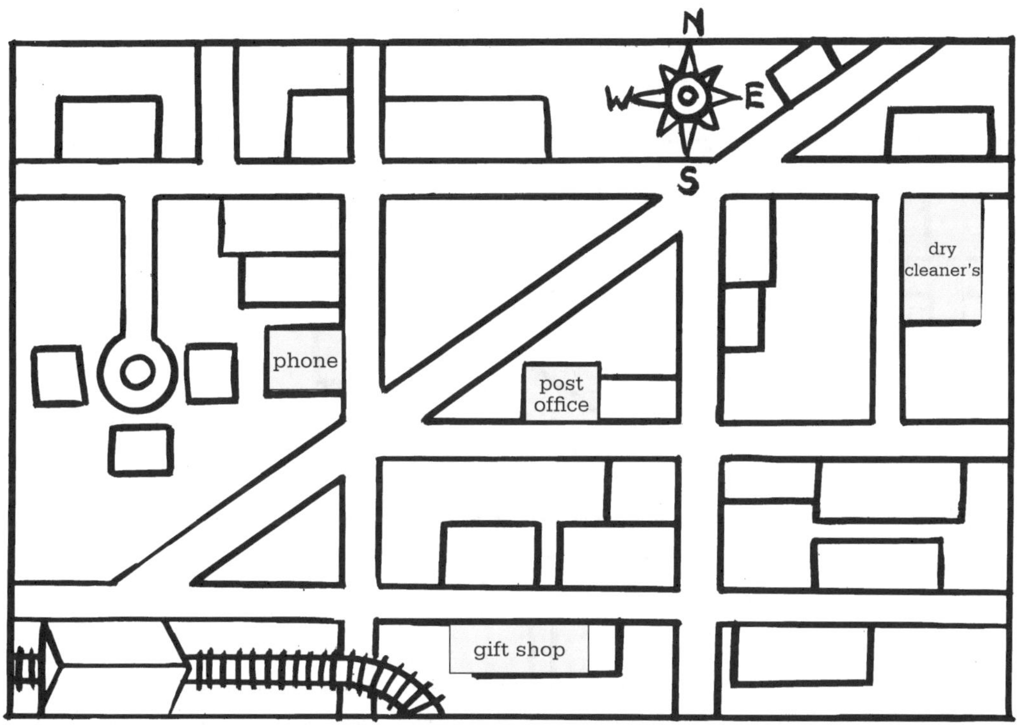

Dinner at the Golden Pagoda

Student B

2 Next, you need to get some money. Give directions from the post office to the bank.

4 You're both a little tired. Invite your partner to have a cup of coffee with you. Give directions from the dry cleaner's to the coffee shop.

6 You would like to buy a news magazine. Give directions from the public telephone to the book shop.

8 From the gift shop, tell your partner to turn left and walk to the corner. Then turn right and walk up two blocks. Turn left at the corner, and then take the next left and walk to the end of the street. The Golden Pagoda Restaurant is the building on your right. Enjoy your meal!

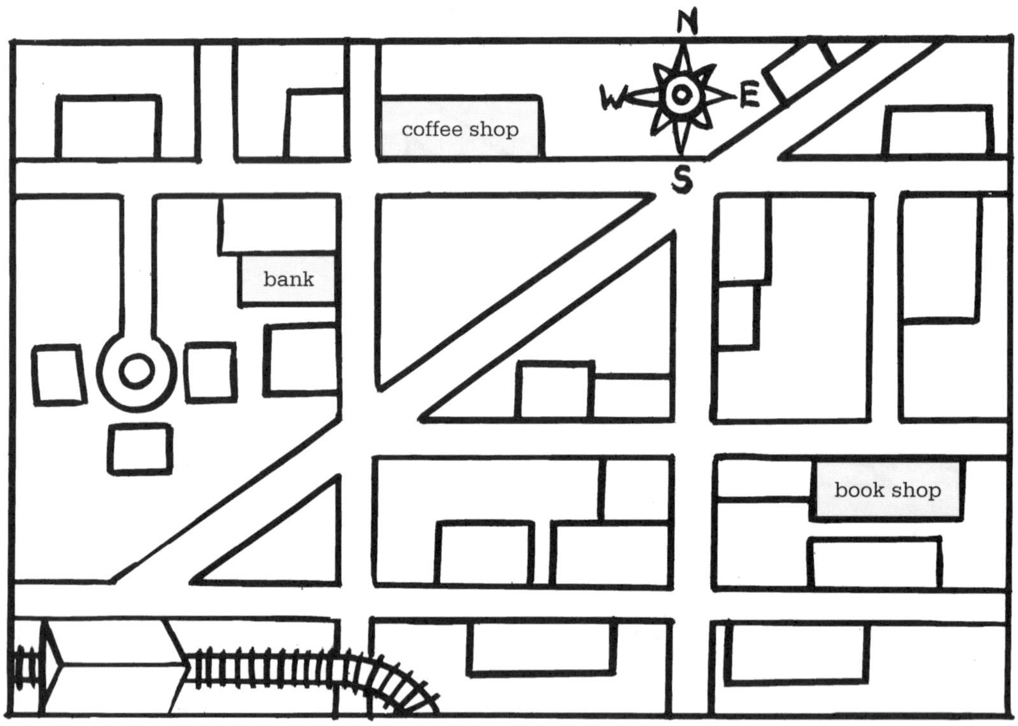

I bet that's a mistake! 7

Get Mail | < Reply | << Reply All | Forward > | New Mail | Delete

To: Anne Bixby <abixby@grfb.com>

From: Jen Kawamura <jenny88@grfb.com>
Subject:
Cc:
Bcc:
Attachments:

Hi Annie Bixby,

How are you doing today? I'm pretty good.

I'm writing in response to request you to a party this weekend at my house. I hope you can come? Just a casual party – pizza and soft drinks, and we'll listen to music and maybe watch a video.

The party will start at 7:00, but it's OK if you come a little later. It's also OK – to bring a freind.

I don't think you've been to my house before, (so I'm attaching a map).

If you have any questions, just email me or call to me on my mobilephone.

I look forward to seeing you! ☹

Best regards,
Jen

Topic: **Mountains**	Topic: **Dessert**
Main point: Main point: Main point:	Main point: Main point: Main point:
Topic: **Water**	Topic: **Choosing an outfit**
Main point: Main point: Main point:	Main point: Main point: Main point:
Topic: **Babies**	Topic: **Fish**
Main point: Main point: Main point:	Main point: Main point: Main point:
Topic: **Cars**	Topic: **Boyfriends / Girlfriends** (Choose 1)
Main point: Main point: Main point:	Main point: Main point: Main point:
Topic: **Email**	Topic: **Coffee**
Main point: Main point: Main point:	Main point: Main point: Main point:

Topic: **Aeroplane flights** Main point: Main point: Main point:	Topic: **Radios** Main point: Main point: Main point:
Topic: **Grandparents** Main point: Main point: Main point:	Topic: **Things that make me laugh** Main point: Main point: Main point:
Topic: **Taking the bus / train** Main point: Main point: Main point:	Topic: **The sun** Main point: Main point: Main point:
Topic: **Flowers** Main point: Main point: Main point:	Topic: **Newspapers** Main point: Main point: Main point:
Topic: **Pizza** Main point: Main point: Main point:	Topic: **Winter** Main point: Main point: Main point:

9a A hiring puzzle

Student A

You and your partner interviewed four people for a job in international sales. Unfortunately, after the interview, your notes got mixed up. You and your partner each remember some of the facts. You remember that the candidates

- are 20, 30, 40 or 50 years old
- have 1, 3, 6 or 9 years of experience
- speak 1, 2, 3 or 4 languages
- are asking for a salary of £40,000, £45,000, £50,000, or £55,000.

Work together to remember which information belongs to which candidate. Take turns to read the clues to your partner, and work together to fill in the chart.

Name	Mr Marks	Ms Singh	Mr Levitz	Ms Salazar
Age				
Years of experience				
Languages				
Salary				

1 The 50-year-old person is a woman.
2 The 20-year-old speaks more languages than the other three people.
3 Ms Singh wants more money than Mr Marks, but less money than Mr Levitz or Ms Salazar.
4 The person who wants £55,000 has more experience than the other three people.
5 The person who speaks three languages has more experience than the person who speaks four languages.

Student B

You and your partner interviewed four people for a job in international sales. Unfortunately, after the interview, your notes got mixed up. You and your partner each remember some of the facts. You remember that the candidates

- are 20, 30, 40 or 50 years old
- have 1, 3, 6 or 9 years of experience
- speak 1, 2, 3 or 4 languages
- are asking for a salary of £40,000, £45,000, £50,000 or £55,000.

Work together to remember which information belongs to which candidate. Take turns to read the clues to your partner, and work together to fill in the chart.

Name	Mr Marks	Ms Singh	Mr Levitz	Ms Salazar
Age				
Years of experience				
Languages				
Salary				

1 Ms Singh is younger than Ms Salazar, and older than the men.
2 Mr Marks speaks only one language.
3 Mr Levitz wants less money than Ms Salazar.
4 Mr Marks has more experience in sales than Mr Levitz or Ms Singh.
5 Ms Singh speaks more languages than Ms Salazar.

Name:

Address:

Email:

Phone number:

Objective:

Education:

Experience:

Skills:

Interviewer role cards	Applicant role cards
Seoul Food Korean Barbecue • needs a Waiter for busy weekend shifts, days and evenings.	**University student; art major** Can only work part-time. Has never worked before. Interests: piano, cooking Skills: cooking, fluent in Korean and Japanese
Kopykit Copy Centre • needs someone to assist customers with photocopying, printing digital photos and sending faxes. Can train the right person.	**University student; business major** Has never worked before. Interests: video games Skills: familiar with common computer software applications; friendly and positive attitude
Trusted Translation Services • needs a bilingual Spanish-English and a Chinese-English Translator. Must have experience.	**English and Spanish Teacher** Experience: • High school Spanish Teacher (in Australia) • Tour guide for international visitors
Gina's Gym • needs a Personal Trainer to help clients at busy gym. Flexible hours.	**University student; health & nutrition major** Experience: Lab Assistant at the university Interests: football, baseball, basketball, lifting weights

Interviewer role cards	Applicant role cards
Creative Designs • needs a Graphic Designer to design websites and magazine advertisements. Must have experience with design software. Experience in advertising desired.	**Computer Software Programmer** Experience: • IT staff for MacroComp • designed advertisements for university newspaper
Music Mania! • needs a Violin Teacher for children for busy after-school programme.	**High school student** Has worked as a Swimming Instructor for children. Interests: piano, guitar, violin
Yarrow Yard Services • needs two assistants to help with mowing lawns, planting and cutting flowers, taking care of trees, general landscaping. Must be healthy and strong.	**University student; land management major** Experience: • Worked on uncle's farm for two summers Interests: gardening, hiking
Fantastic Films • needs Ticket Taker and Cashier. No experience necessary.	**High school student** Has never worked before. Interests: films, TV, video games Personal characteristics: smart and hardworking, never late

11 Photocopiable activities

Student A

What animal is considered lucky for gambling casinos in China? *a bat*	What do people in Turkey believe about a snake in the house?
What number is not found on American lift buttons, and why?	In what two countries are black cats considered lucky? *Australia and Great Britain*
What should you always ask a Nigerian person about when you greet? *His / Her health and family*	What do British people think that it is unlucky to walk under?
If you are invited to a dinner party in Germany, should you eat all of the food on your plate?	What does it mean in Brazil if you flick your fingers under your chin?  *I don't know* or *I don't understand.*
In which of these countries should you take off your shoes when entering someone's house – Belgium; the Czech Republic; Russia? *the Czech Republic*	How do people in Denmark greet each other when meeting for the first time?
Why should you not compliment an Egyptian person on items in his/her house?	In Russia, when you want to point at something, what part of your body should you use? *your whole hand*

Student B

What animal is considered lucky for gambling casinos in China?	What do people in Turkey believe about a snake in the house? *a snake guards and protects the house*
What number is not found on American lift buttons, and why? *13; because it is considered unlucky*	In what two countries are black cats considered lucky?
What should you always ask a Nigerian person about when you greet?	What do British people think that it is unlucky to walk under? *a ladder*
If you are invited to a dinner party in Germany, should you eat all of the food on your plate? *Yes, you should.*	What does it mean in Brazil if you flick your fingers under your chin? 
In which of these countries should you take off your shoes when entering someone's house – Belgium; the Czech Republic; Russia?	How do people in Denmark greet each other when meeting for the first time? *with a handshake*
Why should you not compliment an Egyptian person on items in his/her house? *He/She might feel that he/she has to give them to you.*	In Russia, when you want to point at something, what part of your body should you use?

12 Feedback form

1 What are three important things you learnt in this course?

a

b

c

2 How do you feel about the course? Circle your answers.

1 = a little bit 5 = very much

Useful	1	2	3	4	5
Interesting	1	2	3	4	5
Enjoyable	1	2	3	4	5
Difficult	1	2	3	4	5

3 How much did you like these things? Circle your answers.

1 = a little bit 5 = very much

Working alone	1	2	3	4	5	didn't do this
Working with a partner	1	2	3	4	5	didn't do this
Working in groups	1	2	3	4	5	didn't do this
Listening activities	1	2	3	4	5	didn't do this
Grammar work	1	2	3	4	5	didn't do this
Vocabulary work	1	2	3	4	5	didn't do this
TOEIC® practice	1	2	3	4	5	didn't do this
Homework	1	2	3	4	5	didn't do this
Tests	1	2	3	4	5	didn't do this

4 How hard did you try? Circle your answers.

1 = a little bit 5 = very much

I came to class on time.	1	2	3	4	5
I asked questions.	1	2	3	4	5
I was prepared for class.	1	2	3	4	5
I helped other students.	1	2	3	4	5
I studied outside of class.	1	2	3	4	5

5 Do you have any comments or suggestions for your instructor?

Unit 1. Listen and practise. Introducing a colleague. Exercise 2. (CD1:02)

Tom: Good morning, everybody. I'd like to introduce a new member of our company, Amy Lane. Amy's going to be our new management trainee. She'll be working with Michael in the Marketing Department. Amy graduated last July from the European Business School, and we're very pleased to have her here with us. I'm sure she'll be a great addition to our department. Amy, would you like to say a few words?

Unit 1. Listen and practise. Introducing a colleague. Exercise 5. (CD1:03)

Amy: Hi, everyone. Nice to meet you. As Mr Hayes said, I graduated last summer from EBS. Then I spent about four months doing some volunteer work in Nepal. I've always been really interested in travel and other countries. I'm from France originally, but my family moved to London when I was in primary school. My father is British, actually. Anyway, I'm really excited about working here and getting to know everyone.

Unit 1. Conversation topics. Exercise 2. (CD1:04)

Conversation a

A So, are you from Edinburgh originally?

B: No, actually, I'm not Scottish. I'm English. I came here to go to college.

A: Really? What are you studying?

B: I'm a French literature major. Now, you're Canadian, aren't you?

A: Yes, I am. I grew up in Toronto.

Conversation b

C: Well, it's just really great to meet you.

D: It's nice to meet you too.

C: You must get this all the time, but … you're really tall!

D: Uh, yeah, well … I guess that's pretty obvious.

C: So how tall ARE you?

D: Well, THIS tall, as you can see.

C: I'd guess … maybe 6 foot 4 or 5 … and about 20 stone. Am I right?

D: Uh … I guess I do need to lose a little weight …

C: But young. You don't look a day over 30 years old. Maybe 28 or 29?

D: Yeah, something like that.

Conversation c

E: So, Lynne, are you married?

F: Oh, well, um, no, I'm single. Uh, and you?

E: Yes, I am. And we just had a baby!

F: Really? That's great. Boy or girl?

E: A boy. Name's Justin. He's our first, but I hope we'll have more. I was an only child, no brothers or sisters. I always wanted a brother.

F: Oh, I don't know. I have two brothers and a sister, but as kids, we were always fighting.

E: Yeah, well, you know how it is. So, does your family live around here?

F: No, actually, they're all in Cardiff.

E: Really? So you're from Wales? I was born there, actually. **Newport.** But we moved when I was a kid.

F: Yeah, born and raised in Cardiff.

Conversation d

G: So, Jack, what do you do?

H: I'm in software sales.

G: Oh, that sounds interesting.

H: Yeah, it's OK. How about you?

G: I'm a lawyer. I'm with Tannen and Bowers.

H: Really? A lawyer. That pays pretty well, huh?

G: Oh, you know, it's a living.

H: I'll bet it is! You probably have a big house, drive a really nice car … Now sales – some years it's good, some years not so good. How much do you think I made last year?

G: Well, I don't really know much about sales. You know, I see someone over there I need to talk to. If you could just excuse me for a minute

H: Oh, sure, catch you later …

Conversation e

I: I see they're raising taxes again! This government just loves to raise taxes!

J: Well, yes, but then crime has gone down since they got in and the streets are a lot safer to walk at night. And I love the new library they have just opened down the street.

I: I don't know. I'd rather have more money in my pocket than a library. And I never had any trouble on the street before.

J: Ha! But then you teach karate …

Conversation f

K: What are you doing this weekend?

L: Well, I'm doing my Saturday

job tomorrow at the Italian restaurant where I work. But Sunday, I'm going to church. You should come with me! They love having new people come in.

K: Um ..., that sounds nice, but I play football on Sunday mornings.

L: Oh really! I didn't know you did that. Who do you play for?

K: Oh it's the local club in my town: Banbury FC. I've not been playing for them long, but we've won the last four matches.

L: Sounds great. Would you like to play professionally then?

K: I would love to ...

Unit 1. Making introductions. Exercise 1. (CD1:05)

Conversation 1

Jasmine: Amy, do you know David?

Amy: No, we haven't met.

Jasmine: Oh, OK. Amy, this is David. He's an exchange student. He's studying in Madrid. David, Amy's just started working with me.

Amy: Nice to meet you, David. Where are you from originally?

David: Nice to meet you, Amy. I'm from Greece. Do you know Rhodes?

Amy: I've never been to Greece, but I've heard it's beautiful.

Jasmine: David is really into Rock music.

Amy: Oh, really? Me, too! What's your favourite band?

Conversation 2

Tom Hayes: Amy, I'd like you to meet Michael Young. He's our Sales and Marketing manager for Asia. Michael, this is Amy Lane, our new management trainee.

Michael: Nice to meet you, Amy.

Amy: A pleasure. I'm sorry, what was your name again?

Michael: Michael Young. Please call me Michael.

Amy: It's nice to meet you, Michael.

Mr Hayes: Michael is working on a new marketing campaign for Asia. He's also in charge of our tennis club.

Amy: Really? I love tennis.

Michael: Do you? Well, we would love you to join ...

Unit 2. Listen and practise. Starting a presentation. Exercise 2. (CD1:06)

Lisa: Good morning everyone. Today I want to talk to you about our vision, and our values. My message today is that we need to change, and that we need your help. I'm going to cover three areas this morning. First, I'll talk about our new vision and what it means for our business. After that, I'll talk about the changes we need to make. Finally, I'll talk about how we can work together to grow our business.

Unit 2. Listen and practise. Starting a presentation. Exercise 5. (CD1:07)

Lisa: Are there any questions so far? No? OK then, let me start by giving you some background. As you know, two years ago we expanded our business in Europe and Asia, and we now have production plants in the U.S., France and Japan, as well as in Singapore. Our vision at that time was to become the number two producer of silicon wafers in ...

Unit 2. Presenting information: openings and introductions. Exercise 1. (CD1:08)

Speaker 1: a

A: Good afternoon. My name is Nathan, and I work in the London office. My subject today is our new ...

Speaker 2: b

B: Good morning everyone! Today I'll talk about doing business in China. My main point is that ...

Speaker 3: c

C: Good afternoon. My name is Jun and I work for Berlin Trading Company. Today I want to talk to you about changing our business model. My main point is that business in Asia is changing very quickly, and we need to be more flexible if we want to succeed. My presentation is divided into three parts. First, I want to look at ...

Unit 2. Presenting information: openings and introductions. Exercise 2. (CD1:09)

A: Good morning, everyone, and thank you for coming. My name is Kim, and I work for New Line Investments in Bristol in the UK. Shall we get started?

B: I want to talk about three things this morning. First, I'll show you our new design plans; then, I'll talk about timing for the project; and finally, I'll describe our current situation. Are there any questions so far? OK, then let's ...

C: Hi, my name's Mark, and I'm from Edinburgh, Scotland.

D: The main thing I want to say

to you today is that Seattle is a great place to visit on vacation.

E: My message to you today is this: we need to improve the quality of our service to customers, and we need to start today!

F: My presentation is divided into two parts. First, I'll talk about our new computer training centre; and then, I'll describe the kinds of training we can offer you.

Unit 2. Guiding a visitor: making suggestions. Exercise 1. (CD1:10)

Erika: Is this your first trip to Manchester, Heather?

Heather: Yes, it is. I'm hoping to look around this weekend.

Erika: Would you like me to show you around on Saturday?

Heather: That would be wonderful! Thank you, Erika!

Erika: Excellent! Why don't we go to the Arndale Centre? That's a great place for shopping.

Heather: That sounds great. I need to get some presents for my brothers.

Erika: Then we could go to Chinatown. They have some first-class restaurants. Do you like Chinese food?

Heather: Absolutely! I love Chinese food.

Erika: How about visiting Old Trafford? It's the home ground of Manchester United football team.

Heather: We could do, but I'm not actually very interested in football.

Erika: Oh, we could go to The Printworks. There's a great cinema there and lots of bars and restaurants.

Heather: It's a nice idea, but I'd rather do something a bit more cultural. Are there any good museums here?

Erika: Yes! Why don't we go to the Manchester Museum? It has a great section on ancient Egypt and it also has dinosaurs.

Heather: Sounds great! I've heard the University of Manchester library is a beautiful building to see too.

Erika: Yes, if we have time we can go and see that. Then, how about going to see a play at the Royal Exchange Theatre in the evening if you like?

Heather: I'd love that. I really enjoy going to the theatre ...

Unit 2. Viewpoints. Exercise 3. (CD1:11)

Hiroki

Questioner: What image do you think people from other countries have of Japan and Japanese people?

Hiroki: I guess a lot of people think about Mount Fuji and cherry blossoms. I was so surprised when I travelled to Europe and the U.S.! Many people thought that Japanese people wore kimonos and were like the samurai in the movies. I think young people are different, though. Their image of Japan is like high-tech games and electronics. Oh, and I guess a lot of people think Japanese are quiet and polite, and maybe hard-working. I'm not sure.

Questioner: Do you think these images are correct?

Hiroki: In some cases. Of course, we have Mount Fuji and cherry blossoms, so I guess that's correct. I think it's also true that, generally speaking, we are quiet and polite, but not everyone is like that. Most young Japanese like high-tech equipment, like cellphones, but nowadays, we don't all work so hard.

Questioner: Do you think stereotypes are useful?

Hiroki: Useful? I'm not sure ... I guess not. Like when I visited America, my image was very different from what I found there. I was so surprised! People were so friendly to me.

Markus

Questioner: What image do you think other countries have of Germany and German people?

Markus: I guess the stereotype of Germans is that we are very efficient and punctual, maybe good at manufacturing and engineering. Also, that we drink a lot of beer and eat a lot of sausages.

Questioner: Do you think these images are correct?

Markus: No, I don't think so. Except for being punctual – I think German people are always in a hurry and we don't want to be late for anything.

Questioner: Do you think stereotypes are useful?

Markus: No, I don't. Everyone is different of course. You cannot say Germans are like this or Chinese people are like that – I think it can be dangerous if you have this kind of image in your mind.

Tanisha

Questioner: What image do you think other countries have of America and American people?

Tanisha: Oh, gosh, I don't know –

maybe things like the Statue of Liberty and the Grand Canyon? I think people say we are friendly; I hope so. Oh yeah, and that we talk a lot.

Questioner: Do you think these images are correct?

Tanisha: Yeah, I guess so, but Americans are so different, you know? Like people in New York and people in Texas or California are very different.

Questioner: Do you think stereotypes are useful?

Tanisha: Well, um ... maybe, as a starting point perhaps. I mean, everyone is different, aren't they? People are people. The important thing is to keep an open mind, I guess.

Unit 3. Listen and practise. Running meetings. Exercise 2. (CD1:12)

Hervé Durand: Well, it's just 9:00 now. Is everybody here? Yes? All right, let's get started, then. Does everyone have a copy of the agenda? If not, I have some extra copies here. ... Now, as you know, we need to decide today which conferences to attend this year. I wish we could go to them all, but we don't have the budget! As you can see here, we'll look at three main factors: location, size, and cost. I have my own ideas, of course, but I want to hear from everyone else here, too.

Unit 3. Listen and practise. Running meetings. Exercise 5. (CD1:13)

Hervé Durand: OK, let's discuss the first factor, location. There's the big trade fair in Germany. I think that's a pretty important conference because, really, it's the main one. But this year there's another trade fair in Istanbul, in Turkey, that also looks interesting. In my opinion, it looks like it could be a good place for us to expand our sales into new areas. And then there's a smaller conference in Avignon; of course, that's much closer to us, so that's convenient. And there's the Japan conference. That's an expensive location, I know, but I'd still like to consider it.

So, let's start with the sales team. Patricia, can you tell us what the sales team thinks about these conferences in terms of location?

Unit 3. Meetings and discussions: opening a meeting. Exercise 1. (CD1:14)

Speaker 1

OK, thank you all for coming this morning. Let's get started because we have a lot to discuss today. First, I'd like to get an update on any problems since our last meeting. Then we need to talk about sales plans for the next three months. Sorry, does everyone have an agenda? OK. All right, let's focus on any current issues. Jack – do you want to start?

Speaker 2

Thank you. Let's begin the meeting. This meeting is scheduled until 12 o'clock and we will then be taking lunch together in the main hall. If you have your agenda with you, we will be taking questions after each session for five minutes only. The first report is from José Pinera. José, would you like to start?

Speaker 3

OK, thanks for coming. Can you close the door? Thanks. Um, there's coffee over there if anyone would like a drink – please help yourself. OK, can we begin? As you know, we need to discuss how we can improve our productivity in the marketing department. I want to focus on two issues today. First, let's look at where we can ...

Speaker 4

Right then, is everybody here? OK, let's get started! Does everyone have the agenda, OK? Right, well, as you know we are facing a lot of economic problems at the moment, and I'm afraid that means we need to make some changes to our organisation. This isn't an easy decision but I'm afraid we need to ask you to ...

Unit 3. Meetings and discussions: giving and explaining reasons. Exercise 1. (CD1:15)

a

I think we should have a four-page brochure. For one thing, it's cheaper to produce than an eight-page brochure.

b

If you ask me, we should employ Sylvia Montoya because she's the most experienced.

c

I agree with Diane that we should have the dinner here, because it's more convenient. Another reason is that people won't have to drive or take the bus anywhere after work.

d

We think computer training would be the most useful. The main reason is that many people are still having trouble using the new database.

Unit 3. Meetings and discussions: closing a meeting. Exercise 1. (CD1:16)

a

OK, to sum up, we decided to go

with a six-page brochure, with photos, but black and white – no colour. The marketing department will send me the copy by the 14th, and then I'll check it over and send it to the printer. Thanks, everyone. This was a productive meeting. I'll see you all tomorrow.

b

Well, then, let's review what we've agreed on so far. We agreed that Sylvia Montoya is the most experienced, but we need to know if she speaks Spanish fluently. We also need to know what sort of salary she expects. We didn't like Pat Bolton, so we'll contact him, uh, later with a rejection letter. And we want more information on James Grier, too. We want to know more about his overseas experience. So, our next step will be to call our first two choices and ask a few questions.

c

I guess that's it, then. Let me summarise our decisions. We'll hold the company dinner here, on Friday the 19th, from 6:30 until 9:00. We'll have a barbecue outside – and hope that the weather is good. Ken will take care of hiring some live music for us. I think that will be quite nice. Thank you, everyone.

d

Oh, it looks like we're out of time. OK, let's go over what we've decided so far. We agreed that we'll have two computer training classes, and that the first one will cover the new database. We might have some language training – Michelle is going to get us some more information about that. We'll have a class on giving presentations if we can get Jay to do that for us. And, uh, I'll talk to Jay tomorrow morning about that. And we still need prices for the intercultural training classes. I'll email the company again about that. Let's meet again on Wednesday at, let's say, 10:30, here, and we'll make our final decisions. Thank you.

Unit 4. Listen and practise. Discussing ideas. Exercise 2. (CD1:17)

Sacha: Helena, what do you think about making a TV commercial?

Helena: Well, I'm not sure that will work, and it's difficult to do. What do the rest of you think?

Ken: Mm, let's come back to this later. Any other ideas?

Joe: Well, off the top of my head, why don't we use our website?

Sacha: I like that idea. Then, maybe we could ask people to email us.

Joe: Yes, that's a great idea!

Helena: I think so, too. What do you think, Ken?

Ken: I agree. Excellent!

Unit 4. Listen and practise. Discussing ideas. Exercise 5. (CD1:18)

Ken: OK. Good. Everyone agrees. So, what do you think – shall we have a break now, or do you all want to go on some more?

Helena: Let's go on. We're getting a lot done.

Sacha: Yes, let's go on. We can take a break later.

Joe: Fine with me.

Ken: OK, then. Let's move on to the next topic. Let me see … number four, 'Improving English skills for overseas staff.' Wow, that's a tough one … so what do you think we …

Unit 4. Meetings and discussions: agreeing and disagreeing. Exercise 1. (CD1:19)

Jim: OK, let's get started. As you know, we need to reduce our costs this year by fifteen percent. We already have some ideas on how to do this, but I want to hear your suggestions before we make a final decision. So, what do you think?

Martha: Well, we could move our office – I know this is an expensive area. Maybe we could move somewhere cheaper.

Jim: That's possible, I guess.

Taki: The easiest way is to reduce salaries, maybe by 15 percent?

Jim: Um, no, we can't do that.

Mark: Why don't we cut travel expenses – stay in cheaper hotels, fly economy class, and things like that?

Jim: That's a good idea.

Taki: I know! How about turning off the heating in winter and the air conditioning in summer? It would be good for the environment as well!

Jim: Mmmm, I'm not sure about that. Any other ideas? Kay?

Kay: I think we should reduce overtime work; this will save money and we can also spend more time with our families!

Jim: That's a great idea! Well, thank you all for your suggestions. Let me think some more about it, and I'll let you know what we decide.

Unit 4. Meetings and discussions: agreeing and disagreeing. Exercise 4. (CD1:20)

a

A: Why don't we go to the beach this weekend?

B: No, that's a bad idea. It's going to rain this weekend.

b

C: Maybe we could increase the font size so it's easier to see.

D: I agree; that's a great idea!

c

E: How about this? We could move the TV over there.

F: I don't think that's a good idea – the cable is too short.

d

G: I think we should ask my mother to come and stay with us.

H: Well, we could do that, I suppose. Let's think about it.

Unit 4. Meetings and discussions: moving through a meeting. Exercise 2. (CD1:21)

Jim: All right, all right, is everybody here? Anna? Is Anna here? OK, let's get started, shall we? Now, as you know, next month we have three new people coming, so we need to decide how we're going to reorganise the office space. So, does anyone have any ideas? What do you think, Taki?

Taki: Well, we could move offices again, I guess!

Anna: Can I say something? Let's focus on where people will sit. Then after we decide that, we can look at …

Jim: OK, well, those are some ideas for desk space. We're short of time, so let's move on to other equipment. Do we really need four printers in this office? We haven't heard from you yet, Martha. What do you think?

Martha: Don't ask me – I don't know anything about computers. But I think we have to discuss locker space. We don't have enough room in the women's cloak room for all our coats.

Jim: Well, can we come back to this later? I think we should talk about the printers first. OK, Mark, what do you think about equipment?

Mark: That's a difficult question. Basically, there are three things we need to focus on here. First is the network – now it's difficult to explain, but … other security issues of course. There are two main security issues we need to think about …

Jim: Thank you, Mark, but we are running out of time here, so let me summarise what we've decided. Anna is going to make a plan for desk space, and Mark will find out if … Is there anything else? Great, well, thank you for your time today, and for your suggestions.

Others: Thank you.

Unit 4. Viewpoints. Exercise 2. (CD1:22)

Jun-ha Kim

Because we're a big company, we have a lot of meetings and usually there are 10 or 20 people in a meeting, sometimes more. The meetings are very formal and they usually take one or two hours, sometimes longer. Punctuality is really important – we always start on time. The meeting ends when everyone has finished speaking. Usually, the meeting goes overtime, so we have to schedule extra time when we book a meeting room.

Actually, for me the meetings are not so interesting because we already agreed what to do before the meeting. The purpose of the meeting is just to give information on what we decided. At the meetings the manager speaks and everybody listens to him – it's very formal. There are usually a lot of documents that we go through in the meeting, but everyone has seen them before, so there's no new information. I guess it's a kind of ceremony – everyone can see that we all agree. Anyway, the meeting is not so important. The important work is done before the meeting, when we send documents around to get everyone to agree, and after the meeting, when we have to follow up on the decisions. It takes us a long time to make a decision, but after the decision is made, we can move very quickly.

I don't like speaking out, especially in meetings. I have to think carefully about what I want to say and I worry in case someone disagrees with me, or in case I make a mistake, or my idea isn't very good. I usually wait for someone else to speak first, and if I agree, then sometimes I'll say something. If I don't agree, I don't say anything – I just joined the company, so everyone is older than me, and I need to show respect.

Stefan Weil

I work for a Swiss company. I realise Swiss companies love meetings! When I worked in China, we didn't have so many meetings, and the meetings were usually very long, and only a few people spoke. Here I have lots of meetings every day, but they are very short – 30 minutes or one hour. Sometimes people are late because they have to wait for an elevator or something, or because they are coming from another meeting. Anyway, we have to end on time because usually someone is waiting for the meeting room! Our meeting rooms are small – maybe four or five people at most. That's good, I think, because if it's more than that, then it's difficult to decide anything, and some people don't get a chance to speak.

I think meetings are useful. Face-to-face communication is important, and it's a good opportunity to hear everyone's opinions. We do a lot of problem-solving and a lot of brainstorming, and meetings are very good for that. It's important that everyone gives their ideas freely. It doesn't matter if you're a manager or a new employee – the important thing is to give your opinion. If you don't say anything, then why are you in the meeting?

Honestly speaking, I think we have too many meetings, and sometimes we make decisions too quickly. We don't have time to think about things, and this means that after we make the decision, we sometimes find a lot of problems. Then we have to have more meetings.

Review 1 to 4. Exercise 2. Who are they? (CD1:23)

Lizzy: Hi! I'm Lizzy, Lizzy Brown. Nice to meet you!

Peter: Nice to meet you, Lizzy. My name's Peter, Peter Swain.

Lizzy: Where are you from originally, Peter?

Peter: I'm from Bath, in England.

Lizzy: Really! I've been there! I visited England last summer and we stayed in Bath. It's a beautiful city – I really loved it.

Peter: Yes, it is, isn't it? Where are you from, Lizzy?

Lizzy: Chicago, in the U.S. Have you been there?

Peter: No, I haven't, but I'd love to go there. I heard it's very cold in winter, though.

Lizzy: It really is. But in spring and summer it's really nice.

Peter: OK. So what do you do?

Lizzy: I'm a research assistant for a museum. I'm here looking at some paintings.

Peter: Wow! That sounds interesting.

Lizzy: Yeah, it is. How about you, what do you do?

Peter: Oh, I'm still a student. I'm studying history at the university here.

Lizzy: Oh, OK. And what kinds of things do you like to do in your free time?

Peter: I go rock climbing, and I've just started scuba-diving.

Lizzy: Really? That's amazing! I'm really into scuba-diving! Where do you go?

Peter: Well, I've only been a couple of times, and …

Review 1 to 4. Exercise 6. In my next slide … (CD1:24)

OK, good morning everyone. Let's get started, shall we? This morning I'm going to talk about process improvements and how we can reduce our cycle time. The main thing I want to say is that by improving the way we work, we can cut our costs by 17 percent! Now that's a big savings, as you know.

In my presentation I'm going to talk about three things. First, I'll go over the current situation and how we work now. Then I'll describe the improvements that we are recommending. Finally, I'll talk about the cost-savings we can expect from these improvements.

Are there any questions so far? No? OK then, in my next slide you'll see …

Unit 5. Listen and practise. Leaving messages. Exercise 2. (CD1:25)

Melike: Hi, this is Melike Kayhan in the Istanbul office. Thank you for calling. I'm not at my desk right now. Please leave your name and a message and I'll call you back as soon as I can.

Linda: Oh, hi, Melike, this is Linda from the Munich office. How are you? I'm calling to let you know I'll be in Istanbul next month. Can you call me back?

Unit 5. Listen and practise. Leaving messages. Exercise 5. (CD1:26)

Linda: Um, let me see – I'll be in the office until five o'clock, my time, and then I'll be in the office most of tomorrow. My number is 65-7782-3774. Thanks. Goodbye.

Unit 5. Telephoning: using voicemail. Exercise 1. (CD1:27)

a

Jack: Hi Melike, it's Jack. Listen, I need the sales data for Japan and Korea as soon as possible. Can you give me a call before lunch? I'm in meetings all afternoon. Thanks.

b

Jamir: Hello, Ms Kayhan? This is Jamir from Asia Travel. I'm calling to confirm your hotel reservations for Hong Kong and Taipei. Can you call me back? My number is 206-555-7324. Thank you.

c

Mahmut: Hi, Mom, it's Mahmut I'll call you later. Bye-bye.

d

Jamie: Melike, this is Jamie Selkirk from Finance. I'm returning your call. Can you call me back? I'm leaving the office now but you can reach me on my cell phone – the number is 070-5732-4565. Thanks.

e

Consuela: Melike, this is Consuela Vittorino from Intex. I will be in Istanbul next week, and I wanted to see if you were free for lunch. I'm out of the office the rest of today, but I will call you back tomorrow morning. Thank you.

f

Caroline: Hi Melike, this is Caroline. I have a question about the Munich office. It's not urgent, so I'll send you an email. Thanks. Bye.

Unit 5. Telephoning: using voicemail. Exercise 2. (CD1:28)

a

Jennifer: Hi, this is Jennifer. ... Oh, hi, Ellen. Listen, I'm in a meeting right now. Can you call me back? ... OK. Thanks.

b

A: Leave your message after the tone.

B: Nakano-san, this is Tim from Chicago. Can you call me back this afternoon? Thanks.

c

Please leave your name and number and I'll call you back.

d

C: Hello, Richard Burks speaking.

D: Hello, Richard, this is Addie, from Germany. Are you busy now?

C: Hi, Addie, I'm just leaving the office. Can I call you back this afternoon?

D: That will be fine. Thank you, Richard.

C: OK, talk to you later. Bye now.

D: Goodbye.

Unit 5. Telephoning: using voicemail. Exercise 3. (CD1:29)

a

Yoshiko: Hi, this is Yoshiko Sasaki, from Newmarket Publishing. I'm not here right now, but please leave a message after the tone, and I'll call you back as soon as I can. Thank you for calling.

b

Tom: Hello, this is Tom Johnson. I'm out of the office today, but I'll be back tomorrow morning. Please leave your name and number after the tone, and I'll call you back. Thanks.

c

Michelle: Thank you for calling Pacific Finance. This is Michelle Kong speaking. I'm not at my desk at the moment, but please leave a message after the tone, and I will get back to you.

d

Jamir: Thank you for calling Asia Travel. This is Jamir speaking. Our office is closed today, but please leave your name and number, and we will call you back as soon as we can. Thank you for your call. (Please leave a message after you hear the tone.)

Unit 5. Taking and leaving a message. Exercise 2. (CD1:30)

John: Hello, this is Techno-services. How can I help you?

Jane: Oh, hi. This is Jane Simpson, from BLC. Can I speak to Maggie, please?

John: Just a moment please. ... Hello, I'm afraid Maggie is not here right now. Can I take a message?

Jane: Do you know what time she'll be back?

John: Um, no, sorry, I don't.

Jane: OK, can you give her a message?

John: Yes, of course.

Jane: Please tell her Jane Simpson called, and please ask her to call me back on my cell phone. My number is 088-5592-3779.

John: I'm sorry, can you repeat your number?

Jane: Sure, that's 088-5592-3779.

John; OK. Let me repeat that. That's Jane Simpson from BLC at 088-5592-3779, and you want Maggie to call you back, is that right?

Jane: That's right, thank you.

John: You're welcome. I'll give her your message when she comes back.

Jane: Thank you. I'm sorry, can you tell me your name?

John: Oh I'm sorry. My name is John, John Schmidt.

Jane: OK. Thank you very much, John.

John: You're welcome. Thank you for your call.

Jane: Goodbye.

John: Goodbye.

Unit 5. Viewpoints. Exercise 2. (CD1:31)

A: Thank you for calling Friendly Airlines.

B: Oh, hello, I ... oh

A: If you know the extension of the person or department you wish to reach, please dial it now.

B: Uh, no.

A: For international arrival and departure times, press 1. For domestic arrival and departure times, press 2.

B: What? hang on ...

A: To make a reservation for a flight, press 3. To change ...

B: OK, OK, 3.

A: You have reached Friendly Airlines reservations. To make a reservation for an international flight, press 1, to make a reservation for a domestic flight, press 2. To return to the main menu, press 3.

B: I don't want to make a reservation! Um, this one ...

A: International flight reservations. Thank you for your call. To make a reservation for flights to Europe and Asia, press 1.

B: Aaagh!

A: For flights to South America, press 2. To return to the main menu, press 3.

B: 3, 3, 3.

A: Thank you for calling Friendly Airlines. If you know the extension of the person or department you wish to reach, …

B: OK, OK, come on!

A: … please dial it now. For international arrival and departure times, press 1. For domestic arrival and departure times, press 2. To make a reservation for a flight, press 3. To change a reservation, …

B: Yes!

A: … press 4. To change a reservation for a flight leaving today, press 1. For flights not leaving today, press 2. To return to the main menu, press 3. … Flights leaving today.

B: Yes!

A: Please hold while we connect you to one of our operators.

B: All right!

A: Thank you for flying with Friendly Airlines. All of our operators are busy at the moment. Please hold.

B: What? What?

A: We're sorry to keep you waiting, but all of our operators are busy at the moment. Your call is important to us, so please hold …

B: Not again!

A: … and we will connect you when one of our operators is free. Thank you for calling.

Unit 6. Listen and practise. Checking in. Exercise 2. (CD1:32)

Receptionist: Do you have a reservation?

John: Yes, I do. My name is Vaughan, V-A-U-G-H-A-N. John Vaughan.

Receptionist: Vaughan … I'm sorry, I don't seem to have anything here under that name.

John: Are you sure? I have my confirmation number in my bag … somewhere …

Receptionist: Did someone else make the reservation?

John: Oh, maybe that's it. Try my company name, Microart, M-I-C-R-O-A-R-T, or maybe my assistant, Rivers, Chelsea Rivers?

Receptionist: Oh, yes, here you are. A non-smoking single room for five nights.

John: Yes, that's right. Good!

Receptionist: OK. Could I see your credit card, please? Thank you. Here you go. You're in room 312. The lifts are over there. Is there anything else I can help you with?

John: Yes, actually. Could you recommend a good restaurant?

Unit 6. Listen and practise. Checking in. Exercise 5. (CD1:33)

Receptionist: Sure. What kind of food do you like? There's a really good steak place near here.

John: Actually, I'm a vegetarian.

Receptionist: Well, let's see. How about Thai? I know a Thai place.

John: That sounds good. Is it within walking distance?

Receptionist: Well … I guess you could walk there … but it might be better to take a taxi. You'll be coming back after dark. Here's the address. You can get a taxi at the corner there.

John: Sounds good. Thank you very much.

Receptionist: Have a nice evening.

Unit 6. Asking for information. Exercise 1. (CD1:34)

a

Do you know where the bank is?

b

Can you tell me what time it is?

c

Could you tell me who that man is?

d

Do you know what building this is?

e

Do you know how much tickets are?

f

Can you tell me where the nearest bus stop is?

Unit 6. Giving directions. Exercise 2. (CD1:35)

1

Sandra: Excuse me. Could you tell

me how to get to …? Is it very far?

A: Oh, no, it's really close. Just go up First Avenue for three blocks. Turn left on Pine Street and you'll see it right there. You can't miss it.

Sandra: Thank you.

A: You'll love it – have a great time!

2

Sandra: Excuse me, do you know where … is?

B: Yes … Are you on foot?

Sandra: Yes, I am. But I love walking, and I have my umbrella!

B: OK, well, just go up University Street here until you get to 5th Avenue. Then turn left, and walk, oh, about three or four blocks. It's on the corner of 5th Avenue and Pine Street.

Sandra: Thank you so much.

3

C: Can I help you? Are you lost?

Sandra: Oh, uh, actually … I'm trying to find the … Do you know where it is?

C: Oh, sure, that's a great place. Let's see … it's on the corner of 3rd and Union.

Sandra: So, I can just go up 1st Avenue until I get to Union.

C: And turn right on Union and walk up till you get to 3rd. You'll see it on the corner.

Sandra: Thanks!

C: No problem!

4

Sandra: Excuse me, is there a … near here?

D: Yes, there are several … the closest one is just about a block away. Go to the corner there and turn right …

Sandra: On Union Street?

D: That's right, and then turn left onto Second Avenue. You should see it right there. I forget its name, but it's one of those chains …

Sandra: Thanks so much.

D: You're welcome.

Unit 6. Non-verbal communication: understanding gestures. Exercise 1. (CD1:36)

1

Taxi! Taxi!

2

Um, excuse me …

3

Excuse me, may I have the check, please?

4

Oh, sorry, I don't know.

5

Um, I think there's a mistake here …

6

OK, then go straight here …

Unit 7. Writing emails. Exercise 2. (CD1:37)

a

Jasmine: Hi, Emily, could I ask you a favour?

Emily: Sure, Jasmine. What is it?

Jasmine: Could you check my email to Lisa Ruben? You know, I'm not really used to writing emails in English. It's short – I'm just sending her those reports.

Emily: Sure, no problem. Let me see. … Well, OK, first thing, you need to write something in the Subject line.

Jasmine: Oh, right! I forgot. Like …

Emily: Oh, just say, let's see … Istanbul conference sales reports.

Jasmine: Istanbul conference sales reports. OK.

b

Emily: Then … this is to Lisa Ruben, right?

Jasmine: Right.

Emily: Then you should use her name in the greeting. You only write the department if you don't know the person's name.

c

Jasmine: Oh, OK. So … what … Lisa? Miss Ruben?

Emily: Ms. Ruben, that's 'M-S, full stop, Ruben'. Oh, and you need a comma after her name.

Jasmine: Really? Are you sure? I get emails that don't have commas in the greeting, I'm pretty sure …

Emily: Well, that's very informal English. Normally, greetings should have a comma.

Jasmine: OK, no problem. 'Dear … Ms. … Ruben … comma'.

d

Emily: Then … I think you should explain why you are writing. This just seems very direct.

Jasmine: OK … but what?

Emily: Let's see … something like, 'I'm writing to send you a copy of the sales report from the Istanbul conference, as you requested.' You can keep the rest.

Jasmine: Do you think she forgot that she requested the report?

Emily: No, but you know, it just makes it clear what the purpose is.

Jasmine: I'm writing … to send you … um, Istanbul conference … and then?

Emily: As you requested.

Jasmine: As you requested. OK.

e

Emily: Yeah, the rest of that paragraph is fine. Oh, wait! There's a spelling mistake.

Jasmine: Really? Where?

Emily: Conference. You forgot the 'e'.

Jasmine: Oh, right. F-E-R-E-N-C-E. I didn't even see that.

f

Emily: Then let's see. Your closing is too informal, I think.

Jasmine: Yeah, I guess it is. So … maybe 'sincerely'?

Emily: 'Sincerely' is good, yeah, or 'Best wishes'.

Jasmine: I'll use 'Best wishes'. I can't spell 'sincerely'!

g

Emily: And, uh, you didn't write your name …

Jasmine: Oh, I have my signature file on it. That has my full name and department and everything.

Emily: OK, but you still need to write your name at the end of the email. If your signature file has your full name, then you can just write Jasmine.

Jasmine: Then my name will be there twice.

Emily: That's fine. You need that. Your name above the line, like you 'signed' the letter, and then your signature file.

Jasmine: OK, if you say so! Thanks, Emily. I know it's just a short email, but I want to do it right.

Emily: No, not at all. It's important, I agree with you. Happy to help.

Unit 7. Email vocabulary. Exercise 1. (CD1:38)

Jeff: Hi, this is Jeff White, in IT. Um, you left a message that said you're having trouble with your email?

Emily: Yes, that's right. I can send messages, but I can't receive any!

Jeff: I see. And how do you know that?

Emily: Well, two people told me that they sent me emails, but I didn't get them. Also, my inbox was empty this morning, and that never happens!

Jeff: OK, well let me take a look at your account … What's your username?

Emily: Emilymay92 – that's one word, E-M-I-L-Y-M-A-Y, and then the numbers 9 and 2.

Jeff: And I have to ask you for your password. You can reset it later.

Emily: It's Daisy – D-A-I-S-Y. She's my dog.

Jeff: OK. Uh, you know, that's not really a very good choice. It's better to use something that isn't a real word or name. Just for safety.

Emily: You're right, I know. I'll change it today, I promise!

Jeff: OK, I see the problem. Your mailbox is full. You're going to need to delete some old messages to free up some space. You, uh, you have a lot of really big attachments. Do you need all of them?

Emily: Oh, some of those are old. I don't need them anymore.

Jeff: OK, well, throw away as much as you can, and that should solve your problem.

Emily: And what about the messages that were sent to me? Are they gone?

Jeff: Oh, no, they're still on the server. As soon as there's space, they'll show up. But just call me again if you have any problems.

Unit 8. Listen and practise. Giving a presentation. Exercise 2. (CD1:39)

Katy: If there are no more questions, I'll finish here. Thank you. … So, what do you all think? Can you give me some feedback?

Adam: Well, your content is great, but you need to slow down when you speak.

Katy: Really?

Lucy: I agree. And remember to look at people.

Katy: Oh right. Thanks. Is there anything else I should do?

Adam: Um, yes. Don't wave the pointer around, and try to relax!

Katy: Right. Thanks so much for your feedback. That's really helpful!

Adam/Lucy: You're welcome.

Unit 8. Listen and practise. Giving a presentation. Exercise 5. (CD1:40)

Katy: I really appreciate it – this is my first big presentation and I want to do a good job.

Lucy: Don't worry, you'll do a great job I'm sure. You just need to try to relax, and look confident! The presentation is great so don't worry, you'll be fine.

Katy: Thanks. I need to remember to slow down – when I'm nervous I talk too quickly.

Adam: I'm sure you'll be fine. Do you want to try again?

Katy: That would be great! Do you have enough time?

Adam/Lucy: Of course!

Katy: OK, let's go. Good morning, I'm Katy Watson, and I'm going to talk about ...

Unit 8. Presenting information: giving and receiving feedback. Exercise 1. (CD1:41)

Speaker 1

OK, well, um, thank you, thank you for, um , coming here today, and er, well, I'm, I'm going to, going to talk about, um, the, the results from our survey. The uh, the main thing I want to say, is, um, this. Um, from the survey, um, we need to, to increase the, the, increase our spending on, um training. I'm going to talk about three things: the uh, survey itself, then the um, results, and um finally um, the um recommendations. Right, let's, um, um ...

Speaker 2

Hello everybody I'm Francoise. Good morning. Now if you look at page 7 in your handout, you can see a graph showing our results from the last quarter. As you see here, sales increased in three of our markets. If you go to page 5, no, there – page 5, you can see a breakdown by business area. Now I want to give you some background on this ...

Speaker 3

Right, sorry, shall we get started? My name is Jenny Crawford, sorry – I'm a bit nervous. I'm going to talk about our new project in Germany. My message today, er, is that our results so far are very good, and in fact we are ahead of schedule. My presentation is divided into two parts: first I'll talk about the schedule and then I'll talk about the changes we want to make. Is that OK? Sorry, can you see it? OK, let me go on to the first part then. If you look at this slide ...

Unit 8. Presenting information: delivery: eye contact and voice. Exercise 1. (CD1:42)

a

I'm busy this evening. Around seven friends are coming for dinner.

b

I'm busy. This evening around seven friends are coming for dinner.

c

I'm busy this evening around seven. Friends are coming for dinner.

Unit 8. Presenting information: delivery – eye contact and voice. Exercise 2. (CD1:43)

A: In conclusion, I've talked about our new plans for the Asia-Pacific region. My main point was that we need to improve the way we operate in this market. I talked about changes in our organisation, changes in our management style, and also changes in our recruiting process. Finally, I want to ask for your support. With your help I know we can be successful as we make these changes. Thank you for your attention. Are there any questions?

Unit 8. Presenting information: endings and conclusions. Exercise 2. (CD1:44)

Katy: Let me summarise my presentation today. I've talked about two things: first I described our plans to reorganise the sales team in Lisbon, and second I talked about improving our communication between Lisbon and the Head Office. My main point was that by making these changes, we can raise our productivity and increase the number of customer visits. Thank you for listening. Are there any questions or comments?

Unit 8. Presenting information; dealing with questions. Exercise 1. (CD1:45)

Speaker 1

Speaker 1: Well, thank you very much for listening. Are there any questions?

Questioner 1:Yes, I have a question. How many people took part in these tests?

Speaker 1: That's a good question! Thank you for asking. Well, we wanted to use ...

Speaker 2

Speaker 2: Are there any more questions?

Questioner 2: Yes, I have a question. Why did you choose this method to test how quickly the impurities were dissolved?

Speaker 2: I'm sorry, can you repeat your question?

Speaker 3

Speaker 3: Thank you. Do you have any questions? Yes?

Questioner 3: That was very interesting, thank you. My question is about the next step. What would be the next step in your research?

Speaker 3: Thank you for asking that. Well, the next step is to measure ...

Speaker 4

Speaker 4: Thank you, that's a

difficult question. I don't have that information with me I'm afraid. Let me check and get back to you.

Speaker 5

Questioner 4: Can you tell me something about the study design?

Speaker 5: We started in January and the study took four months. Does that answer your question?

Questioner 4: Yes, thank you. I have another question, what is the ...

Unit 8. Viewpoints. Exercise 2. (CD1:46)

Leila:

I use presentation software a lot in business and I really like it. It takes a long time to learn, but after you get used to it, then it's very easy to use and you can make your presentation very quickly, and it looks very professional.

Before this software, I used to carry so much stuff, even equipment like a screen and projector sometimes; it was so heavy! And it took a long time to make slides and handouts, and it was difficult to make changes. Now I take my laptop with me, and I can change my presentation the evening before if I want – it's so flexible. I don't use handouts now – if someone asks me for a copy of one of the slides or something, then I email the information. It's easy and fast and it saves paper!

Disadvantages? Well I don't think presentation software is good if you want to give a lot of information. You have to make the font quite big so that people can read it, and there isn't a lot of room to put information on the slide. Erm, what else, let me think, um, I don't like watching presentations when they have too much colour or too much animation – it's difficult to focus on what they are trying to say. Oh yes, and I don't like it when speakers read the information on their slides – I don't understand why people do that, there's no point, is there? We can read it!

Young-jin:

Actually I don't like presentation software so much, even though I use it. I also watch a lot of presentations by my colleagues – more than 5 or 10 every week, I guess.

For me, the biggest problem is that people spend too much time making their slides, and not enough time thinking about what they want to say. Sometimes I see very beautiful slides with lots of colour, with photographs or video, and I think 'maybe it took one or two hours to make this slide', but at the same time the presenter hasn't planned how to talk about the information or how to answer questions. I think this is a big problem for people who don't speak English well – they spend 90 percent of their time making their slides and only 10 percent of their time thinking about what to say.

Another problem with this presentation software is too many bullet points. It's easy to use bullet points, so people use them too much – key points, results, recommendations, conclusion, everything. I always tell my colleagues, 'Why do you need so many bullet points?' Just tell me the information!

Good points? Let me see, well, I guess one good point is you can't put too much information on one slide. You know, a good presentation is a good presentation, whether you use presentation software or not. And a bad presentation is a bad presentation. Presentation software is a tool for the speaker, that's all. It's not everything.

Review units 5 to 8. Exercise 1. I'm not here right now. (CD1:47)

a

Hi, this is Jim, how are you doing? Urm, listen, can you call me back later today? I'm in a meeting this afternoon, so can you call me back after 5 o'clock? Thanks. Talk to you later. Bye.

b

Hello, this is Hassan. I'm calling about the soccer game this weekend. I'll call you back later. Bye.

c

Hello, it's Lily. Look, I want to talk to you about the meeting tomorrow. Please call me back. Thank you.

Review units 5 to 8. Exercise 4. Go straight for four blocks. (CD1:48)

City Hall? Sure, no problem. OK, let me see. OK, go straight up here, then turn left at the corner, OK? Go straight for two blocks, then at the intersection turn left; no sorry, turn right and go straight for two blocks. Turn right at the corner of the intersection there and then take the next left. Are you with me? OK. Right, now go straight ahead for, let me see, one, two blocks, then turn left. Go straight for 3 blocks and it's right there on the corner, on the left. You got it? Sure, no problem. You want me to get you a taxi?

Review units 5 to 8. Exercise 7. Thanks so much for your feedback! (CD1:49)

So what do you think? Can you give me some feedback?

Oh right, thanks.

Really? OK, thanks.

OK, thanks.

Of course, thank you.

Right. Thanks so much for your feedback. That's really helpful.

Unit 9. Listen and practise. Discussing job applications. Exercise 2. (CD1:50)

Mr Keen: OK, who's next?

Frances: Jason Park. Let's see ... well, he graduated from Bristol University ... that's a good university.

Mr Keen: What was his degree?

Frances: Business Administration. He studied marketing and international business.

Mr Keen: Well, that's good, of course. And does he have enough experience?

Frances: Well ... I'm not sure. He hasn't had a full-time job yet. The summer before he graduated he interned as an office assistant, and then he worked the summer before ... and it looks like he also had a part-time job while in university.

Mr Keen: Hmmm ... So let's see what he did at his internship. Well, it was a trading company ... oh, and he helped with sales and market research. So that's useful.

Frances: And then before that, uh, sales assistant. I guess he, what, sold clothes?

Mr Keen: Yes, although I think that experience is relevant. I mean, as he says, he was responsible for assisting customers, and that's really what sales is all about, isn't it? You can learn a lot about marketing from working in a shop.

Frances: That's true.

Mr Keen: Now, waiter in a restaurant, I don't know about that.

Frances: But, look, he spoke French and Spanish with customers.

Mr Keen: OK, that's good. He must be very good at languages!

Frances: Yes, he is. Look at his skills – fluent French, and then also Spanish, conversational German.

Mr Keen: That's great for someone in our department.

Frances: And look – excellent computer skills.

Mr Keen: Also good, although it's pretty common, really.

Unit 9. Listen and practise. Discussing job applications. Exercise 5. (CD1:51)

Frances: So. Do we want to interview him?

Mr Keen: Well, I'm not sure. There are some things I really like about him. But he hasn't had a full-time job yet, only the internship and some part-time jobs.

Frances: Yes, but if he's smart and has the right skills ...

Mr Keen: Well, we still have about eight more CVs to go through. Why don't we put his CV in the 'maybe' group, and we'll come back to it after we've looked at everybody?

Frances: OK, that sounds fair.

Unit 9. Reading and writing a CV: supporting opinions. Exercise 1. (CD1:52)

A: Jason has some relevant experience. For example, he worked at a trading company.

A: He speaks several foreign languages, such as French, Spanish, and German.

Unit 9. Reading and writing a CV: supporting opinions. Exercise 3. (CD1:53)

a

Roger: OK, so who's next ...

Annabelle: Let's look at this one. Jeff Zimmer.

Roger: Wait ... where's his photo?

Annabelle: Actually, British people don't include photos with their CVs. It's actually against the law to ask someone for their photo on an application here.

Roger: Oh, yes, that's right. Well, what do you think?

Annabelle: I think he looks good. He's got some good experience. For example, he's working now at Alliance. That company is pretty similar to ours.

b

Annabelle: Oh, dear!

Roger: Well, at least it's different!

Annabelle: Yes, but it's way too informal. Pink paper?!

Roger: And look at this font!

Annabelle: Yes, it looks like a party invitation!

Roger: And the email address ...

Annabelle: justwannahavefun@hotmail.com? That's not very professional.

Roger: Well, I don't think we even need to read this one, do you?

Annabelle: No, I guess we don't.

c

Annabelle: OK ... Jackie, um, I don't know how to pronounce the last name.

Roger: Uh ... do you think she's too young?

Annabelle: Well, the CV doesn't give her age. This is Britain, you know!

Roger: Yes, but if she just graduated last year …

Annabelle: We still don't know how old she is.

Roger: True. But look at her job experience. It's just not relevant.

Annabelle: None of it?

Roger: She's certainly done a lot of things, such as video shop assistant, swimming coach, she's worked in a coffee shop … I don't think she knows what she wants to do!

Annabelle: Well, I guess she won't be working here …

d

Roger: Well, this one looks good.

Annabelle: Hmm … only one job …

Roger: Yes, but look at his education. A double major in Business and German … and he's had some good classes, such as International Law and Contracts. That could be really useful.

Annabelle: Yes, if he learned enough.

Roger: Well, we can ask him in an interview.

Annabelle: You're right. I think we should talk to him.

e

Roger: Well! Very impressive!

Annabelle: Yes … maybe too impressive.

Roger: What do you mean?

Annabelle: Well, I think she's overqualified, don't you?

Roger: Overqualified? What do you mean?

Annabelle: Well, I think she's ready for a higher position than this one. For example, at Williams and Rose, she was a General Manager!

Roger: Yes, I see what you mean. And was that her first job?

Annabelle: Oh, no. British people list their most recent jobs first.

Roger: Oh, right. Still … she might want a much higher salary than we can offer, too. I wonder why she applied for this job. Do you think we should interview her?

Annabelle: I don't know … I think we have enough people already who clearly fit this job.

Unit 10. Listen and practise. Giving key information. Exercise 2. (CD2:01)

Alexandra: Good, well thank you for coming today. I'd like to ask you some questions on your background. Then I'll try to answer any questions you have about the company. Does that sound OK?

Jessica: That sounds fine. Thank you.

Alexandra: OK, good. I have your CV, but can you tell me a little bit about yourself?

Jessica: Yes, of course. Well, I was born in Vietnam but I grew up in France. Right now I'm a student at Rouen University and my major is International Business.

Alexandra: I see. Very good. And why do you want to join our company?

Jessica: Well, I want to work in manufacturing and I want to use English in my career. I looked at your website and it seems an exciting place to work.

Unit 10. Listen and practise. Giving key information. Exercise 5. (CD2:02)

Alexandra: Good, good. When will you graduate?

Jessica: I'll graduate in March of next year.

Alexandra: OK. And why did you choose International Business as your major?

Jessica: Well, I like travel and I like English, and my father worked overseas for a long time, and it seemed an interesting subject.

Alexandra: All right. And, you said you wanted to work in manufacturing. Why are you interested in manufacturing?

Jessica: Well, I want to work in a company that makes things. I'm not interested in working in the finance or service industries. I think manufacturing is important because …

Unit 10. Being interviewed: describing your background. Exercise 1. (CD2:03)

Speaker a

I was born in Canada, in Toronto. I grew up in Canada but I went to Stanford University in California, and I graduated in 2008. My major was Biochemistry and right now I'm a researcher for a pharmaceutical company. In my free time I like to play the cello – I love music, and it helps me to relax after work.

Speaker b

Hello there. I'm from England. I was born in Manchester but I grew up in the South of England, near London. I'm a student – I'm studying Music at Sheffield

University and I'll graduate this year. I'm not sure what I'll do after graduation, maybe I'll be a teacher. In my free time I like making models – radio-controlled models like aeroplanes or helicopters. It's a little bit expensive, but I enjoy it.

Speaker c

Hi! I'm a student at Colorado State University in the United States. My major is Mathematics and I'll graduate next year. I love snowboarding! Colorado has some great ski resorts and in my free time I go snowboarding with my friends! What else? Oh yeah, I was born in San Francisco and I grew up there and went to high school there. That's all, I guess.

Unit 10. Being interviewed; talking about your future. Exercise 1. (CD2:04)

a

Right now I'm a student at medical school in England and I'll graduate next year. After I graduate I'd like to do medical research, I think. Five or ten years from now, I'd like to be researching new drugs for cancer patients. It's an exciting field right now and I want to help people who have serious illnesses.

b

My name is Dimitri and I'm a Construction Engineer. I started working last year after I graduated from university. I work for a construction company and at the moment I am in training. After I finish training I will start working on some construction projects. In five years I want to be a Supervisor on a big project, like a bridge or a pipeline, or subway construction or something like that.

c

Hi I'm Max. I'm 40 years old and I'm from the United States. I work in advertising and my job is to make advertising campaigns for our customers all over the country, so I travel a lot on business. I like meeting new people so I love my job, but I'm planning to change my career after a few more years. Three or five years from now I want to be working for some kind of NGO. I'd like to work in Africa or Asia maybe. After that I don't know. Maybe ten years later I'll come back to the U.S. I'm not sure right now.

Unit 10. Being interviewed: talking about your strengths. Exercise 2. (CD2:05)

May:

Well, I like working with people and I think I'm good at it. When I was a student at university I tutored high-school students for two years. In that job I needed to be well-organised, on time and I needed to motivate the students so that they studied hard. I think I was pretty good at it – all of my students passed their exams!

Yohei:

Let me see, well when I was a student I started my own business and that needed a lot of hard work and management skills. It was kind of of a small business – I imported dried fruit into Japan from the Philippines, but I had to work with shipping companies, and banks, and customers. It was really tough for me, but I enjoyed it and I learned a lot. I managed the business for about three years while I was a student, and then when I graduated from university I sold it to my friend.

Zofia:

My language skills are very good – I speak English and German, a little bit of Russian, and Polish of course. At university I worked in a hotel as a translator for six months, during the summer vacations. I also worked part time in a travel agency for one year. In that job, I had to manage the office, do things like filing and working with the computer and talking to customers on the telephone.

Unit 10. Viewpoints. Exercise 2. (CD2:06)

Fiona: OK, so what do you think Brian – what's the most important thing you look for when you interview.

Brian: Well, I guess I'd say technical skills. Yes, technical skills. If they don't have the technical skills then they can't do the job. Other skills like management or business skills we can teach them after they join, but they need to have the right technical skills before they join. How about you?

Fiona: Well we're a global company and we need people who can work internationally, so we're looking for people who are flexible – flexible in their thinking I mean. Leadership is also very important for us – people have to be confident and show they can work with other people in a team, even if other members are much older than they are.

Brian: I see. You don't worry about the technical or business skills then?

Fiona: Well, not as much, I think. We do look at work experience a lot – what kind of work they have done before, how they have shown leadership, teamwork and that kind of thing. Other than technical skills, what do you look for?

Brian: Work experience is important for us too, of course. And also reliability – our work is difficult and sometimes it can be dangerous. We need people who we know will work hard and will stay with the company for a long time.

Fiona: OK. Anything else?

Brian: Yes, communication skills. We have plants all over the world and our engineers need to travel a lot to install equipment or to train people overseas. They need to be able to communicate their ideas effectively.

Fiona: I agree entirely! Communication skills are really important nowadays, aren't they? I also think that people who have good communication skills are also more flexible, don't you think?

Brian: Well, I'm not sure about that – you may be right though.

Fiona: I really think so. Let me give you an example of what I mean …

Unit 11. Listen and practise. Discussing gifts. Exercise 2. (CD2:07)

Jake: Hi, Eliza, what are you doing?

Eliza: Oh, I'm trying to choose some small gifts for our London office. You know, for the end of the year. What do you think – should I send some Christmas cards?

Jake: Well, not everyone in the London office celebrates Christmas, so ... What else are you thinking about?

Eliza: Well, we have these nice company calendars. They have scenes from nature.

Jake: I think that's a good idea. They're attractive, they're useful, and they're easy to mail!

Eliza: I guess … They're not very exciting, though. What about some local crafts?

Jake: I don't think so. Those would be too expensive. Calendars are fine, and we have plenty of them.

Eliza: You're right.

Unit 11. Listen and practise. Discussing gifts. Exercise 5. (CD2:08)

Jake: So, do you think the London office will send us anything?

Eliza: No, not really. I mean, sometime in December we'll probably all get an electronic greeting card that says something like Happy Holidays or Season's Greetings. But British companies don't usually send gifts. It's just not a custom.

Jake: Well, that's probably a good thing. A few years ago, a new vendor sent our whole office some really expensive gifts.

Eliza: Oh, dear! That could be a problem …

Jake: Yeah, they didn't know that in Singapore, company workers can't accept expensive gifts. It looks like the vendor is trying to buy our business, or something. I know in this case it was just their custom, but still, we had to return the gifts.

Eliza: Ouch! That must have been uncomfortable for everyone.

Jake: Yes, it was.

Unit 11. Selecting gifts. Exercise 3. (CD2:09)

a

Alana: Oh, hi, Yanti. It's Alana here. Listen, can I ask you a few questions about local customs here?

Yanti: Of course.

Alana: Well, I've been invited to someone's house for dinner. I'd like to bring a small gift. Do you think that's OK?

Yanti: Oh, sure, that would be very nice. What are you going to bring?

Alana: Well, I have a nice book about my hometown in Wales, with some lovely photos. And it's even wrapped already.

Yanti: I think that would be great. However, don't expect them to unwrap the gift in front of you.

Alana: Really? Why not?

Yanti: Singaporeans think that looks too greedy.

Alana: Greedy?!

Yanti: Yes, you know, like they want it too much. They'll open it after you leave.

b

Alana: I also thought about bringing some food, maybe dessert or something to drink.

Yanti: Well … actually, it depends on the culture of the people you're visiting. As you know, in Singapore we have a mix of Chinese, Malay, and Indian people. So, for example, it's OK to bring food to a Malay family, but it's not a good idea if the family is Chinese.

Alana: Really? Why not?

Yanti: Well, the host might feel that you think that their food isn't good enough.

Alana: Oh, dear, I don't want that!

c

Alana: Wow, I didn't know it was so complicated. It's very different from Britain! Is there anything else I should know?

Yanti: Um, let's see… well, for Chinese people you should avoid giving four of something

– you know, like four cups or four handkerchiefs.

Alana: Why is that?

Yanti: The number four in Chinese can sound like the word for death, so it's considered unlucky.

Alana: Are there any lucky numbers?

Yanti: Yes, eight is lucky.

Alana: Well, I don't have eight books!

Yanti: I'm sure that's fine.

d

Yanti: And if you're giving gifts to an Indian family, don't give eight of the same item.

Alana: Oh, no. Why not? Is it unlucky?

Yanti: Not the number eight specifically, but Indians think odd numbers are luckier than even numbers. Just the opposite of what the Chinese believe!

Alana: So, seven or nine of something is better than eight …

Yanti: Exactly, or five. For an Indian person, anyway.

e

Alana: Is there anything I shouldn't give to an Indian person?

Yanti: Well, no beef, of course. And also don't give gifts made of leather.

Alana: OK. That's because of their religion, right?

Yanti: That's right. Cows are special in the Hindu religion.

f

Alana: I read somewhere that colours have different meanings in different cultures.

Yanti: Yes, that's right. Let's see … for Malay people, don't wrap gifts in yellow paper. That colour is for royalty – you know, kings and queens. For all three cultures, actually, white is a colour for death, so you shouldn't use white paper either.

Alana: OK … what colour paper is safe, then? Is there a colour I can use that's good for everyone?

Yanti: Everybody? Um … maybe red? That's a lucky colour for Chinese, and Indian people like bright cheerful colours. But Malay people like the colour green, too.

Alana: Well, the paper the book is wrapped in is red.

Yanti: Oh, that's lucky. Well, have a great time!

Unit 11. Explaining a problem or mistake. Exercise 1. (CD2:10)

A: Here, this is for you.

B : Oh, thank you. May I open it now?

A: Please. Go ahead.

B: Oh. Uh … Well, thank you …

A: Is something wrong? It's a plumeria lei, from Hawaii.

B: Oh, it's just that, well, Indians only use this flower for funerals.

A: Oh, no! I'm so sorry!

B: Oh, that's perfectly OK. You didn't know.

A: Anyway, thank you for telling me.

B: And thank you for the gift. It was a lovely thought.

Unit 12. Listen and practise. Reviewing performance. Exercise 2. (CD2:11)

Erik: Come in, Zara. Sit down over there.

Zara: Thank you.

Erik: OK, this is part of your annual performance review. We'll talk about your work over the last year and then we'll talk about your goals for next year and your career development plans. OK?

Zara: That sounds fine.

Erik: Good, so how do you feel about the year? Have you enjoyed working here?

Zara: Yes, very much. I feel good about the year. I've learned a lot and I really like the people here. I think I …

Erik: OK, for job knowledge I've rated you above expectations.

Zara: Good, thank you.

Erik: And I've written here 'Has worked hard to understand her job'.

Zara: Thank you.

Erik: You've done a good job learning about our products and our customers, and I've been pleased with …

Erik: For the next category, I've also rated you above, and I've written 'Pays attention to details (but needs to ask more questions)'.

Zara: I'm sorry, I don't understand. What do you mean by that?

Erik: Well, I mean that it's important to make sure you understand the …

Zara: OK, that's true. Thank you for the feedback.

Erik: You're welcome. OK, let's go on to planning and organisational skills. Here

I've marked you as 'Meets expectations'

Zara: I see.

Erik: And I've written in the comments section 'Needs to make sure she meets all deadlines.'

Zara: I'm sorry, can you explain that a little more?

Erik: Well, sometimes I think you are too careful and you worry too much about details. This means that you miss the deadline for reports or other work.

Zara: Oh I see. Well, can you give me an example?

Erik: OK, well you remember the conference report we …

Erik: And finally interpersonal skills, here you've been outstanding. I've been really pleased to have you as a team member.

Zara: Thank you! I appreciate that!

Erik: I mean it. And I've written here 'Great attitude! Always positive and cheerful'. Now, how do you think you could improve your organisational skills?

Unit 12. Listen and practise. Reviewing performance. Exercise 4. (CD2:12)

Zara: Well, I know I need to improve this. Sometimes I put too much information into the reports and that takes me a long time. Maybe I can take some training courses in time management and writing, or something like that.

Erik: OK, that's a good idea. Is there anything else you can do?

Zara: Um, well, I'm not sure. Do you have any suggestions?

Erik: Well, maybe you could ask other people to help you with this.

Zara: Yes, that's a good suggestion. I know Sonya is really good at writing. Maybe I'll ask her to check …

Unit 12. Responding to feedback and asking for clarification. Exercise 1. (CD2:13)

Zara: OK, that's true. Thank you for the feedback.

Zara: Thank you! I appreciate that!

Unit 12. Responding to feedback and asking for clarification. Exercise 3. (CD2:14)

Zara: I'm sorry, I don't understand. What do you mean by that?

Zara: I'm sorry, can you explain that a little more?

Zara: Can you give me an example?

Unit 12. Checking understanding. Exercise 1. (CD2:15)

a

A: Sales are going down so we need to increase our budget so that we can hire more sales people. If we hire more sales people, we can sell more products and we can spend more money on advertising.

B: OK, let me check that I understand what you're saying. You think that we have to increase our budget and hire more sales people. Then we can spend more on advertising. Is that right?

A: Yes, that's right. If we have more sales people then …

b

C: So these are the problems we have in our Brazilian factories. Can I get your agreement to make these changes?

D: Let me confirm our next steps before we decide. You will talk to the managers in the factories …

c

E: We need to make a decision quickly so that we can start interviewing new people for the position. After that we can decide on training and salary, etc.

F: Can I confirm what you said? The line is not very good.

E: Of course you can, Rob.

F: You said we need to start interviewing quickly, is that right?

E: Well, not really, no. I said we need to decide quickly, so that ...

Unit 12. Discussing performance plans. Exercise 1. (CD2:16)

Erik: OK, I think that's about everything. Do we agree on this then?

Zara: Yes, I think so. Thank you so much for your feedback! This has been really helpful for me.

Erik: You're welcome. Let me confirm that I think you've done a great job this year. I've been really pleased with your work and I hope you have enjoyed working with us.

Zara: Yes, I have. As I said before, I think I've learned a lot here and I really like my job. I will try to improve my time management next year, I promise.

Erik: Excellent! One more thing, I want you to continue working here for the next six months, but after that I am planning to send you overseas for six months so you can get more experience of sales. I'm not sure where at the moment, perhaps in the US, or perhaps one of our offices in Europe or Asia.

Zara: Really! That would be great! That's so exciting!

Unit 12. Viewpoints. Exercise 2. (CD2:17)

Speaker a

I don't like saying to people that they have done a good job or a bad job. People know when they have done a good job, when everyone has worked hard and got a good result – I don't think I need to tell them directly. Also if someone has made a mistake or done something wrong, then usually they know and they will work hard to improve themselves.

I don't think it's a good idea to praise or to criticise one person, unless it's a really serious problem. People need to work well together as a team and have a good relationship with their manager and their co-workers. If someone is praised too much or criticised too much, then other people will feel uncomfortable and they will not work well together. You have to think about people's feelings.

My staff know when I am pleased or when I am angry. I don't need to say it to them.

Speaker b

To be a great manager, giving feedback is really important. People needs lots of feedback, positive and negative. Positive feedback provides motivation and negative feedback lets people know how they can improve. People need to be told when they're doing a great job and when they've done something wrong.

When you give feedback, it's important to be clear, focused, and direct. You need to be specific and to give details and examples of the good or bad behaviour. It shouldn't be personal, however – you need to focus on the behaviour or the problem, not the person.

After you have given feedback to someone, it's important to confirm with them that they understand what you are saying. Then you can focus on what the next steps are, and what changes they need to make.

Review Units 9 to 12. Exercise 3. I enjoy the work, but ... (CD2.18)

I was born in France, in Paris, but I grew up in England, and I went to University in London. My degree was in hotel management, and I graduated last year. Right now I work in a hotel in London – I need to get experience working in different parts of the hotel, so now I'm working on the front desk. It's interesting because I have to do lots of different things such as welcoming guests, accepting reservations, dealing with problems. I enjoy the work, but I work long hours and it's difficult to take a holiday. In my free time I like to go hiking – usually I take a bus or train to the countryside outside London. In the future, I want to go to Australia; I'm saving my money and 5 years from now I want to be a helicopter pilot. I can take lessons in Australia and it's much cheaper than here in the UK.

Review Units 9 to 12. Exercise 7. Don't worry about it. (CD2:19)

A: Aargh, oh no, I'm so sorry. Are you all right? Oh no, all down your shirt! I'm so sorry. Here, let me get a cloth.

B: Um, I apologise, um, I think I, um, just um, deleted all your data. It's just that I pushed the wrong button. You have a back-up, right?

C: I'm really sorry. I forgot the meeting was today. You see I lost my schedule last week. I'm so sorry.

Test 1. Listening section. A. (CD2:20)

N: Listen to the conversation. Tick true or false.

Woman: Hi, I'm not sure we've met.

Man: No, I don't think we have. I'm Mark Bowman.

Woman: Hi Mark. I'm Tina Hall. Are you with Cosmic?

Man: Uh, no, I'm not.

Woman: Oh. A different engineering company?

Man: Well, actually, I'm not working right now.

Woman: Really? So, uh …

Man: Actually, I'm going to school full-time right now. In business.

Woman: Oh, how interesting! My husband teaches business at the university.

Man: Really? Wait … is your husband Thomas Hall?

Woman: Yes, that's right! Are you in one of his classes?

Man: No, I'm not, but I know who he is. I've spoken with him before. He's a great guy.

Woman: Well, he'll be interested to hear that I met you!

Test 1. Listening section. B. (CD2:21)

N: Listen to the talk. Circle the correct answers.

Woman: Good afternoon, everyone, and thank you for coming. As some of you know, I'm Maria Hernandez, and I'm a human resources trainer with North-South Enterprises. And I'm really pleased to be invited here to talk to you all at Global Auto. My subject today is cross-cultural relationships, especially between Mexicans and Americans. We're going to focus on four main areas: relationships between management and employees, relationships between employees, communication with overseas offices, and finally, what you can do to improve your working relationships. Now, let me start by giving you some background.

Test 1. Listening section. C. (CD2:22)

N: Listen to the conversation. Circle the correct information.

Woman: Well, as you know, we're going to talk today about expanding our offices on the third floor. We'll look at two issues mainly: space and cost.

Man: We need to consider how much time this will take, too.

Woman: That is an important point. Let's discuss that after the break, OK?

Man: Sounds good.

Woman: So, then, according to Personnel, they need three new offices.

Man: If you ask me, they have enough space already. They have more offices than any other department!

Woman: Well, the reason for that is that they have more staff than any other department.

Man: I know, but … As I see it, their staff should share offices. Every other department does that.

Woman: Well, one issue is that they deal with a lot of confidential, private information. You know, like everyone's salary, and where they live, and … If you ask me, it's important for them to have their own offices.

Man: I see … well, what does everyone else think?

Woman: Yes, let's discuss this a little bit more, and then take a vote.

Test 1. Listening section. D. (CD2:23)

N: Listen to the talk. Circle the correct answers.

Man: I travel a lot for my job, and I guess one of the main reasons for that travel is meetings. I know, everybody says they hate meetings, but really, they're very useful. We have email of course, and phones, but when I meet someone and we talk face-to-face, we have a different kind of communication. I think it's important to be able to look people in the eye and to see their body language. It's easier to understand what people mean, and not just what they say. In my opinion, face-to-face meetings help us make decisions more quickly. Sometimes I'll discuss an issue for, oh, weeks by email, but when we meet in person, we can make a decision in just an hour or two. So I think that saves the company money in the long run.

Test 1. Listening section. E. (CD2:24)

N: Listen to the telephone call. Tick true or false.

Man: Hello, you've reached the desk of John Sandefer. I'm away on vacation this week, but will be back in the office on May 17. If you need help right away, please call my assistant Angie Walker at extension 173. Otherwise, please leave your name, number, and a short message, and I'll return your call as soon as I can. Oh, and you can also email me at s-a-n-d-e-f-e-r at go global dot com. Thanks for calling.

Woman: Oh, uh, hi, John, this is Kim Walsh. I need to talk to you about next month's schedule, but it's a little complicated. I'll call you next week on Monday or Tuesday when you're back.

Test 1. Listening section. F. (CD2:25)

N: Listen to the conversation. Circle the correct answers.

Man: Excuse me, could you tell me where the concert hall is?

Woman: The concert hall? You mean the Kornblum Concert Hall?

Man: Yes.

Woman: That's it right there. Just across the street.

Man: Oh, really! Thanks. I'm new in town, so …

Woman: Are you going to the concert tonight?

Man: Yes, I hope so.

Woman: Well, if you wait until after 6:30, you can sometimes buy discounted tickets. I think half-price.

Man: Really? That's great … Uh … do you know what time it is?

Woman: Sure, it's … 6:15 now.

Man: Great. Oh, sorry, one more thing … is there a bank around here?

Woman: Yes, there is. Go down Broadway here, and turn left at the light. You'll see a bank right there.

Man: Thank you so much.

Woman: Not at all. Enjoy the concert!

Test 2. Listening section. A. (CD2:26)

N: Listen to the conversation. Tick true or false.

Woman: Hi, Jack. What are you doing?

Man: Oh, hi. I'm setting up a new email account.

Woman: Really? Don't you already have one?

Man: Well, I have my work account, of course. And then I have an old one from my university, but I never use it. But I want one that I can use for my personal email.

Woman: Well, can't you use your university account for that?

Man: Actually, I don't even know how to open it. I mean, I don't remember my password.

Woman: I'm sure there's a way to find out.

Man: I know, but I'm too lazy. I'll just make a new one now. I'm going to use one of those free Web-based services.

Woman: Well, OK … since it's free …

Man: OK, now I need to choose a name …

Woman: What about using your first name and last name? Then it's easy for people to remember.

Man: No, that's boring. I know … 'jack attack'.

Woman: Uh … oh … kay …

Man: Come on, that's great! And now, a password

Woman: Just choose something you won't forget this time!

Man: Oh, it doesn't matter. I'm going to write it down ... somewhere …

Test 2. Listening section. B. (CD2:27)

N: Listen to the conversation. Circle the correct information.

Woman: So, to summarise, I talked about three simple things everyone can do to save the department money. First, I talked about not wasting office supplies, even things you think are cheap, like paper. Second, I talked about using email more often, instead of making so many overseas phone calls. And finally, I talked about saving energy in our offices by lowering the temperature in the winter and raising it in the summer, turning off the lights during the lunch hour, and things like that. Well, thank you for listening. Are there any questions?

Man: Um … yeah … I eat lunch at my desk, you know? And I work at the same time. So do I really have to turn off the light?

Woman: That's a good question. No, of course not. But just keeping the light on for one office isn't so bad.

Man: Well … my office is all open plan. We have about 20 desks in there. There isn't a light just for my desk. So I have to keep the light on for the whole office, even when I'm the only one working.

Woman: I see. Well … is there perhaps a smaller office or room where you could work?

Man: I guess so … I guess I could take my laptop into the break room …

Woman: There you go. There's almost always a good solution if you think creatively.

Test 2. Listening section. C. (CD2:28)

N: Listen to the conversation. Circle the correct answers.

Woman: OK, let's have the next CV.

Man: All right, here we go. Pat Morgan.

Woman: Pat … is that a man or a woman?

Man: Um …. I can't tell from just reading this.

Woman: Well, it doesn't matter. OK, does this Pat have a business degree?

Man: Yes! And graduated with honours.

Woman: Oh, nice. How long ago?

Man: Let's see … two years ago.

Woman: And since then?

Man: Since then Pat has been working at a software company in tech support.

Woman: Well, finally! Someone who's actually qualified for the position! Has he … or, well, has she … has this person been working for two years then?

Man: Let me check the dates … I guess just about one year now.

Woman: Hmmmm … that's not TOO much experience ...

Man: Oh … and guess what?

Woman: Tell me.

Man: We have a Spanish speaker! Pat even spent a year abroad in Ecuador while in college.

Woman: That's perfect. Let's call Ms Morgan … or, of course, Mr Morgan … in for an interview.

Test 2. Listening section. D. (CD2:29)

N: Listen to the talk. Tick true or false.

Woman: Well, let me see. I think I have good interpersonal skills. I really like working with people. I like working as part of a team, like in an office, and I also like meeting customers and clients. I think I'm relaxed and friendly, but I'm honest. If I make a mistake, then I admit it and just try to fix the problem. I think customers respect that. In college, I worked as a server in a busy restaurant. I know that's not an office job, but it takes a lot of people skills. You have to make your customers feel relaxed and comfortable, and also make them feel special. So I think I could use that experience to help me in a busy office like this one.

Test 2. Listening section. E. (CD2:30)

N: Listen to the conversation. Circle the correct information.

Woman: Hi, Peter. Could I ask you for some help?

Man: Sure, what's up? Something with work?

Woman: No, no. I need to buy a graduation gift for my nephew. He's graduating from university. And I have no idea what to get him!

Man: Well, what does he like?

Woman: I have no idea, really. I don't know him very well. My sister lives in another town, so …

Man: OK. Do you know if he plays sports? Or … has any special hobbies?

Woman: I have no idea. I know, I should pay more attention to him, but I have such a large family, and they live so far away and ...

Man: Hey, you don't have to explain it to me!

Woman: I just thought, you know, since you're a young man.

Man: I'll see what I can do. Umm. how about cash? Every young man needs money!

Woman: I know, but I think that's not special enough.

Man: Hmmm … some DVDs, or some music CDs?

Woman: That's a good idea, but … it's too difficult to guess what he'd like.

Man: Then why don't you get him a gift certificate? Like for one of those online music stores. Then he can download whatever he wants.

Woman: That's a great idea! I knew you'd be able to help! Thanks, Pete.

Man: Hey, no problem.

Test 2. Listening section. F. (CD2:31)

N: Listen to the conversation. Circle the correct answers.

Woman: OK, I think that's everything. Do you have any more questions or comments?

Man: Not really, except thank you. This has been really helpful. You know I'm never quite sure if I'm doing a good job.

Woman: Well, remember, we did say that you need to work on your self-confidence!

Man: Right! I will! And I will ask questions when I don't understand.

Woman: Yes, that's a great plan. Really, there's nothing wrong, ever, with asking questions. That's the best way to learn!

Man: And I'll also take that training course in business writing.

Woman: Yes, I think that's a very good idea. Writing is hard for a lot of people, not just you. But if you practise, I'm sure you'll improve.

Man: So, for the next year, I'll still be working in the same office …

Woman: Yes, that's right. Is that a problem?

Man: Oh, no, not at all. Although … one reason I applied to this company is because it has offices in Europe. And I do speak German, so …

Woman: Well, when you have some more experience, that's something we can discuss. We don't usually transfer new hires overseas. However … I guess I didn't realise you speak German. Are you fluent?

Man: Oh, yes. My mother is German, actually.

Woman: Really? Would you like to help out with translating some documents occasionally?

Man: Oh, yes, that would be great.

Woman: And really useful for us. I'll make a note of that.

Man: OK, then, I guess that's all. Thank you.

Woman: And thanks for coming in.

TOEIC® practice listening

Unit 1. Practice for the TOEIC® test. Listening A: Photographs. (CD2:32)

1

A

It's a formal situation.

B

They're in the office.

C

It's a business training program.

D

The people are at a party.

2

A

The woman is giving a presentation.

B

The man is making an introduction.

C

The people are not comfortable.

D

She's meeting an old friend.

Unit 1. Practice for the TOEIC® test. Listening B. Sentence – Response. (CD2:33)

3

Cara, would you like to say a few words?

A

Hi, everyone, it's nice to meet you.

B

Actually, I'm an only child.

C

No, we haven't met.

4

So, where are you from?

A

I'm studying business.

B

Actually, I'm not married.

C

I was born in Australia.

5

Yeah, I like sports. I play a lot of baseball.

A

Really? My husband plays baseball too.

B

I see. Who's your favourite singer?

C

That's interesting. What's your major?

6

So, what do you do?

A

Fine, thanks, and you?

B

I'm in sales and marketing.

C

I'm going to a meeting.

Unit 2. Practice for the TOEIC® test. Listening: Short conversations and talks. (CD2:34)

Questions 1 to 3 refer to the following talk.

Good morning, everyone. I'm Carolyn Menzel from Personnel. I'm going to talk today about how every one of the staff here can help improve customer service. My message is that we need to make some changes – but the good news is that I think a few simple changes will make a big difference. Now, today's presentation is divided into two parts. For the first hour, I'm going to talk about three important improvements we can make in dealing with customer complaints. Then after lunch, I'm going to talk about some things we can do to improve the order process. OK, then, let me start by giving you some background information. Uh … can everybody see this slide? This shows …

Questions 4 to 6 refer to the following conversation.

A: So is this your first visit to Chicago, Ann?

B: No, I've been here once before. But it was a few years ago. I don't remember it very well.

A: Is there anything special you're hoping to see? A baseball game, maybe?

B: Well, the Art Institute, of course. I love art museums. And I really want to go shopping, too.

A: Well, I'm not so interested in shopping, but I'd love to go to the museum with you.

B: Well, why don't I go shopping in the morning tomorrow, and then we could go to the museum in the afternoon?

A: That sounds great. Why don't we meet for lunch downtown? I know a great Chinese place.

Unit 3. Practice for the TOEIC® test. Listening A: Photographs. (CD2:35)

1

A

They're looking at the brochure.

B

The man has a video camera.

C

The people are welcoming a visitor.

D

They're having a meeting.

2

A

She's making copies of the agenda.

B

The woman is giving a presentation.

C

The meeting has finished.

D

The woman is showing a film.

Unit 3. Practice for the TOEIC® test. Listening B: Sentence – Response. (CD2:36)

3

We need to decide when the meeting will be.

A

OK, how about some time next week?

B

I think it should be about two hours long.

C

I still haven't decided yet.

4

So, should we hire some more sales staff?

A

I don't have a copy of the agenda.

B

I think we should accept everyone's suggestions.

C

First we need to consider whether we have enough money.

5

Why do you think we need a new brochure?

A

I agree with Mike and Jean.

B

The main reason is that the old one is hard to understand.

C

If you ask me, I think we should buy it.

6

Well, it looks like we're out of time.

A

We should order some more, then.

B

It'll probably take an hour.

C

OK, I'll see you tomorrow, then.

Unit 4. Practice for the TOEIC® test. Listening: Short conversations and talks. (CD2:37)

Questions 1 to 3 refer to the following conversation.

A: OK, here's an idea. Why don't we put an order form on our website?

B: I think that's a great idea. It would be convenient for customers, and we'd probably get more business.

A: We could offer some discounts for ordering online.

B: I'm not sure about that. We're already not making a very big profit.

A: OK. We can come back to that idea. Now, what about the overall look? Everyone agrees that our current pages are hard to read.

B: Yes, that's true. Just off the top of my head, I think we should have more photographs and fewer long paragraphs.

A: Good idea. And maybe add some more links. You know, move some of the writing to another page.

Questions 4 to 6 refer to the following talk.

Meetings? Yeah, I guess my company has a lot of meetings. My section has a general meeting every Monday morning, just for an hour. We go over our plans for the week, talk about any problems or challenges, that kind of thing. But I always have other meetings during the week – at least twice a week with people from other departments, or with customers … it varies. The people I work with say we have too many meetings, that we should use email more, but I prefer meeting face-to-face. I think that's really important. You need to know what people are feeling, not just what they are thinking, and you can't see people's faces through email. The only kind of meeting I don't really like is a teleconference, you know, with a lot of people on the phone. I never know who is saying what. And like I said, I like to be able to see people's faces.

Unit 5. Practice for the TOEIC® test. Listening A: Photographs. (CD2:38)

1

A

He's not at his desk right now.

B

The man is writing a message.

C

The man is in a meeting now.

D

He isn't sitting down.

2

A

She's leaving a voicemail message.

B

The woman is typing a report.

C

A: She's working at her desk.

D

The woman is using a cell phone.

Unit 5. Practice for the TOEIC® test. Listening B: Sentence – Response. (CD2:39)

3

Can you ask him to call me back?

A

Yes, I'll call you back.

B

Sure, I'll give him the message.

C

Of course. Please call him back this afternoon.

4

Let me confirm. We'll meet at 10:00, is that right?

A

Yes, I'd like to leave a message.

B

Thanks. I'll call back in half an hour.

C

Actually, it's 10:30, in my office.

5

Can I take a message?

A

Certainly, I'd be happy to take one.

B

No, that's OK, I'll call back.

C

Yes, please leave a message with me.

6

I'm not at my desk right now, so please leave your name and a message after the tone.

A

Hi, Katherine, this is Mark.

B

I'm sorry, I'm on vacation now.

C

Yes, thank you for calling.

Unit 6. Practice for the TOEIC® test. Listening: Short conversations and talks. (CD2:40)

Questions 1 to 3 refer to the following conversation.

A: Excuse me, can I help you?

B: Uh, yeah, I'm a little lost. I'm looking for the Park Central Hotel. Do you know where it is?

A: Oh, dear, I'm not sure. Maybe … Is it a big hotel?

B: I don't really know. I know that it's next to a park …

A: Well, I do know how to get to the park … To get there, just go up this street till you get to the first traffic light. Then turn right and walk for, oh, about 3 or 4 blocks. You'll see the park on your left. It's not a big park, so if the hotel's there, I guess you'll see it.

A: Great, thanks so much.

Questions 4 to 6 refer to the following talk.

Are you planning a trip to Las Vegas? Whether you're coming for business or pleasure, you'll love staying at the Golden Sands Resort Hotel. We offer 35 floors of single, double, and deluxe rooms. There's something for everybody! If you're looking for a romantic getaway, you'll love our fine dining in one of two upscale restaurants. Here with the family? We have casual dining too! Kids are welcome. And, to stay in shape, visit our 24-hour gym. Business travellers will appreciate our copy centre, large conference rooms, and free wireless access in every room. And, from September through November, stay two weekend nights and receive either Friday or Monday night free! But call now – rooms will fill up fast. We look forward to seeing you soon at the Golden Sands Resort Hotel!

Unit 7. Practice for the TOEIC® test. Listening A: Photographs. (CD2:41)

1

A

The train was very late today.

B

The flight back was delayed.

C

They're sending an email.

D

They're driving slowly in the rain.

2

A

It's an outdoor market.

B

Please fax us the report.

C

I work in sales and marketing.

D

They're looking at shoes and shirts.

Unit 7. Practice for the TOEIC® test. Listening B: Sentence – Response. (CD2:42)

3

How was your flight?

A

It was OK, but I have a little jet lag.

B

They were very productive, thanks.

C

I'm sorry I couldn't be there.

4

Let's see, what's your password?

A

Oh, I see the problem now.

B

Actually, I can't remember it.

C

I'm using a different account.

5

Did you send me the report yet?

A

No, I didn't use any emoticons.

B

Yes, I met with the design team.

C

Yes, I emailed it as an attachment.

6

Did you delete that old report?

6

A

Yes, I threw it away.

B

Yes, it's on the server.

C

No, there wasn't enough space.

Unit 8. Practice for the TOEIC® test. Listening: Short conversations and talks. (CD2:43)

Questions 1 to 3 refer to the following talk.

Well, let me summarise my presentation today. I've talked about three things. First, I talked about some ways that we can improve communication among all of our offices in Europe. Second, I talked about some staffing changes that will affect France and Germany. Finally, I talked about the upcoming conference and our plans for that. My main point was that we need to make some changes in our European offices in order to improve sales. It won't be easy, but I think we can do it if we all work together. Thank you for listening. Are there any questions or comments?

Questions 4 to 6 refer to the following conversation.

A: So, are you ready for your presentation on Friday?

B: Oh, sure, I think so. I mean, I know what I'm going to say, so …

A: And have you prepared all your slides?

B: Slides?

A: Yes, aren't you using presentation software?

B: No, I'm not. I prefer, you know, just talking. It's more personal. And then I know people are paying attention to me, not just reading something.

A: I know what you mean, but … sometimes it's nice to have everything written out clearly. I don't like to take notes during a presentation.

B: Oh, don't worry. Everything important is on my handout.

Unit 9. Practice for the TOEIC® test. Listening A: Photographs. (CD2:44)

1

A

The customers are leaving the store.

B

The man is on the phone.

C

They're talking to the sales clerk.

D

She's interviewing the man.

2

A

They're using presentation software.

B

She's working with a tutor.

C

The women are preparing a contract.

D

They're walking together.

Unit 9. Practice for the TOEIC® test. Listening B: Sentence – Response. (CD2:45)

3

Do you think he has enough experience?

A

He didn't include a photo.

B

No, it's against the law.

C

Yes, he's been working for four years.

4

Well, he's worked at several companies, but I don't know if he has the right skills.

A

The position has some good benefits, though.

B

I know. His experience doesn't seem relevant.

C

He didn't include a lot of personal information.

5

Do you think we should interview her?

A

Let's read a few more résumés first.

B

I don't know. It's not a full-time job.

C

B: That's not very professional.

6

Oh! She used to work as the general manager of Human Resources.

A

It sounds like she's overqualified.

B

Yes, I see what you mean.

C

That's a pretty good school.

Unit 10. Practice for the TOEIC® test. Listening: Short conversations and talks. (CD2:46)

Questions 1 to 3 refer to the following conversation.

A: So, Anne, tell me a little about your background.

B: OK, uh … where should I start?

A: How about with your education? What was your major in college?

B: Well, I graduated with a Business degree. But I also took a lot of classes in international relations.

A: So you're interested in …

B: International things, yeah. I took Spanish for four years. I'm pretty fluent. So I'd love a job that involved travel, like to Spain or South America.

A: Well, we do have offices in Brazil, Argentina, and Mexico. However, this position doesn't involve any travel. Have you worked as an administrative assistant before?

B: No, not really. But it seems really interesting.

A: I see. Well, as the announcement stated, we're looking for someone with some solid experience.

Questions 4 to 6 refer to the following talk.

Well, let's see. I'm a very patient person. I don't get angry or frustrated easily. I think that helps me a lot working with other people. I don't mind explaining things or taking time to talk things through, you know, to reach a consensus. So I'm a good team worker. On the other side, well, I guess some of my technical skills aren't as good as I'd like them to be. But I'm taking some classes now, and I'm working on that. I'm also a little shy, so it's hard for me to give presentations and things like that. I guess I just need more practise.

Unit 11. Practice for the TOEIC® test. Listening A: Photographs. (CD2:47)

1

A

They're opening the box now.

B

He's buying her something at the store.

C

The gift is still wrapped.

D

She ordered some flowers.

2

A

I know he likes stuffed toy animals.

B

It's a gift made from leather.

C

I'm choosing some small gifts.

D

It's a little too fragile.

Unit 11. Practice for the TOEIC® test. Listening B: Sentence – Response. (CD2:48)

3

Why don't you order some flowers?

A

Because I didn't have enough time.

B

Thanks, that's a good idea.

C

Don't wrap them in red paper.

4

Do you think I should send the office some gifts?

A

Well, they probably won't send us anything.

B

Actually, the number eight is unlucky.

C

Different colours have different meanings.

5

May I open it now?

A

Yes, it's wrapped.

B

No, that's OK.

C

Sure, go ahead.

6

Here, this is for you.

A

Yes, it's over there.

B

Oh, thank you.

C

That's perfectly OK.

Unit 12. Practice for the TOEIC® test. Listening: Short conversations and talks. (CD2:49)

Questions 1 to 3 refer to the following conversation.

A: Well, what kind of goals do you have for the coming year?

B: Let's see … I'd like to work on some of the international projects. Perhaps some of the Asian campaigns …

A: Well, that's certainly possible … do you mind traveling?

B: Oh, no, I love to travel. And you know I've been studying Chinese this year, so …

A: That's right, I'd forgotten about that. Well, that's certainly a relevant skill. Let me put you in touch with Harry Chan. He might be able to involve you in some projects.

Questions 4 to 6 refer to the following talk.

I think I saw a great example of high and low-context communication in the coffee shop, actually, when I was living abroad in an Arab country, in Morocco. Now, I'm American – at home, when I go to a café, I go alone, and you know, I just have a cup of coffee. I sometimes bring my laptop and do some work, or I might read the newspaper. But in Morocco, I noticed that people went to the café to socialize. They expected to meet their friends and to talk. It would be considered rude to bring work and just sit by yourself. To a lot of Arab people, friends are more important than just work. And you know, they might have a point there …

BEC practice listening

Unit 2 (CD2:32)

Karen: Good morning, Karen speaking. How can I help you?

James: Hello, I'm ringing from a company called L & C Limited. I'd like to place an order, please.

Karen: OK. Could I have your name please?

James: Yes, it's James Wilstead. That's spelt W-I-L-S-T-E-A-D.

Karen: And what's your email address?

James: purchasing@LandC.com. I'll give you my direct phone number too.

Karen: Right.

James: It's 0-1-double 9-8, 3-7-6, 2 double 7.

Karen: Thank you. And what would you like to order?

James: We want three laser printers, and the reference number on your website is GK 57.

Karen: OK.

James: Then some wall calendars for next year – five of them, please, with the number PIL double 4-8.

Karen: They're the calendars that show the financial year.

James: Yes. And finally two noticeboards, reference HT 31.

Karen: That's the grey ones.

James: Yes.

Karen: Right. Let me just calculate the total price ... OK, that comes to four hundred and nine pounds 35.

James: That's what I calculated. How soon can you deliver them? I hope it can be this week.

Karen: We can get the goods to you by the end of the week at no extra charge, but if you want them tomorrow there's a delivery charge of £15.

James: The end of the week will be fine.

Karen: Right, so that's Friday, June the 15th.

James: Good. Thank you.

Unit 5 (CD2:33)

1 Which item does Beth still need?

Man: Do you need anything for your new desk, Beth?

Woman: Let me think. I've taken my laptop and there were already some shelves on the desk. There isn't a desk lamp, though.

Man: OK, I'll arrange to get you one.

Woman: Thanks.

2 How do they decide to negotiate with their new supplier?

Man: Our new supplier has just telephoned. I think the negotiations with them are going to be difficult. Maybe we should go to their office and talk.

Woman: We're too busy at the moment. Let's arrange a teleconference. That's almost as good, and we won't waste time travelling.

Man: I'd rather talk face-to-face, but I suppose you're right. OK, let's do that.

3 Which chart shows the company's sales this year?

Woman: Asia is our fastest growing market, with sales now a third of the total. Middle East sales have fallen, though it remains our leading market. Our sales in Africa are still lower than in other regions, however.

4 What does the man want Jane to do?

Man: Jane, it's Malcolm. I'm calling about Wednesday's meeting. I'm afraid I can't attend, so can I send you a written report instead? If that's OK, it'll need to be attached to the minutes. Sorry to give you extra work.

5 Which graph shows the company's payments to suppliers?

Woman: Our expenditure on raw materials is high this year, isn't it?

Man: Yes. There was a steady increase in the first quarter, because the price of metal rose, and we needed to purchase large amounts. Expenditure then fell slightly, before starting to rise again. At least there was a sharp decline in the final quarter.

6 When will Hilary travel to the conference?

Man: Shall I book your flight to the conference, Hilary?

Woman: Yes please. I want to travel on the 17th of September.

Man: But that's the date the conference starts. I thought you wanted to go the day before.

Woman: I'm only interested in the topics being discussed on the 18th, so I don't need to go on the 16th.

7 Why does David want a meeting with Becky?

Becky: Becky speaking.

David: Becky, it's David. We need to meet and talk about our next advertising campaign.

Becky: OK.

David: The agency wants to know what we think of the advertisement they've designed. It's very different from the current one, so I'd like to talk about it with you before we see them.

8 Which product will they sell at a reduced price?

Woman: Armchairs are selling fast, so we clearly got the prices right. There are still plenty of sofas in stock, though, so we'll see if a half-price special offer helps sales. If that works, we'll consider reducing the prices of tables.

Unit 9 (CD2:34)

Right, I'll go through the plans for Monday's job interviews, as you're both involved. We're seeing three people, and they're due to arrive in reception by 10 am. Cathy, could you wait for them there, please, then take them to the Corner Room for some refreshments – the canteen won't be open at that time. I've booked some refreshments. Then could you show them round the business park – take them inside some hi-tech units, and maybe the restaurant, too. You need to finish up in the information centre, where the interviews will take place. Ben, we'll meet them there at 11.30. The interview team will consist of us three and an HR officer – either Jack or Hazel, whoever's free.

Remember our advert simply mentioned vacancies in finance, so the applicants are pretty varied. Gillian Brown works for a publishing company, where she's responsible for salaries. She's also been a college lecturer in finance, and she looks like a strong candidate..

Peter Collingwood is in the local council's budgeting team. He's interested in a job where he plays a major part in developing strategy, so we need to focus on that in his interview.

The third candidate is called Soraya Hamilton. She isn't actually a finance specialist – in her current job she designs websites – but she wants to be a programmer, and write financial software. I thought she'd be worth interviewing.

In each interview, I'll start by telling them about the plans for developing the business park, then we can all ask about their current and past jobs. After that, Ben, could you concentrate on finding out what skills they have, please. I've made a list of ones that we need. Cathy and I can also join in with some questions. Then when that's finished, Cathy, I'd like you to focus on ...

Unit 12 (CD2:35)

Woman: Well, Gary, you've had a month in this store. Do you think you've learnt everything about the job yet?

Man: Most of it, I think. I didn't know much about sports clothes before I started, so I've spent a lot of time finding out about them. But I don't really understand how you decide which items to put on special offer. I think I know what I need to do in my job, though, and I try to do my best.

Woman: One thing I'm very pleased with is that several customers have sent emails saying how polite you are. And you're always punctual – that's important. It's a shame you can't work overtime, but I understand your home situation.

Man: Thanks.

Woman: Don't forget, though, that if you need help, it's OK to ask any of the other staff – unless they're talking to customers, of course.

Man: Right.

Woman: What do you think of your organisational skills?

Man: Well, I'm not very efficient at setting my own objectives – it's much easier if someone else sets them. But I always make sure I meet deadlines, even if it means working really hard. I need to manage my time better – I spend too long on some things.

Woman: OK. Now how about your interpersonal skills? You don't have a problem chatting to customers.

Man: No, I find that quite easy. I don't always listen enough, though, especially if I can't understand straight away what they want.

Woman: Do you think you work well as a member of the team?

Man: With the other staff, you mean? Well, it's sometimes difficult.

Woman: Right. So what would you say is your biggest strength?

Man: Well, I always think about how one thing affects everything else – I try to see the big picture.

Woman: Yes, I've noticed that. It's a very useful skill.

Man: But that can make it hard for me to make a decision, because there's so much to consider. And when I've made up my mind, I'm not always flexible enough to change it if I need to.

Woman: Yes, I think you're right. So do you want to work in a store, when you've finished your training, or in head office?

Man: Well, I don't really want all the responsibility that you have as store manager. I don't think I'd be very good at purchasing, either – I can never predict what's going to sell well. I want to specialise in human resources – recruitment, dealing with employees' problems, that sort of thing.

Woman: That's good to know, in case a vacancy comes up in future. Now, I can arrange for you to attend a course before you go to head office. What would you be interested in? I don't think you need to improve your communication skills!

Man: Thank you. I suppose finance would be useful.

Woman: Yes, but you'll have training in that at head office. How about a general course covering all aspects of retailing?

Man: Yes, I'd like that.

Woman: OK, I'll organise it. Right. Let's stop there for the moment and discuss your progress again later on.

Man: Uh-huh.

Woman: You're going to work in head office in two months' time, so shall we talk again in a month from today, on the 19th?

Man: I've arranged to take some leave then, I'm afraid.

Woman: Oh yes, I'd forgotten. Then we'll wait until after you come back to work – say in six weeks' time.

Man: Right. That's fine.

Macmillan Education
4 Crinan Street
London N1 9XW
A division of Macmillan Publishers Limited
Companies and representatives throughout the world

ISBN: 978-0-230-46355-4

First edition published 2009
This edition published 2013

Designed by Carolyn Gibson
Page make-up by MPS Limited
Illustrated by Val Saunders
Cover design by Carolyn Gibson

Jaimie Scanlon would like to thank Morris and Rei for their tireless support and the staff at Macmillan for their expert editorial guidance.

Printed and bound in Thailand

2018 2017 2016 2015 2014
10 9 8 7 6 5 4 3 2